# THE
# REALLY ROUGH HOLIDAY
# GUIDE

**Other books by the same widely travelled authors:**

The Complete Revenge Kit
The Return of the Complete Revenge Kit
The Ultimate Revenge Kit
The Office Revenge Kit
The Official Politically Incorrect Handbook - Volumes 1 and 2
How To Be a Complete Bastard (with Adrian Edmondson)
How To Be a Complete Bitch (with Pamela Stephenson)
The Book of Revelations
The Naughty 90s
How To Be a Superhero
The Book of Stupid Lists
How To Be a Real Man (with Julian Clary)
Back to Basics (with John Major)
Roy Chubby Brown Unzipped! (with Roy Chubby Brown)
Rolf Harris's True Animal Tales (with Rolf Harris, of course)
The Extra-Terrestrial's Guide To The X-Files

# THE
# REALLY ROUGH HOLIDAY GUIDE

Mark Leigh and Mike Lepine

**BEER BELLY BOOKS**

First published in Great Britain in 1997 by
Beer Belly Books
332 Ladbroke Grove
London W10 5AH

Printed and bound by Mackays of Chatham PLC, Chatham, Kent

# About the Authors

**MARK LEIGH** visited 112 different countries in the course of research-ing this book and hated every single one of them (particularly those beginning with 'M' and those in which a chewed Bic biro is viewed as a status symbol).

During his extensive travels he was personally responsible for caus-ing fifteeen jihads, eight coup d'etats, ten armed insurrections and eigh-teen emergency convenings of the United Nations.

Surprisingly, despite his loathing of smelly foreigners, Mark is a firm believer in the principle 'When in Rome, do as the Romans', and he likes visiting Italy just so he can pinch girls' bums.

He agrees with the maxim that travel broadens the mind - but points out that travel to any Third World kharzi also broadens your chances of ending up with typhoid, Hepatitis A, B, C, D, E, F *and* G, not to mention beri-beri and the deadly (but ridiculously named) Green Monkey Disease.

Mark currently presents the weekly TV holiday programme, *Wish I Wasn't Here.*


**MIKE LEPINE** is one of Britain's most accomplished travel writers. His achievements include the rudest and most insulting sentence ever com-posed in the English Language (*Traveller's Turkey*, 1994) amd provoking the Buddhists into issuing their first-ever fatwah (*Tibet for Masochists*, 1993).

To ensure the absolute accuracy of information in this book, Mike travelled to the four corners of the earth (no mean feat when you con-sider that the earth is a sphere). On his travels he picked up scores of invaluable tips, a wealth of experience and a gastric infection that pre-vents him from ever again mingling in polite society.

After his epic journey, he can truthfully say that there really is no place like home – especially since he lives in a corrugated iron igloo shaped like an inverted pyramid.

His ambition now is to travel to Mars and complain about the lack of adequate toilet facilities.

# THE REALLY ROUGH HOLIDAY GUIDE

# INTRODUCTION

*So you're thinking of going abroad on holiday this year.*

*Don't!*

That is the essential message of this invaluable guide book. In fact, if you heed that one simple word of advice, you don't need to read the rest of the book. Give it to someone else who's considering going abroad. It may have cost you £6.99, but it's saved you hundreds of pounds and several feet of gastric lining.

Britain is the best holiday destination for the true Brit. Everyone speaks English (except for Wales and parts of Scotland), everyone eats normal food (except for Wales and parts of Scotland) and the entertainment revolves around fun pubs, amusement arcades and pleasure beaches instead of strange practices with sheep (except for Wales and parts of Scotland).

If you really must go abroad, then study this book carefully. Over a hundred of the world's most popular and exotic holiday destinations are dissected and laid open in these pages as a stark warning to those foolhardy enough to consider going there.

If that doesn't put you off and send you scuttling away to book two weeks in Blackpool, then God help you. You're on your own.

*Just remember one thing.*

*We once had an Empire stretching all around the world.*

*We owned countries on every continent.*

*And we gave them all back.*

*We must have had a bloody good reason.*

## SPECIAL ADVICE TO TRAVELLERS READING THIS INTRODUCTION IN THE AIRPORT DEPARTURE LOUNGE

1. Check your booking. Can you still cancel and get your money back?

2. If not, go to the nearest pharmacy and buy all the Diocalm you can carry

3. Go to the nearest public toilet and steal every toilet roll you can get your hands on

4. Buy lots of books to read

## THE LANGUAGE BARRIER

If you can, always choose a holiday destination where English is the first language. This isn't just a question of being understood. It's also a fairly good guarantee that the water will be drinkable, the food safe and no-one will be offended if you turn down the chance to have sex with a favoured quadruped.

Never, ever take a phrase book on holiday with you. Have you ever heard a foreigner trying to speak English? They sound mental, right? Do you want to sound like that when you attempt their language? Of course not. Only ever speak English when abroad. That way, you sound fluent and they sound like idiots, making you look and feel superior.

A good rule of thumb to employ when trying to communicate with the natives is: if they can't speak English they're probably not worth talking to.

If you really have to speak to someone with little or no English, perhaps because you want your shoes shined, you can usually make yourself understood by speaking slowly but very very loudly. Punctuate your words with little finger jabs into the foreigner's ribs to help him understand where the emphases fall.

Finally, it is a well-known fact that all Frenchmen speak English – but refuse to do so. Fine. Our advice is not to bother talking to them at all. Arrogant bastards.

## CHOOSING YOUR AIRLINE

Travel operators will tell you that, today, one airline is much the same as another. This is untrue.

*When you book your flight, follow these simple safety precautions:*

\# Never choose an airline with a non-British animal as its mascot

\# Or one that flies Dakotas over the Andes

\# Never fly in a plane with non-English lettering on the tail

\# Never use an airline that flies from Dar es Salaam to Ouagadougou

\# Avoid airlines whose idea of 'in-flight entertainment' is drumming

\# Never, ever use an airline that only ever takes off during the hours of darkness. This is either because they can't afford much aviation fuel (taking off during hot daylight hours requires more fuel) or because they don't want you to see the Sellotape on engine number 3

\# Never be taken in by seemingly impressive slogans like 'Uzbekistan's Favourite Airline'

\# Competent pilots do not usually wear nose jewellery at the controls

\# Or rub a lucky rabbit's foot just prior to take-off

\# Be suspicious of any operator who says 'goats travel free'

\# Or chickens

Finally, if you really absolutely have to use one of the world's least favourite airlines be sure to carry lots of cash. These companies often owe airport operators considerable sums of money for fuel and landing rights and may be refused permission to take off. Unless you want to be stuck in some nightmarish masquerade of an airstrip, give generously when the pilot asks for a whip-round.

## HOLIDAY BROCHURES – WHAT THEY SAY AND WHAT THEY REALLY MEAN

If you believed everything the holiday brochures told you, you'd end up in the Garden of Eden every year. Before you make the same mistakes you made last year, study this useful guide to 'Brochure Speak'. Go on. You know your GP told you your sphincter couldn't take another shock of the same magnitude two years running.

---

### THE LOCATION

UNSPOILED - Squat toilets only

CHARMING - Dull

PICTURESQUE - Even more dull than 'charming'

RELAXED - Comatose

UNPRETENTIOUS - Barbaric

LIVELY - Full of drunken electricians vomiting on their cut-down jeans

NEVER SLEEPS - Loud disco music will keep you awake at all hours

UNTOUCHED - Unpopular

MIDDLE EASTERN INFLUENCES - No concept of sanitation

BUZZING - The police get called out every five minutes

PARADISE - Anywhere with a beach bar that sells a Diet Coke for three quid

STRIKING - Largely volcanic and barren

ENERGETIC - The rave capital of the area

PEACEFUL - Dead as a doornail after 6pm

TRADITIONAL - Food poisoning a certainty

CHARMING FISHING VILLAGE - Fuck all to do

EXOTIC - Weird

BEAUTIFUL - Shite

---

### THE LOCALS

UNHURRIED - Bone idle

FRIENDLY - Liable to pester you for money morning, noon and night

COSMOPOLITAN - Rude and arrogant

GENTLE - Dim
EXTROVERTED - A pain in the arse
UNPRETENTIOUS - See nothing wrong in excreting right
in front of you
WELCOMING - Greedy
STRAIGHTFORWARD - Surly
CHARMING - Greasy
SIMPLE - Can't speak English
ACCOMMODATING - Hate the Brits
NATURAL - See 'UNPRETENTIOUS'
LIVELY - Watch your personal belongings
GOOD-NATURED - Uneducated
VIVACIOUS - Mental

## THE HOTEL

CONVENIENT LOCATION - For the ring road
MODERN - Prefabricated
IN KEEPING WITH
LOCAL ARCHITECTURE - Ugly
COMFORTABLE - Basic
PLEASANTLY
DECORATED ROOMS - If your taste runs to Woolworth's
nick-nacks
IMPRESSIVE - A high rise
ELEGANT - Old as sin
ABUNDANT FACILITIES - An overpriced mini mart, postcard rack
and a noisy disco bar full of drunken
Northerners having a punch up
HIGH STANDARD - In comparison with the country's normal
tawdry standards
FRIENDLY - Small
SPACIOUS - Tiny rooms, but a huge lobby
CENTRAL LOCATION - Miles from the beach
INTERNATIONAL - Thronging with fat Kraut holidaymakers
SIMPLY FURNISHED - Dirty
FAMILY HOTEL - Full of out of control children yelling
'wanker!' off the balconies
QUIET LOCATION - The warehouse district
RELAXING - Nothing to do

RIGHT ON THE
WATERFRONT - No beach
AUTHENTIC - Dirty and serves unhygienic food
WELL-APPOINTED - Within driving distance of a beach
SOCIABLE - Popular with pensioners' outings
HELPFUL STAFF - Greasy spotty lotharios who want to sleep
with your teenaged daughter
EVENING
ENTERTAINMENT - Something ethnic involving fire, tom-toms
and very stupid costumes
VALUE FOR MONEY - See 'SIMPLY FURNISHED'
ROOMY - Uncluttered with superfluous furniture
AIRY - No air conditioning in hotel
INTERNATIONAL
CABARET - A singer with stretch marks, a dreary
novelty act which involves puppets and
juggling and a crap magician
EXTENSIVE CHILDREN'S
ENTERTAINMENT - See above
RELAXING TV AREA - Airless, dank room containing a 14-inch
portable and 38 chairs, where people dump
their luggage on the last day
FREE - Between the hours of 6.00am and 8.00am

## HOLIDAY ILLNESSES

**THE WORLD'S TOP 20 DIARRHOEA HOT SPOTS**
According to the latest figures from the Critical Bowel Injury Ward
at The London Hospital, March 1996. (Last year's positions in brackets)

| | |
|---|---|
| 1. Turkey (1) | 11. Myanmar (7) |
| 2. India (4) | 12. Chad (10) |
| 3. Pakistan (11) | 13. Mongolia (14) |
| 4. Spain (5) | 14. Portugal (16) |
| 5. Egypt (2) | 15. Tunisia (18) |
| 6. Mexico (19) | 16. Morocco (12) |
| 7. Greece (3) | 17. Brazil (17) |
| 8. Sri Lanka (9) | 18. Honduras (13) |
| 9. Thailand (8) | 19. Zimbabwe (20) |
| 10. Nigeria (15) | 20. Isle of Wight (6) |

## HOW TO AVOID HOLIDAY DIARRHOEA

1. Stay in Britain (except for the Isle of Wight. See above)
2. Drink only bottled water
3. Bring all your own food with you, and keep it in an airtight container
4. Avoid inhaling next to locals
5. Clean your teeth with bottled water
6. Never eat out
7. Avoid ice in drinks
8. Wear a quarantine suit (Level 3 BioHazard type recommended)

## DIARRHOEA EMERGENCY

If you are stricken down with terrible diarrhoea, don't bother to contact the British Embassy for help. They'll just make a disgusted sound and slam the phone down on you.

Local doctors can be expensive and unreliable. Your best bet is to pack plenty of Diocalm before you travel. This handy diarrhoea medicine can help, at least up to a point.

Be sure to take several packs with you. In many holiday destinations, ounce for ounce, Diacalm is more expensive than gold. At some Spanish hotels, for example, where an outbreak of food poisoning has occurred, you often see frantic 'Diocalm' auctions where cynical Diocalm 'dealers' charge desperate holidaymakers hundreds of pounds for a few hours blessed relief.

Do not try to undercut them with your own 'stash'. The 'Diocalm Mafia' as they are known are totally ruthless and will think nothing of making you disappear.

## LAST-MINUTE BARGAINS

You know in your heart that 'last minute specials' are the holidays that no-one else wanted. Two-week prison sentences inside crumbling musty villas with overflowing drains sited precariously halfway up a volcano, or hotels officially on the tour company's books but not featured in the brochure after all the litigation.

These are the places you see on *Watchdog* rather than *Wish You Were Here*, dives so dire that they have to be booked completely unseen.

Be sensible with your money. Put it down on the ground and then set fire to it. That way at least, you'll get to spend your holiday in England and won't need to use a colostomy bag for the rest of your natural life.

*If, after this warning, you are still tempted by the lure of a bargain holiday at an unspecified resort, just remember: the phrase 'last resort' had to come from somewhere ... and probably refers to where you'll end up.*

## ERRORS AND OMISSIONS

By its very nature, a guide to the world can never be fully complete and up to date. If your choice of holiday destination is not featured in this book, it's either because it doesn't matter, we ran out of pages or else the guide book to it had already been borrowed from our local library.

# A

## ALBANIA

There are many reasons for not visiting a foreign country but 'Norman Wisdom' rarely features as one of them – unless you happen to be thinking about visiting Albania. It has long been a puzzle to comedy connoisseurs how (and more importantly, why) certain comics achieve demigod status abroad while being viewed as 'talentless cretins' in their own country. Stalin was a great fan of George Formby, Jerry Lewis is still a cult figure in France while Norman Wisdom is the equivalent in this South-eastern European republic.

To the long-suffering Albanians, Norman Wisdom represents their arduous struggle for independence. They identify with his comic persona – the fight of the little man against his oppressors in the face of all odds. To Albanians, *Man of the Moment* (1955) is an allegory for their 400-year oppression under the Ottoman empire – as well as a hoot. Likewise, Norman's character of Pitkin in *A Stitch in Time* (1963) is symbolic of the country's 1912 revolt against the Turks led by Ismail Qemal and his band of Albanian patriots.

What this means for the visitor is a constant bombardment of images of Norman Wisdom – there's just no escaping his presence. In the capital city, Tirana, portraits of Norman hang in every public building. There are two state-run TV stations 'Wisdom 1' (which shows his old films 24 hours a day) and 'Wisdom Gold' (which shows his even older films 24 hours a day).

A 20-foot tall bronze statue entitled 'Meksi Grimsdali' ('Mr Grimsdale') faces the People's Assembly building. His character Norman Puckle and the diving suit scene from *The Bulldog Breed* (1960) is captured in an 80-foot high fresco overlooking the main square in the port of Durres on the Adriatic coast, where it confuses visiting sailors.

If your trip to Albania should coincide with a state visit from Norman Wisdom, then be prepared for long delays as a Lada motorcade grinds its way from the airport to the State Parliament building. The five-mile journey can take several hours to complete.

Even the State police have been influenced by 'Wisdomania' and their uniforms include cloth caps and jackets pulled down behind their backs. What they lack in comic timing though, they more than make up for in systematic brutality and club-wielding skills.

### The Albanian People

Imagine a race of Eric Cantonas and you've got the entire Albanian population in one go (except they're not as proficient at football and aren't on a $500,000 retainer from Nike – and they're not French). They're surly, rude, quarrelsome and above all, ready and willing to pick a fight with anyone – or any country.

Throughout its long history Albania has argued and fought tooth and nail with the Romans, Goths, Visigoths, Huns, Bulgars, Normans, Serbs, Turks, Greeks, Macedonians, Russians, all Eastern European states, Yugoslavians, Chinese, Americans and nearly all Western European states.

*If you're looking for trouble this is the place to go.*

### Albania – stupid name capital of the world

*Fact!*
It was once ruled by King Zog (1928 – 39) – the monarch formerly known as 'Ahmed Beg Zogu'

*Fact!*
There are two types of Albanian, the Ghegs (to the north) and the Tosks (to the south)

*Fact!*
Albania has the only river that rhymes with a famous Monty Python character – the Shkumbi.

**DID YOU KNOW?**
*The national anthem of Albania is*
*'Don't Laugh At Me ('Cos I'm A Fool)'*

---

## DICTATORS AND THEIR FAVOURITE COMEDIANS

Joseph Stalin - George Formby
Pol Pot - The Grumbleweeds
General Pinochet - Hope & Keene's Crazy Bus
General Franco - Arthur Askey and Richard 'Stinker' Murdoch
Adolf Hitler - Charlie Chaplin
Nicolai Ceausescu - Bobby Davro
Erich Honecker - Jimmy Clitheroe
Fidel Castro - Sid Ceasar and his Show of Shows
Idi Amin - Hydrogen

---

# ALGERIA

Algeria hides its light under a bushel and is actually the tenth largest country in the world and the second largest in Africa. However, that in itself is not enough of a reason to visit it when you consider that 98 per cent of the country is actually the Sahara Desert – a region not known for its many and varied tourist attractions.

Some travellers think the idea of traversing the Sahara Desert to Algeria is romantic in an Indiana Jones sort of way. Man verus the elements. Taking on Mother Nature and punching her on the nose. Car 1, Sand 0. It isn't. The chances are your car will get sand in the carburettor half an hour out of Mali, and you'll get sand under your foreskin after half an hour trying to fix it. Both are equally troublesome for the traveller.

Just as the Eskimos have twenty words for snow, the Saharan nomads, the Tuaregs, have eleven words for sand, depending on whether it's fine, coarse, wet, dry, hard, soft, blowing, static, in dunes, under the foreskin or in those little glass lighthouses that you buy on the Isle of Wight.

*If you insist on trying to cross the Sahara, you'll come across five main hazards:*

**SOFT SAND:** Hit a patch of this and your your vehicle can sink within minutes, giving you barely enough time to escape with your life, your supplies and all the Esso tokens stuffed in the glove box.

**SANDSTORMS:** Severe storms can totally ruin your windscreen - something to bear in mind when you consider that the nearest Autoglass depot is probably 3,000 km away and if you phone them expecting an emergency call-out they'll tell you to 'piss off' and slam down the receiver.

**ROAD-RAGE CAMELS:** Keep your cool when stuck behind vast caravans of these ambling, ill-tempered and surly beasts. Sounding your horn will only provoke an international incident which will leave you with serious dents in your hired Land-Rover and spittle all down your windscreen.

**GIANT WORMS:** These come bursting out from the sand dunes just like in that terrible film featuring Sting in his underpants.

**RUNNING OUT OF WATER:** Thirst is your greatest enemy. Be careful not to run out of water, or else you may have to resort to lapping up camel spittle off your windscreen to survive. The desert is littered with the bones of men who took the easy way out...

(OK, so we lied about the giant worms but it's still dangerous, all right?)

## WHERE TO GO

### In Salah
After driving for 1,000 km you'll be glad to stop at this town in the centre of the desert, if only to visit the toilet-come-civic auditorium there. It's difficult to leave straight away since the locals do not get many visitors and will insist that you visit 'La Musee de Sable', a museum devoted to sand which contains the biggest single piece of sandpaper in West Africa, an illustrated history of the dune and a sandcastle replica of Mohammed's house.

### Djanet
One of the few towns in West Africa containing a girl's name (apart from NDebbie in Chad and M'Sharon in the Congo), this is near the Tassili National Park in the south-east of the Sahara, home to thousands of rock paintings dating from 6,000 to 4,000 BC. These are very crude and only worth a detour if you've got nothing better to do. Erich von Daniken claims that the strange figures in these paintings are proof that intelligent life once visited the earth. Nonsense. No intelligent life would travel millions of light years and then choose to land in the Sahara. It's not even worth getting on a plane from Manchester Ringway to go there.

## Algiers

The capital city, famous both for its unimaginative name and its walled marketplace, the kasbah – a visit to which is not recommended. Imagine being in a Pound Shop that's staffed by 100 dirty, noisy, conniving, ill-mannered staff (it's not hard), who are serving 1,000 dirty, noisy, conniving, ill-mannered customers, all of whom are passing the time by vigorously hawking phlegm while waiting to be served (ditto). Now imagine that the Pound Shop sells absolutely nothing that you will ever need but if you did, you'd be short-changed and, as you made your way out, you'd be fingered, groped and propositioned by toothless, lecherous old men with one good eye, who fart all the time. Well, multiply that by a factor of ten and that's what it's like to shop in the kasbah.

---

*Why the Algerian struggle for independence from France was odd...*

### *FACT!*

The leader of the first nationalist movement was Abd El-Kader, who ruled the country's Mascara region (which sounds like it should be south of the 'Eyeliner Rift' and 'Foundation Valley')

### *FACT!*

The nomadic Tuaregs were defeated by the French in 1902 at the Battle of Tit (historians claim their attacking manoeuvres were a flop and they should have stood firm)

### *FACT!*

The French residents in Algeria were known as 'Colons' (although most native Algerians probably called them 'arseholes')

### *FACT!*

The 1962 Evian Peace Talks involved President De Gaulle agreeing to Algerian independence. It was not an attempt to resolve the long-standing argument over which bottled water was best, still or sparkling

---

**DID YOU KNOW?**

*The best slogan the top advertising agency in Algeria could come up with to promote the kasbah was 'The kasbah – it's bloody horrible'.*

# ANGOLA

Scenic, picturesque, charming, vivacious, relaxing, exciting – unfortunately, none of these words can safely be applied to Angola. The place is a dump. If Walt Disney, in a moment of madness, had decided to build 'Dumpland' instead of Disneyland (or indeed had been christened 'Walt Dump' and had no other choice but to call his dream 'Dumpland'), it would have been remarkably like Angola (except the hamburgers would have been ten times more expensive and some six-foot rat would have come along to scare your children – instead of several three-foot ones).

*This is not a popular holiday destination.*

Angolan politics are complex. Like many Third World hellholes, Angola is split by a ferocious civil war. However, unlike many Third World hellholes, the factions here are constantly fighting to decide who *doesn't* have to run the country. There are no less than three warring parties, all of whom would rather not run the country; the FNLA (National Front for the Liberation of Angola), the Marxist MPLA (Angolan People's Liberation Movement) and UNITA (National Union for the Total Independence of Angola.)

For many years, all three successfully stayed out of power until a massive drive against UNITA saw them pushed back into the parliament building where they had no choice but to run the country for several years before they could muster the strength to break out and escape back into the bush. Despite determined MPLA efforts to track them down, round them up and make them propose a budget, UNITA rebels remain in isolated pockets in the bush to this day.

To fill the power vacuum, the United Nations did attempt a series of democratic elections, but these collapsed under widespread intimidation, with threats of 'Vote for us and you die'.

Quite rightly, Angolans are deeply ashamed of their country and their nationality. So much so, in fact, that you will very often find them pretending to be fellow tourists. On arrival, the first thing you will notice (apart from a strange smell that resembles giant burning tyres made entirely of onions) is a huge crowd of Angolans hanging around the airport terminal looking at imaginary wrist watches and checking the destination boards for planes they are not booked out on. 'Soon be going home' they say to each other. 'Away from this terrible country, ha, ha!' This explains why the biggest status symbols to own in Angola are a sombrero and a straw donkey.

Even the Angolan United Nations mission were too embarrassed to admit where they came from. It was several years before anyone noticed that there were two Norwegian delegations in the General Assembly.

Some Angolans speak Portuguese. The others are too ashamed to talk and just make little clicking noises as they desperately avoid making eye contact with you.

There are few tourist attractions worth seeing. However, if you have nothing better to do, the empty parliament building in Luanda is worth checking out. It is covered with graffiti saying 'FNLA Rules OK' – written by the two other warring factions, either out of spite or optimism. The docks contain a number of shameful reminders of Angola's past as a centre of Portuguese slave trading, including a small colonial memorial to all those Angolans who died fighting to secure a place on the slave ships.

Souvenirs are almost impossible to buy. This is because they have all been purchased by the native Angolans to help them pose as tourists.

## DON'T SAY...

*A list of the greatest insults you can use in Angola...*

Are you an Angolan?

Do you live in Angola?

Were you born in Angola?

Is that your house over there?

## MAKING FRIENDS

*Small talk Angolans respond positively to...*

You must be a tourist here yourself

Aren't you that bloke from Kenya?

When do you go home to another country entirely?

This country is awful. You must be so glad not to live here...

## DID YOU KNOW?

*When the national anthem is played in Angola, people stay seated and pretend they don't recognise it.*

# ARGENTINA

Argentina is the spiritual home of corned beef – which tells you all you need to know about Argentinian cuisine and culture. It is also the spiritual home of Eva Peron – Evita – patron saint of Slappers.

Let's be honest. The Falklands might be almost fifteen years ago, but we still hate the Argies. Britons won't forget – especially as The Falklands was the only thing we've won since 1966. You don't want to go there, and they don't want you there – mainly because we make them cry.

Argentinians would like very much to be macho, but don't have the temperament for it. Hot-blooded Latinos to a man, they are frequently bursting into floods of tears. The mere sight of a victorious Brit reduces them to uncontrollable sobs and the tearing out of hair. No wonder then that Argentina is the single largest importer of Kleenex (there is another reason, but there is no need to go into that any further here).

It is hard for us to understand why they are so fiercely patriotic when their own government killed far more of their young men than the British ever did. Many thousands of Argentinian students were rounded up and made to vanish off the face of the earth. They were made 'invisible'.

Still today, their parents refuse to let the authorities forget. If you stand outside Buenos Aires' most notorious prison you will see the 'Mothers of the Missing', dancing with their 'invisible children' to get the message across to the authorities.

This is a solemn and dignfied, intensely moving spectacle, and as a bystander you are well advised to use tact at all times.

- ❏ Do not tap a Mother on the shoulder in mid-dance and ask if you can cut in

- ❏ Do not hold up scorecards as if you were judging *Come Dancing*

- ❏ Do not try to get the Mothers to do 'the twist'

- ❏ Do not try to get a conga line going

- ❏ Do not dress up as a skeleton, trot into the square and say, 'so Mum, do you still want that dance?'

❏ Do not dance holding the imagined hands of someone eighteen inches high. When the Mothers ask what you are doing, do not say 'my cat Tiddles went missing last week and I dance to remember'

❏ Do not dance on your hands and knees. When the the Mothers ask what you are doing, do not say 'my keys are missing'

'Dancing with the Missing' is not the only form of protest still going on. Throughout Argentina, parents regularly stage other events. In the parks, for example, you will see them playing 'Chess with the Missing' (or at least waiting for white to make the first move) or 'Football with the Missing' (current score Parents 574, Missing 0).

Argentinians excel at very little. However, they do lead the world in cheating. From Maradona's handball to the notion that there is any beef in corned beef, the Argentinians excel at dishonesty. While staying in Buenos Aires be sure to check out the Museum of Duplicity, in which Argentinian lies throughout the ages are proudly kept in display cases. (Many of these items are not the originals, but forgeries.) A new 50-acre wing will be completed by 1998 - lazy Argentinian builders permitting. Argentinian gauchos – or cowboys – are also particularly proud of their finely woven ponchos and hold an annual 'Festival of the Poncho' in Catamara where poncho-related celebrations go on for days. There is a fashion show, a poncho parade, a singing contest to promote new songs about the poncho, seminars on dyeing and weaving and the use of rhinestones and a lot of deep existential despair. Tourists with an interest in the poncho are advised to seek urgent psychiatric help. Or get out more.

## SPECIAL ADVICE FOR STUDENTS
Students are not liked in Argentina. Do not visit. No matter how many times you fawningly call the Falklands the Malvinas, you are still more than likely to be stripped naked and thrown out of the back of a Hercules.

## HOBBIES
Argentinian milk cartons feature photos of 'The Missing'. These are hot collectable items and swapped and traded in the playground by the Argentinian children who weren't taken, with the aim of collecting the full set of 80,000, including the very rare premium card of Hector Luis Vargez.

'The Missing' – have inspired a number of toys including a special edition 'Missing Barbie' and her missing friends which became the fastest-selling empty boxes in Argentinian retail history. 'Missing pogs' were also briefly fashionable.

**DID YOU KNOW?**

*The same songs have been in the Argentinian Top 10*
*for five years now.*
*They include 'She's Not There' by The Zombies,*
*'She's Gone' by Hall and Oates, 'Missed Again' by Phil Collins,*
*'Missing You' by John Waite, and 'Lonely This Christmas' by Mud.*

# AUSTRALIA

A country where Kylie Minogue and Paul Hogan are considered intellectuals; where real academics like Mark Little and Rolf Harris are persecuted and hounded out just for having an IQ over 90; where poisonous spiders hide under toilet seats; and where the national pastime is 'drinking yourself stupid'. In the words of one of its most famous sons, 'Can you tell what it is yet?'

Yes, it could only be Australia, the Essex of the southern hemisphere. The country that no-one gives a XXXX about. As a general rule of thumb, the best holiday destinations are not usually those which were once a dumping ground for hardened criminals. If this were so, then Alcatraz or Devil's Island would be ideal places to stay – as would Liverpool.

The early British settlers were disappointed when they first landed, and so will you be.

### Aborigines

As the original inhabitants of Australia, this race is believed to have amassed much wisdom from living in harmony with their environment. However, any people who believe that the sun is a beautiful woman that sleeps in a cave during the night, that fire originated from the rainbow bird and that the world rests on the back of a giant turtle have probably got a few of the fundamentals wrong and probably spent too much time in the sun.

### The Hole in the Ozone Layer

For reasons known only to her, Marie Curie used to put radioactive material in her mouth. She didn't live to a ripe old age and neither will you if you spend too much time out of doors without factor 200 sun cream and a big hat – or better still, an environmental suit and a Geiger counter. The biggest hole in the ozone layer is over Australia and 'catching the rays' now refers to the 'gamma' variety.

## Australia and the Arts

If your choice for a holiday destination is influenced by your interest in the arts then you won't want to  come within 500 miles of here (or any-where else in the southern hemisphere for that matter).

There are museums in Australia but they're only of real interest to people wishing to get out of the sun or for those wanting to experience what a really good echo sounds like. Some of the best Australian muse-ums are:

## The Perth Art Collection

Claiming the finest collection of Australian art, this brownstone building near the port houses many works by Rolf Harris and Ken Done. However, endless variations of a sunset over Ayers Rock painted with a 5-inch emulsion brush, or cute koalas in primary colours, are not worth the admission price of nothing.

## The Canberra Museum of Australian Culture

There are few visitors to this museum, because tourists refuse to believe it even exists. Those in its immediate vicinity often walk straight past, thinking that it's a heat mirage.

This is sad, but better than going inside. It does exist, as Australians are intensely proud of their heritage and keen to show it off. Among its four floors of exhibits visitors will find:

- ❏ 47 varieties of plastic boomerangs

- ❏ 845 varieties of stuffed kangaroos

- ❏ A T-shirt with the slogan, 'No flies on me, cobber'

- ❏ A set of three ceramic flying emus

- ❏ A complete set of scripts from *The Sullivans* and *Young Doctors*

- ❏ Sunglasses with lenses the shape of Australia

- ❏ A hat with corks hanging from it

- ❏ Paintings of a doe-eyed dusky maiden gripping a tree

❏ A plastic model of Father Christmas sitting on a deckchair and wearing sunglasses

❏ A film poster of *Crocodile Dundee* signed by Paul Hogan

❏ A film poster of Mad Max *Beyond the Thunderdome* signed by Mel Gibson

❏ A still from *Tinga and Tucka* signed by Auntie Jean

## Australia and Science

A continual absence of Government funding (and interest) has had a direct effect on Australia's lack of achievement in the sciences. This means, to date, that the country's greatest technological achievements are the boomerang, the gas barbi and the ring-pull, all of which are on display in the Adelaide Museum of Science and Technology, a rather austere steel and glass building. The difference between British and Australian attitudes to science can be summed up as follows:

A British scientist discovered penicillin
An Australian scientist discovered that it cured VD

A British scientist defined gravity
An Australian scientist invented bungee jumping

A British scientist split the atom
An Australian scientist got pissed, fell over and split his head open

## The Sydney Olympics 2000

Sydney has been selected to host the Olympic Games in the year 2000, and the country is preparing itself for a huge influx of visitors, all eagerly awaiting the introduction of some new sports in track and field.

The Urinal Slash Dash
Contestants down eight tinnies and dash to the toilets as fast as they can. It's skill and not just speed that counts as points are awarded for creative toilet use:

| | |
|---|---|
| Leaning your head against the urinal wall in a drunken daze while slashing | 2 points |
| Vomiting and urinating simultaneously | 5 points |
| Drenching your shoes | 5 points |
| Drenching the shoes of the athlete next to you | 8 points |
| Drenching the shoes of the athlete furthest away | 15 points |

| Smirking at the athlete next to you and saying, 'I wouldn't get that out in public if it was mine, mate!' | 5 points |
|---|---|
| Facing the wrong way completely | 5 points |
| Picking a fight with the cobber next to you | 8 points |
| Picking a fight with yourself | 2 points |
| Forgetting entirely what you came into the toilet for, stumbling back to the Olympic Village and then relieving yourself over your own bed | 20 points |

## 4 x 100m Team Cubicle Relay

This is in a wholly different class to the Urinal Slash Dash and requires real team co-operation. Competitors start with a six pack of Castlemaine which they drink as they run 100m. They then hand this to the next runner who does the same until the last team mate has to finish what's left, then down a huge Vindaloo and lock himself in a toilet cubicle. Points are awarded for the first to finish and for being truly disgusting...

| Managing to bang your head against all four sides of the cubicle before sitting | 2 points |
|---|---|
| Stuffing the whole bog roll down the toilet for a laugh | 5 points |
| Getting excreta all over the door handle | 5 points |
| Somehow getting it all over the door as well | 8 points |
| Writing abusive graffiti about the sheila who just dumped you | 5 points |
| As above, but including her home phone number as well | 8 points |
| Falling asleep and being woken up by a representative from the International Olympic Committee five hours after the event | 12 points |

## Hurling

A variation on throwing the hammer. Athletes down two steaks on a barbi washed down by sixteen cans of Fosters. If they can find the hammer they pick it up and spin round and round with it. The vomit reaching the furthest distance wins.

## Music

Concertgoers to the Sydney Opera House will find that Australian interpretations of classical symphonies bear little, if any, resemblance to the original works. Hearing Mozart's 'Eine Kleine Nachtmusik' on the wobbleboard, Tchaikovsky's 'Swan Lake' on the Stylophone or Schubert's Unfinished 8th Symphony on the didgeridoo take some getting used to.

## Aborigine Hunting

Tourists to Western Australia are able to take part in the sport of hunting aborigines. These expeditions are most popular out of Kalgoorlie, up into the Western Desert. At night an Aborigine caught in the glare of a jeep's headlights makes an easy target and the sight of one or two tied to a fender are a common sight by daybreak.

## Ayers Rock

Situated in Uluru National Park, this 350-metre high rock might be sacred to the Aborigines but it's deadly dull to tourists. You can walk round it from east to west. You can walk round it from west to east. You can walk up it. You can even walk down it. It changes colour during the day but then so does a chameleon and you can see them in London Zoo any time.

## The Great Barrier Reef (off the NE coast of Queensland)

Australians proudly tell visitors that this is the world's biggest collection of coral. What they neglect to say is that it's also the world's biggest collection of the venomous scorpion fish, the equally venomous stonefish, the not venomous but still quite painful box jellyfish and the not venomous at all but still very dangerous, shark. There are some sights in the world which are worth getting injured for, but coral is not one of them.

### DID YOU KNOW?

*Toilets in the outback can be as much as 2000 km apart, which is why Aborigines can be seen standing on one leg for days at a time.*

### DID YOU KNOW?

*Generations of Australian schoolchildren in the remote outback have been taught by teachers over the radio. To this day, many of them still believe that the country was discovered by 'Captain James Sqwaaak-Crackle-Crackle Cook' and that the first British penal colony was at 'Botany Crackle Bay Over'.*

## DID YOU KNOW?

*Contrary to popular belief, 'Waltzing Matilda' is not the Australian national anthem. It is in fact a rather rude song when you realise that an Australian's 'Matilda' is his pet name for his penis. To 'waltz it' therefore means something quite different to what you might expect, and the line 'You'll come a-waltzing Matilda with me' takes on a whole new dimension. In fact the whole song has deep hidden meanings, as a quick examination of the first verse demonstrates:*

*Once a jolly swagman (gay person) camped (minced) by a billabong (gay club) under the shade of a coolabah tree. Up jumped a Jumbuck (swarthy Greek man) and stuffed him in his tucker bag (colon), singing 'you'll come a waltzin' Matilda with me.'*

---

# AUSTRIA

Just as modern Germany refuses to admit it took part in any World War (let alone lost both of them), Austria vehemently denies it's the country where Naziism flourished or indeed that it's situated anywhere remotely near Germany.

The locals are so paranoid about guilt by association that the whole country goes on the defensive when questioned about even the most innocuous topics:

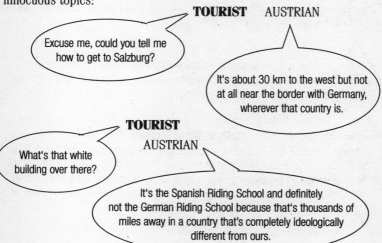

**TOURIST**   AUSTRIAN

Excuse me, could you tell me how to get to Salzburg?

It's about 30 km to the west but not at all near the border with Germany, wherever that country is.

**TOURIST**   AUSTRIAN

What's that white building over there?

It's the Spanish Riding School and definitely not the German Riding School because that's thousands of miles away in a country that's completely ideologically different from ours.

**TOURIST**

AUSTRIAN

Where's that beautiful singing coming from?

That's the Vienna Boys' Choir who sing in Church and don't parade in black shirts and report dissident friends and family to the Gestapo, I mean police.

Where can I catch a riverboat along the Danube?

Hitler was never Austrian, it's all a Zionist lie!

**TOURIST**   AUSTRIAN

This 'collective denial' is also evident in the roadsigns you'll find throughout Austria:

 **Deviation to the left** (and never ever to the right)

 **Cattle** and not slave labour being herded into trucks and sent off to the labour camps

 **Elderly couple crossing** (who might not meet the Aryan ideal but are still entitled to a long and dignified life)

 **Low flying aircraft** and not a Stuka divebomber, which was never manufactured in Austria. Whatever a Stuka is

 **No U-turns**, like retreating from Stalingrad in 1942

 **Danger** (and not a graphical representation of Hitler's genitals, who wasn't born here anyway)

**Vienna**

The only city in Europe to be named after a sausage (apart from Bangor, in Ireland, but that's spelled wrong, and Frankfurt which is bloody close), Vienna is famous for being both the birthplace of psychoanalysis and Naziism.

The *Sigmund Freud Museum* on Berggasse 19 is a must for the tourist and is easily recognised by the line of 20-foot high phalluses thrusting out of the paving stones leading up to the entrance. Locals claim these are just 'lamp posts' and likewise, the vegetation outside the gate is just a 'hedge' not rich, thick pubic hair and that button on the door is a 'buzzer' and not a clitoris, hard with sexual excitement.

Whatever the interpretation, Austrians love to witter on about psychoanalysis to tourists and, if you give them a chance, they'll talk the pants off you (and then tell you what that means). However, Freudian analysis is filled with technical terms that can be quite confusing. To maintain credibility, try and avoid the following commonly made faux pas:

Oedipus Complex - A modern art gallery in Paris similar to the Pompidou Centre

Latency - Closet homosexuality

Repression - The main feature of the Sandinista regime

Electra Complex - Luton's answer to 'The Metro Centre'

Phallic Symbol - Part of a drum kit

Auto eroticism - The car as a penis substitute

Libido - Where you go to swim and sail boats

If that's too dull, then the *Citadel of the Order of Teutonic Knights* on Singerstrasse 7 might be worth a visit. Austrians claim that this order was a medieval rotary club – one that just happened to adopt secret occult ceremonies, high-kicked marching, black uniforms and a right-handed salute.

### DID YOU KNOW?

*If you do happen to mention the war, Austrians will automatically take that to mean the Austro-Prussian war of 1866. And they proudly point out that they were on the opposite side to the Germans. So there.*

# THE BAHAMAS

The Bahamas used to be a rich man's playground. Nowadays it is so expensive that even the super-rich cannot afford to go there, and the only regular visitors are young thugs from Britain on a fortnight's rehabilitation holiday with their social worker at ratepayers' expense. Scandalous? Maybe. Still, before you get too angry remember that, if they weren't out in the Bahamas they'd be in your bedroom shitting on your duvet or on a daytrip to Whipsnade knifing small children.

The prevalence of British young offenders probably explains why the Bahamas has the fifth largest incidence of drug-related offences, the second highest rate of theft and the second highest murder rate in the world, as well as a huge problem with alcohol abuse. It certainly explains why every car in the Bahamas is either on fire or upside down in a ditch.

The Bahaman authorities turn a blind eye to transgressions by their visitors, because they bring in much needed cash. A tube of glue costs nearly £90, while a Stanley knife can sell for over £300 in the street markets – so there is big money at stake.

If you want to visit the Bahamas, try putting an 83-year-old in intensive care or setting fire to Nottingham city centre. If you get let off with a warning, try again until the authorities have no option but to send you on an all expenses paid luxury holiday. You will never be able to afford to visit the place yourself. Last year they deported Donald Trump for vagrancy.

Most visitors to the islands just like to lie around on the splendid sandy beaches with a plastic bag full of UHU over their heads and a slow trail of dribble running down their Fred Perry tops. More active types can look forward to a host of other activities including smashing shop windows, pissing in people's gardens and fighting. Organised gang fights and stabbing incidents are laid on at most five star hotels for guests. Check before you go. The most popular hotel for Brits to stay at is the Five Star

Paul Gascoigne on Grand Bahama, which prides itself on catering for the very lowest forms of human behaviour. The Hotel Vinnie Jones on Long Island is also popular, as synchronised swearing is held around the pool every morning, and its staff are remarkably easy to duff up.

*Most of the native population can be found in the upland mountain areas, hiding.*

# BANGLADESH

Whoever it was that said that 'no good deed ever goes unpunished' need look no further than Bangladesh to prove their case.

To say that Western aid has completely transformed Bangladesh is an understatement. The influence of aid programmes has made this country one of the strangest on earth. Because of the damage they have done, the media in Britain have not reported the appalling after-effects of their meddling but the tourist visitor will soon become all too aware of the cultural chaos gripping one of the most densely populated lands on earth.

Nominally a Moslem country, the vast majority of Bangladeshis have learned over the years to turn to the West for help and comfort and now instead worship the holy trinity of Peter Purves, Valerie Singleton and John Noakes. Minarets that once echoed with the wails of the Immam calling the faithful to prayer now resound with the *Blue Peter* theme five times a day, calling the faithful carrying cases out of old seed trays and elastic bands to come and assemble Action Man.

Fundamentalist *Blue Peter* worship has now firmly taken hold in the country. Failing to face the West twice a day while doing things with sticky-back plastic and chanting 'Danshep, Danshep' is an offence punishable by death, while it is considered incumbent upon every Bangladeshi to find tortoises and put them into cardboard boxes full of straw, wherever they might be. The most popular children's names are now Shep, Goldie and Petra.

The teachings of *Blue Peter* are spread by word of mouth. In particular, The parable of Bleep and Booster is very popular (although not widely understood).

In the superstitious rural areas (which accounts for 99 per cent of Bangladesh – there are only three cities and two of those are partially submerged), if you are young, white and look like a twit, you may find yourself being worshipped as a '*Blue Peter* Presenter'. *Blue Peter* presenters are said to have power over all the beasts, particularly kittens and golden retrievers, the ability to summon up massed marching bands out of thin air and can make time stand still so that it still appears to be the 1970s.

If mistaken for a '*Blue Peter* Presenter', you may even be invited to marry the local headman's daughter. Do not give in to temptation. Your hosts, although friendly and respectful, will expect you to bungee jump, abseil, handle large poisonous reptiles and recount the origin of the Cub Scout movement.

If you have won a *Blue Peter* badge, take it with you. You will be regarded as a most faithful and holy man and wherever you go people will carry your bags (and not run off with them).

Aside from the obvious cultural havoc wrought upon the country by successive *Blue Peter* appeals, deep environmental scars have also appeared on the landscape. The countryside is now littered with vast mountain ranges of old milk bottle tops, Christmas cards and keys dutifully despatched from Britain, which no Bangladeshi has any idea what to do with.

If a Bangladeshi says to you 'Mount Lesley Judd', for example, they are not making an obscene suggestion but pointing out a 40,000 foot snow-capped peak of old odd socks which has rendered several thousand square miles downwind completely uninhabitable. Despite their unsightliness, most of these rubbish tips are regarded as holy places and pilgrimages are made to them by the devout twice a year. Some travel from as far as a thousand miles away on foot to pay their respects and stay squatting on the keys or bottle tops for at least a week, humming the *Blue Peter* theme all the time. This is enough to drive most tourists insane and you are well advised to stay away.

**ALSO BE WARNED.** The west of Bangladesh is not safe for tourists as it is in the midst of a civil war between ruling *Blue Peter* worshippers and a heretical splinter group who follow the ways of *Magpie* and the teachings of Susan Stranks, Mick Robertson and Tony Bastable.

Finally, it will be very evident to any tourist that apart from *Blue Peter*, the BBC itself has also had a very powerful influence on Bangladeshi business. Wages are starvation level, no-one has a clue what they're doing and the top slogan of Bangladeshi industry is, for some reason, 'we hate the Tories'.

# BARBADOS

*'Oh, I'm going to Barbados' starts the popular song.*

Not if you've got any sense you're not.

The Barbadians are more British than the British. They have always modelled themselves on us. For many years, this meant drinking afternoon tea with an almost religious fervour, playing cricket and being polite. Now it means routine knifings, filthy streets and an addiction to *Neighbours*.

The once sparkling beaches are now smeared with dog's muck and embedded with lolly sticks, Coke cans and used condoms. Expensive changes to the island's sewer system have been made to ensure that the effluent now ends up on the beaches and not out to sea. Calypso rhythms have been replaced by Radio 1 blaring out over poor-quality speakers on the beach fronts.

Popular beach sports now include picking fights, pissing in the water and seeing who can play their radio the loudest.

*Traditional Barbadian shops are now a thing of the past. In the capital, Bridgetown, every fourth shop is a Halfords or a Mr Byrite and it is next to impossible to buy something that you couldn't find in even the dreariest English market town.*

Hotels have now become far more expensive and the staff have undergone rigorous training to destroy any last vestiges of their natural politeness and courtesy. Training courses for hotel staff last for fourteen days and include a half day devoted to the shrug and a further day and a half devoted to the supercilious sneer. Staff are also trained how to deliver the incorrect morning newspaper, ignore 'do not disturb' signs and get your bill entirely wrong.

Quite rightly, this has put many holidaymakers off. Why should they travel thousands of miles when they could get exactly the same thing in Great Yarmouth?

Barbadian authorities are aware of the problem, and questions have been raised in the Barbados parliament (in exchange for cash). With no cultural identity of their own though, it is difficult for Barbados to stop emulating all things British. This problem will correct itself when British culture is itself swallowed up by Europe, at which point the Barbadians will probably suddenly find Jerry Lewis funny, lose all musical taste and start trawling in other people's fishing grounds.

# BELGIUM

As empty, hollow and lacking as any Queen lyric, Belgium is every bit as boring as you feared it might be when you decided 'to go somewhere a bit unusual this year'.

Why Belgium is soooo boring is an easy question to answer: it's full of Belgians. Were it full of Spaniards it would be different. It would be lively. Smelly, but lively. Then of course, it wouldn't be Belgium. It would be Spain, so further speculation down this avenue is pointless.

Why Belgians as a people are so tedious is another question altogether. They do not think themselves dull but, to outsiders, they appear as a race of ambulatory coma patients. Belgians seem to thrive on the boring, grey and uninteresting, which is why Brussels is home to the European Community and its attendant bureaucracy. The EC seems to have captured their collective imagination − such as it is − and made them among its leading proponents.

Enough about the Belgians, because there really isn't much more to say. What about the country itself? Belgium is largely flat and featureless, like its population, and contains several cities which can be enjoyed with the lowest of expectations. In the port cities of Ostend or Zeebrugge, for example, you can find some amusement in viewing the containerised goods of all nations, while Antwerp is a city favoured by lovers with no romantic streak. Brussels is OK if you have a good book, and Bruges is fine if you want to go to bed early and catch up on your sleep.

Belgium is definitely not geared up for tourists. However, despite this, the country can boast a number of small tourist attractions which are well worth a miss. These include:

### EURO-CHOCOLATE WORLD
The story of the European Community, told in chocolate. Crowded in winter. Closed in high season when exhibits melt and go all white and blotchy.

School parties and unaccompanied children have recently been banned after an unfortunate incident in which Jacques Poo got licked.

Look out for the 'Parade of Praline Presidents', probably the only confectionary-based celebration of senior statesmen in the world. The rendition of the Maastricht Treaty made from noisette whirl is also worth a look, unless it's a hot day when the text becomes illegible.

## RADIO RADIO
The world's largest (and most frequently ignored) collection of radiograms.

## THE COMFY CHAIR MUSEUM
Armchairs and recliners from all over the world, lovingly reupholstered and gathering dust in a museum complex no-one ever goes to. Currently hosting the 'World of Chintz 1896–1914' exhibition, which you should be paid to see.

## WINDOWBOX GARDEN FESTIVAL
The best of Belgian windowbox floral displays. Belgians lead the world in windowbox displays, mainly because no-one else can be bothered. Well worth visiting if it's raining outside and there's nowhere else to shelter.

## MUSEE DE HURDY–GURDY
The world's nastiest musical instrument, celebrated with genuine examples, audio-visual displays, performance theatre and *son et lumière*. Someone has too much money. A popular destination for tourists who don't know what a hurdy-gurdy is.

## TIN TIN LAND
A celebration of Belgium's most famous cartoon character, bringing his vaguely exciting adventures to life. Tin Tin lookalikes – ridiculous teenagers with even more ridiculous and heavily lacquered quiffs – roam the park begging you to take their photograph, while children ask, 'who's Tin Tin? Is he a Power Ranger?' Watch out for the Snoweys. They bite.

## HOSEPIPE WORLD
Long, short, old, new, green, blue – they're all here. A comprehensive collection of Belgium's favourite gardening utensil from the nineteenth century to the modern day. All that's missing are the visitors. A new extension – Sprinkler 2000 – is currently under construction.

## BELGIUM HALL OF FAME
A celebration of great Belgians past and present. Allow at least seven seconds for your visit.

# BOTSWANA

*Move over Las Vegas – here comes Botswana!*

At least, that's how the advertising from the newly established Botswanan Tourist Board reads. (Actually, they've mispelled 'Las Vegas' – and 'Move', 'over', 'here', 'comes' and 'Botswana', but that's what they mean.)

Firmly in the shadow of its more opulent neighbour South Africa, Botswana is desperate to attract foreign tourists and the money they bring. However, being a seriously dull country with nothing to offer even the most undemanding of holidaymakers, it has recently decided to turn itself into one huge gambling paradise in an effort to tempt the world's high rollers away from Las Vegas and Sun City.

Botswana cannot hope to match Las Vegas for its opulence and gaudy spectacle. There is no electric light, for one thing, and the hotels are altogether less lavish affairs. You can stay at Caesar's Hut, which is remarkably similar to its Las Vegas counterpart except that it's made of mud and sleeps four (less in the lambing season) or a number of other luxury hotels-cum-casinos-cum-agricultural-fertiliser storehouses lining 'the strip', where licensed gambling goes on all day and all night.

Sadly, Botswana also cannot afford the roulette wheels, croupier's card tables, slot machines, dice or packs of playing cards so prevalent in the West. Botswanan ingenuity, however, has found a way around the problem by replacing Las Vegas style games of chance with ones requiring less specialised equipment.

Now, big time gamblers from the West can challenge a croupier to a game of 'paper, scissors, rock' (this is an easy game to win, because most Botswanans are unfamiliar with paper and scissors) or play in a high stakes game of 'Simon says' or 'pin the tail on the donkey'.

If you intend to visit Botswana to gamble, our advice is not to waste your money on 'I-spy'. The game is played in Bantu and you will never guess that 'something beginning with M' is in fact the sky. You should also avoid 'musical chairs', as in high season there can be a long queue to get a game, since there are only five chairs in Botswana and one of those collapses if you sit on it.

If you do want to gamble, 'charades' is your safest bet. Put your money down when the movie category appears. It's a sure thing that the mime is *Those Magnificent Men in Their Flying Machines* as this is the only movie ever to be shown in Botswana.

---

*Note that, according to Bantu tradition, gamblers on a lucky streak are considered to be possessed by the devil. After three consecutive wins you will see your croupier flee in terror, waving his arms above his head. You will get your winnings, but an exorcism is required before you will be allowed to gamble again.*

---

Just like Las Vegas, Botswana is also striving to stage top shows to attract the punters. Top of the bill is the Botswanan *son et lumière* show where, shortly after dusk, someone comes out with a torch and shines it around a bit (batteries permitting). Be polite and don't boo. He is trying his best.

The acts performing in Botswanan nightclubs are all household names (at least in Botswana). While the nation cannot afford David Copperfield, it did manage to briefly stage 'M'Bingo's Magic Ball' and 'Cup Spectacular'. However, this was abandoned after the first night as it caused all the waiters to flee in superstitious terror. Zele M'Tingi's 'Paper Doll Show' also came to an unfortunate end when he revealed his chain of paper dolls and was attacked by the staff for stealing their souls. Nowadays, Botswanan casino owners go for the safer bet of cabaret singers, who will thrill you with romantic ballads about the Impala. (If you are watching a floorshow, note that the lions are not part of the act. They have wandered in to see what all the fuss is about.)

Again like Las Vegas, the casinos all promise particularly cheap food and all-you-can-eat buffets. These are superb value, but may be suspended during periods of drought or locust blight.

### DID YOU KNOW?
*Avoid anywhere signposted 'Craps'.*
*This is not the popular dice game, but an emergency room for visitors who have eaten local delicacies.*

# BRAZIL

They say there's an awful lot of coffee in Brazil. There's also an awful lot of nuts. Thankfully, these are mainly British pop stars out hugging trees in the depths of the Amazon. Brazilians themselves are a remarkably sane and pragmatic people, notwithstanding that they choose to speak Portuguese and think doing the bossa nova is not embarrasing.

They know that the only way out of the terrible poverty gripping this huge country is to plough down the Amazon jungle – and no super-rich Geordie plank who can do it for eight hours at a stretch is going to tell them any different.

Amazonia is one of the most important places on earth, as it supplies almost half the world's supply of oxygen. It also supplies almost three-quarters of the world's self-assembly shelving, fitted kitchens and mahogany-finish wardrobes, which bring in far more money to the Brazilian treasury than fresh air…

In the early 1980s, a compromise was attempted. Development in Amazonia would be halted and the area preserved as a tourist attraction to help offset the losses to the furniture industry. This failed, because the Amazon is singly the most boring place on earth. There are 18,000 different species of trees and plants, the overwhelming majority of which all look green and totally unremarkable to the naked eye. If you like trees, you will be in heaven here. If not, you will join the vast majority of tourists who give it a miss. Ten out of ten for the conservationists for trying to attract visitors, with such noble projects as 'Tree World', 'Shrubland Fun Park' and 'Vine and Creeper Wonderland' – but it's no go. Amazonia is also not the place to go if you have hay fever, as pollen allergies are the second biggest cause of death here after boredom.

The furniture barons have now set about raping and pillaging Amazonia with a vengeance. Local tribes are either bribed off their traditional land with the promise of a sideboard, or simply bulldozed out of the way when they try to hold out for matching cupboards. Southern Amazonia is in the grip of bloody 'Credenza Wars' between rival manufacturers while 'Footstool Warlords' have carved up much of the western territories. The brutal use of 'traditional finish toilet seat killings' keep the natives there in check.

For tourists, Brazil usually only means one thing – Rio. And, more specifically, Rio during carnival, when everyone gets drunk enough to enjoy the Samba. The Rio Carnival has proved so popular a tourist attraction that it has now been extended for a further week. Avoid the second week of carnival though, when Alka-Seltzer replaces rum as the drink of choice and any samba band insensitive enough to start up is unceremoniously stoned by hung-over revellers.

You would be well advised to stay sober and keep your wits about you during carnival, as Rio is one of the most dangerous and crime-ridden cities on earth. Criminals are everywhere you look. Note the large numbers of police. They're all criminals for a start. Then there are the infamous 'street children', orphans reduced to fending for themselves in this brutal dog-eat-dog city. Every year these desperate children start out younger on a life of crime. Many steal before they can walk. Some are proficient enough to rob you before their first birthday (although these usually say 'ta' after they've lifted your wallet and are easily apprehended before they can toddle off into an alley). It is hard not to feel sorry for them — until one of them knifes you in the kidneys.

The other big criminal element in Rio is comprised of the ex-pat British contingent of bank robbers on the run. You can easily spot them because they all look like Phil Collins, they all sound like Frank Butcher and they've all been married to Barbara Windsor. They are generally friendly towards British tourists and are desperate for news of back home. Watch out for leading questions like 'can you drive?' or 'have you got a tasty shooter?' as old habits die hard.

# BULGARIA

Bulgaria stayed loyal to the USSR for the longest time. This has meant that, out of all the former Eastern Bloc countries, it has taken the longest to adopt progressive Western attitudes and shake off state socialism.

Tourists visiting the country will therefore find themselves in a land where time has stood still. A country where the ultimate fashion statement is a pair of high waist tartan baggies and a stripey tank top and where the Bee Gees are national heroes (Maurice Gibb was awarded the 'Freedom of Sofia' in 1995 while Barry and Andy Gibb are both freemen of Bansko in the Pirin Mountains).

## Bulgarian Top 10: w/c 10th March 1997

| | | | |
|---|---|---|---|
| 1 | (1) | Stayin' Alive | Bee Gees |
| 2 | (3) | Movie Star | Harpo |
| 3 | (4) | Tragedy (re-entry) | Bee Gees |
| 4 | (8) | Seven Tears | Goombay Dance Band |
| 5 | (5) | More Than A Woman | Tavares |
| 6 | (-) | Jive Talkin' (re-entry) | Bee Gees |
| 7 | (9) | Could It Be I'm Falling In Love | Detroit Spinners |
| 8 | (6) | Native New Yorker | Odyssey |
| 9 | (2) | The Night Chicago Died | Paper Lace |
| 10 | (-) | Massachusetts (re-entry) | Bee Gees |

## ENTERTAINMENT

If you hate gypsy music then don't eat out. If you really hate it, don't go out. And if you really despise it, don't go to Bulgaria in the first place.

Bulgarian restaurant managers labour under the misapprehension that all tourists love gypsy music and no sooner are you sitting down to a bowl of lukewarm boiled vegetables and dessicated black bread than you're assaulted by a clump of violinists and guitarists, all smiling inanely and wearing ridiculous ethnic clothing.

Before you've had a chance to take one mouthful, the band leader will approach your table and solicit requests (and a big tip). It is considered bad manners to decline this offer, although you might want to consider this traditionally understood response: 'Fuck off gippo.'

*How to spot the difference between genuine gypsy musicians (like you find in Bulgaria) and other gypsies (like you find at fairgrounds)*

GENUINE GYPSY MUSICIANS
Play the fiddle

OTHER GYPSIES
Are on the fiddle

---

GENUINE GYPSY MUSICIANS
Claim to be direct descendants of fourteenth-century gypsy musicians

OTHER GYPSIES
Claim the dole

---

GENUINE GYPSY MUSICIANS
Travel around the country in small caravans with a wood burning stove

OTHER GYPSIES
Travel around the country in £20,000 motorhomes
with satellite TV

---

GENUINE GYPSY MUSICIANS
Keep time

OTHER GYPSIES
Do time

---

GENUINE GYPSY MUSICIANS
Have a natural ability to change time signatures

OTHER GYPSIES  Have a natural ability to change their own signature
(especially when they're down at the DSS)

---

GENUINE GYPSY MUSICIANS
Keep the beat

OTHER GYPSIES  Keep a vicious Alsatian-brown bear cross breed

---

GENUINE GYPSY MUSICIANS
Can read music

OTHER GYPSIES  Can't read

---

GENUINE GYPSY MUSICIANS
Are pains in the arse, accosting you at the table for a request

OTHER GYPSIES  Are pains in the arse, accosting you in the street
to sell you lucky heather

---

GENUINE GYPSY MUSICIANS
If you cross them, they'll invoke an old gypsy curse

OTHER GYPSIES  If you cross them, they'll attack you with 4 x 2 bits
of timber and lengths of heavy chain

---

GENUINE GYPSY MUSICIANS
Can use a violin to steal your heart

OTHER GYPSIES  Can use a screwdriver to steal your car radio

---

## The Black Sea Resorts

Any place called a resort is just that, usually – a place you 'resort' to when everywhere else is fully booked. The Black Sea resorts are no different.

The resort of Varna is known as 'The playground of the Black Sea'. However, in reality you'd have more fun on a piece of council waste ground with a see-saw, climbing frame and a big foaming dog snapping at your heels. Being remote from the thriving youth scene in the capital Sofia, Varna and the other Black Sea resorts have developed their own social scene which includes cruising the promenade in a Vauxhall Viva, a sporty Hillman Avenger or even on a bright orange spacehopper. After a long day playing rotaskip or twister, it's nice to end with a milkshake or two, dancing the night away doing the bump, the locomotion or even the frug.

---

# BURUNDI

If you think that people in Chad or The Gambia are poor, then they're the Rothschilds of Africa compared to the people of Burundi. This East African republic has long endured its reputation as 'one of the world's poorest countries' (as described by the UN) and 'one of the world's shittiest' (as described by everyone else).

So bad was its reputation that it even underwent a name change in the 1960s in a misguided attempt to throw off this negative image – and get it nearer the front of holiday guide books. Unfortunately, unlike the successful transition from Marathon to Snickers, changing the country's name from Urundi to the rather unimaginative Burundi failed to convince the rest of the world that it had a new, revitalised and growing economy, and its stature (or lack of it) in international affairs has remained the same ever since.

Proof of its deeply-rooted undesirability is the eagerness of the colonial powers to get rid of Burundi almost as soon as they've occupied it –

even before they even had a chance of plundering its minerals. The only African nation not to be exploited by the white man and firmly left on 'the continental shelf' as it were, Burundi has endured over a century of looking on enviously at its occupied neighbours.

Today, Burundi is in dire straights economically, and would dearly love to become a colonial territory and not have to fend for itself. It even went to the drastic length of recently advertising in the small ads section of 'United Nations News':

**WANTED. SBN seeks SWN.**
East African republic seeks colonial engulfment, leading to full loss of sovereignty. Pleasantly located with imposing views over Lake Tanganyika and Zaire. In need of some refurbishment but room for potential. Hardly used by two previous owners Germany and Belgium. Would suit first time imperialist with GSOH. N/S preferred. No reasonable offer refused; all letters answered. Please send recent photo of your country. Box number F863, Bujumbura.

When it comes to entertainment, Burundians take a leaf out of Trini Lopez's book – but rather than hammering, they drum. They drum in the morning. They drum in the evening. They drum all over the fucking land. But especially when it's 2.00am in the morning and you're lying all sweaty in your un-airconditioned hotel room thinking 'Jesus Christ. Won't that syncopation ever stop!' Paul Simon may like the Burundi drummers (he featured them on 'Graceland') but he only had to put up with them in a recording studio for a few hours. For tourists, every day is like living in the speakers at an Adam and the Ants gig.

Burundi has one state-run TV station but so preoccupied is the country with drumming, that it pervades every aspect of culture. A typical Saturday night's TV line-up is this:

6.00    Pro-Celebrity Percussion

7.00    Metronome (chat show). Tonight's guests include
         Cozy Powell and Bill Bruford

7.30    Who's Rhythmic Counterpoint Is It Anyway?
         (drumming improv.)

8.00    Film: The Little Drummer Boy

9.30    The Phil Collins Story (rpt)

10.30   'Whooops! I thought You Said "Harmonic Timbre!"
         (sit com)

11.00   Eat to the Beat: cookery and drumming made simple

11.30   Bang Your Drum! Topical debate. Tonight,
         'Polyrhythms - Do they have a place in Burundi politics?'

12.00   Late night film: Backbeat

1.45am  Video Juke Box: Tonight: 'Beat It'
         (it's not about drums but it sounds like it could be)

2.00    Early morning movie: Carry On Drumming

3.00    Open University: Metrical Superimposition Module 58b

## DEALING WITH THE LOCALS

As strange as it might seem, there is a more serious threat to your health in Burundi than incessant drumming – the country's political unrest.

Burundi is blessed with three ethnic groups. The smallest are the Twa – which is not really surprising since they're pygmies and account for just 1 per cent of the population in numbers and 0.005 per cent in volume. Unless you're three feet tall, a shade taller than this but particularly weedy or have recently been abducted by Grays, there's nothing to fear from the Twa – although it can be a bit disconcerting trying to hold a conversation with someone who's staring at your groin. Don't worry. They're not cannibals. Whatever your feelings towards pygmies, you are unlikely ever to meet a Twa person during your stay as they prefer to stay in the bush and only occasionally venture into town to purchase a new pair of platform shoes or a stepladder.

The chief ethnic groups are the Hutu and the Tutsi, both of which have been responsible for numerous massacres in Burundi's volatile political history – most of which have been caused by someone taking the piss out of their ridiculous names. (Following the 1972 Hutu uprising, the UN banned the singing of 'Tut-Tut-Tutsi Goodbye', describing it as 'a gross act of provocation'. Unless you want a machete in the head or responsibility for a civil war, tourists are advised to respect this ruling.)

### DID YOU KNOW?

*Burundi's principal import is the drumstick. Its principal export is bugger all.*

## THINGS NOT TO SAY TO THE TWA PEOPLE, SHOULD YOU MEET ONE

Shouldn't you be in school?

Would you like a lollipop?

Isn't it past your bedtime?

Does your mummy know you're out?

## THINGS YOU'LL NEVER NEED TO SAY TO A TWA PERSON, SHOULD YOU MEET ONE

Haven't you grown?

I want you to join our basketball team

Heads down in front…I'm trying to watch the movie!

# CAMBODIA

Cambodia is a poor peasant nation. However, what the country lacks in wealth and sophistication, it more than makes up for in landmines.

There are estimated to be several million such devices still lying undiscovered around the country, as a legacy of its bitter civil war and the Vietnamese incursion. This is one good reason not to visit. This is also one very good reason not to consider a walking holiday here.

If you have to visit Cambodia, try to remain still for as long as possible. Stay in your hotel until it is time to go home. If you really must go outside, do what others do. You will notice 'trains' of experienced tourists patiently walking along directly behind a native Cambodian, in his footsteps, to ensure that he triggers any mine before they do. This is fine, as long as he is going somewhere useful, such as the bank or tourist office. However, he is usually just going home, and before you know it, you and several dozen other tourists will be in his house. Being Buddhists, the Cambodians are a very hospitable people and will insist you stay for supper, which will include nothing remotely edible.

Most tourists visit Cambodia to see the legendary temple of Angkor Wat, which is many hundreds of miles from anywhere. This is a daunting proposition because it will cost you an arm and a leg to get there, if not in financial terms than very probably quite literally. Stay in your hotel and instead buy a postcard of the damned place.

Cambodia is irretrievably scarred by the events of 'Year Zero' when Pol Pot's murderous Khmer Rouge managed to slaughter a million people who were considered intellectuals because they could write their name in the ground with a stick. (It is only a pity that these events didn't happen in modern day Britain, as casualties could have been far lighter).

Even though the Khmer Rouge (who incidentally gave themselves a French name in the hope that it would help them get more girls) are now a spent force, their legacy remains. No-one in Cambodia has an IQ over

75. Consequently the Kampuchea Broadcasting Company shows *Lucky Numbers* and *Wheel of Fortune* five times a night.

The arts have suffered too. Cambodian finger-painting has almost completely died out and Cambodian dancing is not what it was, with on average three-quarters of the troupe struggling to balance on one leg (sometimes between them).

As a tourist, you will find that you are a source of endless fascination for Cambodians – not because you are white or own more than one pair of trousers, but because you have all your limbs. Do not offend your hosts by ostentatiously counting them in public. Other frowned upon activities include clapping your hands together or crossing your legs. Indeed, as a gesture of politeness and understanding, you should consider hopping.

If you are unlucky enough to find yourself in a remote country region, do not give any indication of your intellectual prowess, as elements of the Khmer Rouge still operate there. Whistling old 'Bros' numbers and claiming you come from Essex should fool them, in an emergency.

---

### SOME SIMPLE SAFETY PRECAUTIONS DURING YOUR VISIT

---

Walk around as little as possible

Do not play hopscotch

If some child suddenly says, 'See! I have found a funny metal Frisbee buried in the ground', do not play the hero...

Do not wear glasses in case some wandering Khmer Rouge unit thinks you are an intellectual

Cambodians are mortally afraid of Sooty. Do not bring any Sooty-related materials into the country

### ESSENTIAL ITEMS TO PACK

Mine detector.          Tourniquet.

Stilts.                        Plasma.

Large signed picture of Jim Davidson
(to prove you are not an intellectual)

**ESSENTIAL PHRASES TO LEARN**

Do kok lik ta ko wa-shi-wa -
(Do not put your foot there, you white fool)

Wa chi do iama wu kok sak Buddha ko -
(You have stepped on a 'Bouncing Betty'. Stay perfectly still
while I pray to Buddha)

Diko lo chi wu kok wu hai? -
(Can it be sewn on again?)

# CAMEROON

Recently released ABTA statistics reveal that up to 20 per cent of visitors booking holidays to Paris never actually arrive there – they only think they have.

Now the scandal has been exposed for what it really is – a gigantic con-trick perpetrated by a desperate Cameroon Tourist Board and the French Government, who (for some reason) still feel slightly guilty about pillaging the resources of this ex-colony.

*Be warned, tourists are still being tricked today.*

It starts when gullible tourists boarding night flights to Paris are diverted. Instead of landing at Charles de Gaulle they arrive at Douala airport in Cameroon and are greeted by a huge banner that says 'Bienvenue a Parris' – a pretence that the Cameroons try and maintain for the duration of the stay, and would be greatly assisted if they managed to spell the name right.

Now, French might still be one of the official languages of Cameroon and the currency might still be the franc but, for the keen-eyed traveller, that's where the similarities start and end.

The Cameroons, however, have gone to a lot of trouble to recreate the sights of Paris in this pathetic West African dustbin. If you don't have your wits about you – and, let's face it, we are speaking about the French here – you may not immediately spot the difference. Here are the 'give-aways' to ensure you are not being ripped-off...

## HOW TO TELL THAT YOU'RE IN CAMEROON AND NOT PARIS

❏ The Eiffel Tower is not twenty feet tall and is not made from eight palm trees lashed together with ropes

❏ The Arc de Triomphe is not fifteen feet tall and is not made from three bamboo poles lashed together with a few more ropes

❏ The Palace of Versailles is not made from wooden tea crates and it does not have a hand-painted cardboard sign saying 'Palase der Verseyes' nailed above the doorway

❏ The Metro is not one of those trolleys used by railroad workers to inspect tracks, operated by rocking a lever up and down

❏ Bistros are more likely to serve mussels and oysters, not baked snake or fried grasshoppers

❏ Disneyland Paris does not consist of a plank of wood used as a slide ('Space Mountain'), a shopping trolley with three wobbly wheels ('The Thunder Mountain Railroad'), a cave with some bones in it ('The Haunted Mansion') or a see-saw made from a tree trunk ('Adventure Land')

❏ The artists quarter at Montmartre does not consist of a bunch of people naked apart from thongs and berets with only a tin of watercolours and a balding paintbrush between them

❏ The Louvre is not a mud hut containing a photocopied page from a book about Leonardo da Vinci

❏ The Champs-Elysées is not a dirt track lined with run-down souvenir shops selling leather belts, clay pots and wicker baskets, even though they might have a sticker saying 'I ❤ Paris' on them. Few cows are ever herded down this grand avenue in the genuine city

❏ The Cathedral of Notre Dame is not a squat toilet

❏ The Moulin Rouge does have bare-breasted dancers but they don't perform the cancan to the rhythms of 12 Bantu drummers playing in unison

❑ Despite what you might have been told, there are no piranhas in the Seine

❑ The Pompidou Centre is not a Portakabin with a vacuum cleaner hose glued to the outside

❑ Although it can be quite warm, Paris is never 35°C in the shade

❑ In the Cameroon-fake Paris, the drivers are considerate and the people friendly

## DID YOU KNOW?

*The most cunning trick perpetrated by the Cameroons is to dress up 80 smelly monkeys in stripey jerseys to represent Parisians.*

# CANADA

Now that the USSR is no longer one big happy family, Canada is the largest single country in the world – but, like waistlines, debt and boils on the end of your penis, it's another case of 'biggest' definitely not being 'best'.

Known as the 'Belgium of the Americas' – or 'that boring bit on top of the USA'– Canada is extremely dull. Compared with the US it has virtually no internationally acclaimed landmarks except the Niagara Falls – and even these have to be shared between the two countries. Instead, what it has is Tundra, thousands of square miles of it, along with some frozen permafrost and Arctic waste. Tundra excites no-one, so Canada has to go to great lengths to promote its other physical features.

Only Canada could call five landlocked stretches of smelly, stagnant water 'The Great Lakes' in a feeble attempt to make something of them and attract tourists. To their credit (and proof of the gullibility of visitors), the name has stuck, which is more than can be said for some fir trees in Alberta ('The Gargantuan Forest'), the hilly bits around Vancouver ('The Colossal Mountains') or the far north ('TundraWunda-Land').

To entice visitors to what are just large expanses of untreated water (and let's face it, a large expanse of water is pretty much like any other, no matter where you go), the Canadians have taken a leaf out of the

Scottish Tourist Authority's book and made astonishing claims about each lake. Tourists are advised to treat these with some scepticism...

## Lake Huron

This is supposedly the home of the famous Lake Huron monster. Serpent-like, locals claim it lives hundreds of feet down and only surfaces for a few weeks each year (which, coincidentally, is just when the tourist season starts). It has been photographed, but the fact that it resembles nothing more than some old half-tyres roped together and dragged behind a speedboat is, we are told, nothing but a strange coincidence of evolution.

## Lake Superior

Locals warn visitors not to go too near to the water's edge, for this is where the 'Creature from Lake Superior' lives. Some think it to be the last survivor from a race of hideously mutated half-fish, half-men with the power to shoot radiation beams from their eyes. Others say it's an otter.

## Lake Erie

The name says it all. Home to the terrible 'Erie Rectangle', claimed to be 25 per cent more scary than the infamous Bermuda Triangle. Tourists certainly seem to vanish – less than 24 hours after booking into their hotels.

## Lake Michigan

This is the gateway to the Lost Continent of Atlantis (well, according to the Canadian Tourist Office it is). Others not sharing this view see the Lake as a just another dreary place to fish.

## Lake Winnipeg

Beware as you venture on to this lake, for lurking in its murky depths is a giant squid, with tentacles two hundred feet long, eyes the size of a child's paddling pool and a beak that can snap through a steel hull as if it were tin plate. When pressed as to how many ships have fallen victim to this denizen of the deep, the man at the same tourist office starts speaking in French then slams the phone down.

## OTHER PLACES TO VISIT

*if you must*

**VANCOUVER** - dull

**LABRADOR** - lifeless

**NOVA SCOTIA** - uneventful

**CALGARY** - dreary

**OTTAWA** - prosaic

**TORONTO** - mundane

**NEWFOUNDLAND** - pedestrian

**NEW BRUNSWICK** - plodding

**MONTREAL** - full of French

### DID YOU KNOW?

*The Canadian police force are not all homosexual. They might be nick-named 'Mounties' and they might all 'get their man' but that is where the similarities end.*

### DID YOU KNOW?

*Posters proclaiming 'Canada Dry' are promoting a famous ginger ale. They are not part of a campaign from KY Jelly.*

### DID YOU KNOW?

*The famous 'Calgary Stampede' is a rush by tourists to get out of the most boring city in western Canada?*

# CHAD

Chad has no natural tourist attractions, so it has, quite unashamedly, made them all up.

Tourists in Chad can now visit the birthplace of Beatrix Potter (located close to the Gettysburg Battlefield on the Libyan border) or the grave of George Washington, for example. You can also stand on the exact spot where Columbus discovered America, or where Jesus had his fifth birthday party. All sites of world historical interest are commemorated with a mud brick souvenir shop-cum-latrine where you can purchase post-cards or catch malaria.

Especially worth avoiding is the fourteen-day 'In the Footsteps of Moses and James Brown' package holiday and the re-enactment of the Battle of Waterloo on the actual battlefield which, if the Chad Tourist Board is to be believed, was fought between two dozen apathetic cattle herdsmen with blunt sticks and a little boy sitting on a malnourished cow.

Attempts to lure tourists by this method have met with only very modest success (anyone that stupid goes to Malaga). This has not deterred the Chad Tourist Board. In the last few years, Chad has suddenly announced to a largely disbelieving world that it was once home to a lost race who vanished in pre-history and took all their architectural wonders with them, lock, stock and barrel.

The Chad Tourist Board is now busy selling the country as 'the cradle of civilisation' and offers package tours of all its lost wonders. All tours are overpriced and last considerably longer than necessary. Just outside the capital N'Djamena is the site of the lost city of Mpanza (now completely not there). Visitors are also taken south to Moundu to see the site of the fabled step pyramid of Ch'Bonga, which once stood where a goat pen is today, and the once-fabulous jewelled temple of N'Dingi which vanished, foundations and all, sometime in the sixth century BC. On an extended tour, you can also not get to see the amazing hanging cliff city of Dingi, famed for being absent, and the gold-encrusted Palace of B'Dongo, which was apparently stolen by thieves just the previous day before you got there.

The most modern wonder in Chad, according to the tourist board, is the 'Museum of Invisible Things' in N'Djamena Square, where all kinds of priceless invisible art and archaeological treasures are on display. Apparently. Definitely not for the faint of heart, the nearbye 'Zoo of Ghosts' is claimed to contain the largest collection of spirits in captivity.

Chad has also tried to capture a slice of the family market. For the kids, there's always the suspiciously mispelled Dinseyland Fun Park in Am Timan, where they can swing from an old tractor tyre or take the 'Space Mountain Water Slide' – actually an old tin tray that ends up in a crocodile-infested pool. Caring parents should take steps to go anywhere else.

# CHINA

The Chinese don't like tourists. A thousand years ago, they built the world's largest structure just to keep them out, and for centuries Beijing has remained 'the forbidden city', off-limits to 'round-eyed foreign devils'.

Today, little has changed. All tourists disembarking at Beijing Airport are scrutinised by the keen-eyed secret police, who will greet you with the incantation, 'Why you here? What you want? When you go?' In particular they are on the lookout for British TV camera crews sneaking in disguised as tourists and determined to film their abominable human rights travesties. (In fact, if you arrive with a packed lunch and less than fifty quid in your pocket, Chinese authorities will automatically assume you're from the BBC and put you on the next flight out.)

*If you make it through customs, there are two channels to go through: a green one marked 'Chinese Residents only' and a red one marked 'piss off' with deliberately slippery floors.*

Taxi drivers outside the airport are no more friendly. Tell them your destination and they'll say, 'You no want to go there. You want go home. I take you back to terminal. You go home now!' Persevere, and you will find that the state-run hotels are also less than welcoming. It doesn't matter if you have a confirmed reservation, you will be met with a stony glare by the matron behind the desk, who will tell you, 'We have no room. You go home. I call you cab. Next plane you go.' Get past this formidable obstacle, and the boy taking your bags to your room will turn to you in the lift and say, 'I take them down. Put them in cab. You go home now. No need unpack.'

Is everyone in China a rabid xenophobe? Of course not, but everyone you're likely to come into contact with is in the pay of the Chinese intelligence services, determined to deter you from staying if they can, and to prevent you from getting a look at the real China.

*Strange things are going on in China today and the authorities are determined to keep it quiet...*

If you manage to stay in the country, you will soon find yourself availed of a friendly 'official guide'. Make no mistake. He is not pleased to see you – that's a .38 in his pocket. His job is to make sure you never see anything you want to see. 'Why you want go see Tiananmen Square? Nothing there,' he'll tell you. 'No dead students. No people got squishy-squashy under tank. All made up. Capitalist plot.' Instead, he'll insist on taking you to China's biggest HB pencil factory to see 'glorious nib-whittling by artisans and patriots' or to the world's fifth largest pig-iron smelting plant to see 'honest sweat cross noble brow of fulfilled Chinese work hero who no believe we squishy-squashy students under tank'. He is almost certain to take you to see a child, proclaiming proudly, 'See, this is girl-baby. Parents love her. No left to die. See, we have girl-baby happy in China! We have dozens girl-babies. Asleep at moment, so sadly cannot see to check, but true!'

The one place of interest your guide may well take you to is the Nanking factory complex which represents China's leading manufacturing activity – producing hugely unstable and dangerous fireworks. Products like the Beijing Mighty Skyraider and The Chinese MiG Spectacular were banned in Britain until recently under the Trade Descriptions Act, but are now available again as the Chinese have agreed to change their names to more accurately reflect their performance. You can now visit the actual factory that makes the 'Nanking Finger Remover' and the 'Shanghai Blow Your Face Off' and 'Set Your Hair Alight' – if it's not on fire that day. Free samples are given to visitors and are the third most common cause of death in China behind coital heart attacks and too much ribbon waving.

If you can slip your 'official guide', try to meet the real Chinese. They're an interesting people, even if they do talk like cartoon characters. They smoke more cigarettes than any other race on earth. They also have sex more than any other race on earth. These two facts may be linked. All Chinese also share a love of gambling which may, again, be linked to their love of cigarettes.

The Chinese authorities are finally waking up to the huge problem of overpopulation and are taking drastic steps to sort the situation out – steps so drastic that Western visitors would be appalled if they saw the truth – hence all the secrecy. Peasants are now offered the equivalent of two months wages to have their testicles crushed between two house bricks, or can trade in their penises for new hoes at any government ironmongers.

Homosexuality is also being actively encouraged, and there are generous grants on offer to any man willing to work with fabrics. Posters of men in provocative poses are everywhere accompanied by official slogans that translate to something like 'Premier Dung Xiao Ping declares this the year of the heavenly man's bottom' and 'Just look at the sexual allure of this Red Army Ramrod, fellow men'. Accompanying this are wall posters bearing anti-women messages. Typical approved slogans say 'Dung says they're short and talk about shopping. Do not lie with them' and 'Breasts are catching, and by sleeping with a woman you may get breasts too'.

The most drastic step – and the one which the Chinese are most anxious to keep secret – is the introduction of compulsory masturbation under the slogan 'let's all pull together for China'. Members of the civil service and other official bodies are required to masturbate at their desks three times a day to relieve their sexual urges. Special breaks are provided, as are novelty origami tissues shaped like horses. This could be very disconcerting to the foreign tourist who just wants his passport stamped, so the customs men at the airport are trained to do it surreptitiously. It is lucky that their eyes look slitted and strained at all times, so the vinegar stroke does not become apparent. The Red Army is not exempt either, and regimented masturbation is an integral part of every parade (except during formal inspections by visiting heads of state). Ordinary members of the population join in too. Walk in the parks in the morning. You think all those people are doing tai-chi? Take a closer look. Or perhaps not.

### DID YOU KNOW?

*If a Chinese shopkeeper offers to give you your change in 'dongs' he is not referring to a type of coin. Severed animal penises are held in high regard for medicinal purposes and are as valuable as cash. Spend your 'dongs' before leaving the country, or you could find yourself locked up in a British mental hospital for life.*

### DID YOU KNOW?

*The Great Wall of China is the only man-made object that can be seen from space – although Roseanne Barr is catching up fast.*

## ADVICE TO STUDENTS

After Tiananmen Square, the Chinese Authorities are naturally suspicious of students. However, since no British student has ever been pro-democracy, you should find yourself welcomed.

# COLOMBIA

Colombia is a country in the grip of fear. It is terrified that it will one day become Nigeria. Where this idea came from no-one knows, but it is a fearsome fate to contemplate. If that wasn't bad enough, the country is also terrorised by the vicious cocaine drug barons.

The capital, Bogota, is exceptionally quiet. This is because the Cali and Medellin drug cartels have threatened to kill anyone who talks. Don't ask directions to your hotel, for example, because people are too scared to answer you and you might well be shot for saying too much. The only human sounds you will hear are thumps and deep baritone groans. This is because all Colombians also walk around with their eyes tightly shut to avoid 'seeing too much'. (The deep baritone groans of pain as they carom off buildings or cars are a desperate attempt not to be accused of squealing).

Many native Colombians also wander around with earmuffs on, even in the height of summer. This is so that, when they are questioned by drug lords as to what they've heard, they can swear on the lives of their children that they've heard nothing.

*Be especially careful if you are a university graduate. The drug cartels see anyone who knows too much as a very real threat. They recently assassinated the entire staff of the Colombian Encyclopaedia for this very reason.*

'Smelling too much' is not considered a threat, which is lucky, because that's what most of the Colombians seem to do. You'd sweat too, if you had to live there.

If you keep your eyes open, you will see lots of Americans everywhere, in smart suits and dark glasses. These are either CIA operatives or drug smugglers. Or both. Many drug-busting operations sponsored by the Americans have failed because the CIA have told themselves they are coming and have time to hide from themselves to avoid arrest.

*What a stupid country to choose to visit.*

Finally, be aware that UK customs officials are very interested in anyone returning from Colombia. You are certain to be stopped and have several customs officers and a drug-sniffing dog inserted into your jacksie to make a thorough search.

**TIP**

Never go for a ride on a mule.
A 'mule' is what the drug barons call someone who
smuggles drugs for them
and you could be arrested as an accessory,
even if it is just an innocent piggyback.

# THE CONGO

Like 'The Gambia', prefixing this country's name with the word 'The' gives it an assumed sense of importance – one that it definitely does not deserve.

Although you wouldn't think so by visiting it, The Congo is one of the wealthiest African countries – although, of course, this is all relative. A country where people enjoy an annual income of £62.50 and where the average life expectancy is 58 might be high by African standards but it's jack shit as far as any Western tourist is concerned.

*Apart from its high standard of living,*
*the Congo has achieved fame as a centre for*
*African music and art.*

## AFRICAN MUSIC

Almost an oxymoron, African music owes more to grunting and hitting things than it does to harmonies and a tune. The Congo prides itself in being the African centre of world music and the home of many fine artists such as Pierre Moutouari, Youlou Massengo and Tshala Muana. In Africa these are household names whereas in the West they just look like anagrams.

## AFRICAN ART

For most Westerners, art involves using skill to create an aesthetically pleasing image – it is not the ability to weave a cane basket or make a clay pot with two handles. Inhabitants of The Congo seem unable to distinguish between art and crafts and many tourists are disappointed when they visit the National Art Gallery in the capital Brazzaville and mistake it for a jumble sale, whose prize exhibits include the following:

❏ Some grubby rugs woven from smelly savannah grass

❏ Some mis-shapen carved wooden figures that might be a woman and child, a kangaroo or the Elephant Man

❏ Picture of an antelope painted on to a decomposing papaya skin

❏ Five carved wooden devil masks that resemble the Nolan Sisters

❏ Fertility symbol woven from hemp that looks like it's been sat on

❏ Bit of bark that looks like a bit of bark

❏ Clay pots that have never been within 50 feet of a kiln

❏ Room of Sandals

❏ Rafia table mats that are all curling at the edges or coming undone

❏ Some blue beads threaded on a bit of fuse wire

## DEALING WITH THE LOCALS

The first European tour groups to visit The Congo donated biros to the underdeveloped and underfunded schools in the country. Rumours of this magical writing implement from overseas soon spread throughout the country and even today, young children accost visitors with the cry of 'Any pen? Any pen?' Tourists are therefore recommended to stock up on pens since these can be useful not only as gifts for friendly youngsters, but also as useful implements for jabbing in the eyes of persistent nuisances. Adults love them as well as children (as a gift that is, not in the eye).

As a guide, a Bic will ensure your waiter gives you his full and undivided attention, a Platignum will ensure the maid cleans your room and changes your sheets every day and a Papermate to the hotel manager guarantees a constant supply of electricity to your room (health of treadmill monkeys permitting). Owning a Sheaffer or Mont Blanc will make you chief in some of the villages along the east banks of the Congo River.

## HOLIDAY ROMANCES

In the West, the attributes women traditionally find attractive in men are personality, sense of humour, a flat stomach, tight bottom, wealth and trouser bulge. In The Congo, size of herd is more important than size of either wallet or girth. To impress the girls, rich young Congolese hang out in the swank (ish) nightclubs, with their full herd of animals around them. (Congolese nightclubs really are cattle markets!) Others drive their livestock up and down Brazzaville's main strip, hoping to catch girls' eyes.

The more animals you own, the sexier you are. Someone with 90 sheep and 60 cows would certainly have a lucrative career ahead of him in hard-core Congolese pornography!

*If you've neglected to bring your livestock on holiday with you, forget any chance of a pull.*

# CUBA

After almost forty years, and despite all America's best efforts, Cuba remains as fiercely communist as ever under its leader Fidel Castro. Castro swept to power after a bloody communist uprising in 1959, spoiling America's attempts to turn Cuba into one large, conveniently situated brothel. Still, Cuba's loss was the Philippines' gain...

Today, Cuba would dearly like to attract tourists to bring in much needed foreign currency. Unfortunately, it does not have the first idea how to attract them. Potential visitors are promised spectacular 'spontaneous street marches by the gallant workforce', as well as tours of the Karl Marx Memorial Cementworks, The Vladymir Ilich Lenin Sugar Refinery, The Leon Trotsky Memorial Missile Silos and the Arthur Scargill offal-reclamation plant. Unmined beaches are few and far between.

There is more to Cuba than that. March is a good month if you like seeing fists punched in the air, while April is excellent for sporadic gunfire and cries of 'ay, ay, ay!' August is traditionally the time of harvest for the sugar crop, and is therefore popular with those who like to see muscular Latino men sweat a lot.

If you decide to go to Cuba, grow a beard first. The country is so poor that the beard is worn as a sign of wealth and status. No-one is allowed to have a fuller or longer beard than Castro himself, in case he is humiliated and made to feel less masculine. (Having got wind of this, the CIA sent in a team of Navy Seals to shave him in 1962. This failed because they forgot to bring any soapy water. In 1992, the CIA landed ZZ-Top at the Bay of Pigs in an attempt to inspire a beard-led revolution. This failed because locals refused to believe their beards were genuine and the unfortunate rock group were forced to flee back to their submarine under much pulling and tugging.)

Women visting the island are also advised to try to grow a beard, especially if they want a holiday romance, because Cuban men find heavily bearded women attractive (it reminds them of their mothers).

Cuba is also home to vast tobacco plantations, and fine Havana cigars are renowned throughout the world for giving rich men lung cancer. It's probably a communist plot...

**DID YOU KNOW?**
*The only thing ever invented on the island was the Cuban Heel,*
*a reaction to the Puerto Rican Toecap and the Cayman Odour Eater.*
*The Cuban Heel is now banned in America and anyone*
*caught wearing one can be heavily fined.*

# CYPRUS

Cyprus, with its long-standing tradition of deep enmity between the native Greek and Turkish populations, has a bitter history of violent and bloody conflict. On arrival at Limassol, you could be forgiven for thinking that hostilities have broken out again as you will see the bodies of soldiers lying openly in the streets. Don't worry, these are just British squaddies sleeping it off.

For many years, the island has played host to the British Army, who use it as both a staging post and a place to hold exercises. At any one time, most regiments posted there are engaged in combined manoeuvres, sweeping across the island from bar to bar. During the war games, tactical assaults are staged on simulated enemy positions, 'dagos' and 'anyone who looks a bit poofy', and a tank is considered to be 'knocked out' when its crew have filled the turret three-quarters full of vomit and driven it into a ditch. Whoever can remember his own name at the end is declared the winner (and then beaten up by his fellow squaddies for being a poof).

Because of the prevalence of British troops on the island, much of the entertainment has been set up to meet their needs. There are, for example, over 45,000 disco bars and only one bookshop. The biggest single event on the island, sponsored by the British Armed Forces, is the infamous 'Jack the Biscuit' competition. You don't want to join in – or even hear what it is.

Most visitors to the island make a point of seeing the passing out parade of the 1st Gordon Highlanders, held outside Tudors nightclub after closing time, and the inspection of the Royal Engineers by the military police for poppers and e's (Bailey's nightclub, 8 til late). Cyprus is also famous for keen performances of the military two-step, carried out shortly after a visit to one of the island's numerous Balti houses.

Avoid the southernmost part of the island which is a firing range, off-limits to visitors. Shooting, however, is confined to the late afternoon when everyone's got over their hangovers and can see straight. The Turkish side of the island is mercifully free of British troops, but then again there are lots of Turks there, so either way you can't win.

Cyprus is unjustly famous for its wines, which can match any sparkling Argentinian controllee for saltiness and lack of wit. The island particularly prides itself on a syrupy red which has the consistency of ketchup and the bouquet of a Turkish labourer. Cypriots have traditionally used their wines to fend off invaders over the centuries. This has failed to deter the latest invasion – by the British Army – as the islanders did not reckon on the undiscriminating palates of a horde of highly trained sixteen year-old car thieves from Essex who consume vast quantities of the stuff with no more ill effect than the occasional renal failure.

Of late, there have been moves to eject the British Army from Cyprus, but the economy is so dependent on the soldiers that it is likely to collapse completely if they were to pull out. Some 75 per scent of the Greek islanders are employed as bar staff and vomit sweepers, and they would all lose their livelihoods, as would the estimated two thousand emergency medical staff in the stomach-pumping unit at Limassol General.

**DID YOU KNOW?**

*Every shop doorway in Limassol is actually a public toilet – at least according to the British forces stationed there.*

**DID YOU KNOW?**

*The most frequently performed military tattoo on the island is the word 'Mum' in a heart.*

# DENMARK

*Only three types of people choose Denmark as a holiday destination:*

❏ those who want to see a live sex show featuring two blondes and a donkey called 'Lars'

❏ those who have lived all their life as 'Steven' but all along have felt they should really be 'Stephanie'

❏ those who are great fans of Lego.

This small Baltic peninsula, apart from being the warmest (and cheapest) of the Scandinavian countries, is as liberal about sex and sex changes as it is about the beer given away at the end of the Carlsberg brewery tour (see below).

## WHERE TO GO

### Copenhagen
There's a song that goes, 'Wonderful, wonderful Copenhagen' but don't get the idea that Copenhagen is stunning. It's OK as cities go and was only used in the song since it's one of the few capitals with four syllables. (Well, the song could hardly have gone 'Wonderful, wonderful Mogadishu' or 'Wonderful, wonderful Ulan Bator' could it?)

## WHAT TO SEE

### Probably the best Tourist Attraction in Denmark

More satiating than a night at the 'Bosom-A-Go-Go' club, there's only one sight worth visiting in Denmark and it's the Carlsberg brewery. Free tours take place Mon – Fri but there's a downside – before you get to the unlimited free lager at the end you've got to endure 40 minutes hearing about fermentation, distillation and a load of other processes that you won't recall when you're lying in your own vomit outside the main entrance.

## OTHER SIGHTS

Try not to spend a weekend in Copenhagen, since that's when the Carlsberg brewery is closed. However, if there's no way of avoiding this you might choose to visit one of the following:

### The Little Mermaid

This bronze statue overlooking the harbour is based on a Hans Christian Andersen character, but it's nowhere as sexy as the Disney interpretation with her flame hair, tight buns and pert breasts. The statue has come to symbolise Copenhagen. If you want to get a good look at it, see it at midday when the sun shines directly upon it, rather than late on Friday night when there are hordes of drunks just out from the Carlsberg tour all clinging to it and trying to give it one. Giving the Little Mermaid one is against the law, not to say quite sexually unfulfilling. (If you doubt this, and intend to spend lots of money going to Denmark with the express intent of shagging a statue, have a practice one with the statue of Edith Cavell near the National Gallery, or Arthur 'Bomber' Harris, near Parliament, before you book. Sex with national monuments is nearly always greatly overrated, and few people ever truly take pictures of the Pyramid of Cheops out of their wallet, elbow their mates and say, 'I've had that'. More say, 'I've been there', but they don't mean it in the same way.)

### Tivoli Gardens

Imagine Chipperfield's circus performing at the end of Great Yarmouth's pleasure pier and you've got the idea of the sort of entertainment on offer. Now imagine a down payment for a Ferrari and you've got an idea of the admission price. A juggler is a juggler is a juggler wherever you see one, and so is a performing palomino pony.

## Legoland

In the town of Billund, over two million plastic bricks are used to create a huge model village containing some of the world's most famous monuments and landmarks. Constructing the village took two thousand workers nearly eighteen months. Not so much 'how?' but 'why?'

## SHOWS

All the biggest Broadway or West End stage shows are faithfully adapted for the Danish audience. At the time of writing, in Copenhagen you could choose between 'Les Miserables' (featuring King Dong), 'Seven Brides For Seven Inches', 'Starlight Excess', 'Phantom of the Orifice', 'Greased' and 'Lots of Sex Please, We're Danish'.

# ECUADOR

People can take pride in their country when it's famous as the world's leading source of oil, uranium, gold, diamonds – even bauxite. But when it comes to balsawood, there's no credibility whatsoever – and such is the case with Ecuador.

The source of this 'wooden gold' (as it has been known to generations of aero-modellers) is the forests and jungles that cover 40 per scent of this South American republic. These forests are a utopia for big, hairy anti-road campaigners (who would love to live there) and big, hairy, poisonous spiders (who do). Apart from balsawood, Ecuador's other main gift to the world is mangrove bark and straw hats – products which the West is also, reassuringly, not reliant on.

## FIVE THINGS YOU NEVER KNEW ABOUT BALSAWOOD:

One man can lift a whole tree just by himself

You can cut 6" x 6" joists with a pair of round-nosed scissors

It's very good for making rafts

But not very good for making doors for bank vaults

Or bulletproof vests

Ecuador is so named because it's situated on the equator. Unlike the International Date Line, where you can lose or gain an entire day just by hopping over it, nothing as significant happens with the equator. Unless you count that bath water drains clockwise and counter-clockwise depending on which hemisphere you're in (and probably straight down, if you're exactly on the equator). While this, in some circumstances, might be construed as amusing, it is not a reason in itself to visit Ecuador.

## THE GALAPAGOS ISLANDS

These are located off Ecuador's western coast but are really overrated and not worth a trip on a dodgy Ecuadorian ferry. They're known as a 'living laboratory' but there's no sentient Bunsen burners, carbon-based conical flasks or centrifuges with a DNA helix common to ours in sight – just a considerable amount of old volcanic rock. Biologists rave about the unusual native animals here but they're not that unusual. The way the Ecuadorians go on about the Galapagos Islands, you'd think you were about to enter Jurassic Park. Nothing could be further from the truth.

Take the so-called giant tortoises. They're not giant, not in the least. If they were giant, they'd be 160 feet tall, and scaling the Empire State Building (a feat which would take them about three years), snapping with their beaks at aircraft, then retreating into their shells as the aircraft open fire, and falling off the side of the building. The creatures on the Galapagos Islands should really be called 'quite big tortoises' or 'overgrown terrapins' but 'giant tortoises' – no way.

Then there's the so-called 'giant iguanas'. When you use the phrase 'giant iguana', it conjures up something like Godzilla or some Stegosaurus hybrid. What you actually see is just a fat newt.

Just because Charles Darwin visited a place once, doesn't mean it's automatically brilliant. If this was the case then the Royal Geographic Society would be brilliant when we all know it's deadly dull.

## HAT PRIDE

When it comes to feelings of nationalism, most countries attach importance to their language, their monuments or their borders. In Ecuador they're more concerned about their straw hats. Ecuadorians are incensed that although this headwear was invented in Ecuador, they became known as 'Panamas' and it is not wise to rub their flat noses in it by saying things like, 'Call this a straw hat, it's not as good as the ones invented in Panama or 'If you invented it, why isn't it called an "Ecuador Hat" then? These hats might be useful in keeping the heat off you but there's a more than likely chance that if you continue to wear them on your return home, you'll end up looking like a wanker, a 1920's gangster or that umpire twat from the Yellow Pages commercial.

## WHAT TO EAT

When it comes to food, Ecuador is 'Fruit Central'. (An example of why English should be a universal language is exemplified by the fact that in Ecuador, lemons are called 'limas' while limes are called 'limones'. This might not seem important but if you were violently allergic to limes (or lemons) – like one bite paralysed you from the feet up – you might think twice about visiting the country).

Ecuadorians love their soups as well, but in the light of recent BSE scares, one local dish to stay well clear of is 'yaguar locro'. If you're mental, and wish to try it then you'll be enjoying a soup containing the heart, liver, kidneys and intestines of a cow, sheep or pig. To make it even more appetising, the surface of the soup is sprinkled with the animals' dried blood to give it the appearance of dry animal blood.

When you also consider that the traditional delicacy called 'cuy' is actually whole roasted guinea pig, you'll be relieved that fruit (albeit misnamed) is so plentiful.

# EGYPT

Few tour companies offer travel insurance for visitors to Egypt, as the chances of being killed by an Egyptian taxi driver (either as a passenger or pedestrian) are extremely high. Their vehicles are among the most unroadworthy in the world, and a cab with seatbelts, tyres that have tread, brakes that work or an MOT that's less than four years out of date is harder to find than an honest driver. None of the meters in Egyptian cabs work, and tourists have to be on their guard not to be ripped-off.

### *How to know if you're being ripped-off by an Egyptian cab driver.*

❑ It doesn't cost £200 for the first mile and £400 for each subsequent mile

❑ The fare from the Valley of the Kings to the Temple of Karnak is not £5,000

❑ They do not have a personal letter of recommendation from Fred Housego

❑ They smile at you

## Cairo

If you do survive your journey from the airport to your hotel, the first thing that will strike you is that how strange it is that a nation whose ancestors built the Pyramids have no concept of how to build even the simplest of sewage systems. The city's sanitation arrangements are an exact replica of those used in London – at the time of the Great Plague – with waste flowing directly into the Nile. (It's only due to strong currents that the Blue Nile and the White Nile are not joined by the Brown Nile.) The reason that Arab women cover their faces in this city is not due to modesty or religion – they find the smell every bit as offensive as you do.

## The Cairo Slums

'Squalid' is just one of the words which sums up the Cairo slums. 'Pitiful', 'Desperate' and 'Worse than Barratt Starter Homes' are others that come just as easily to mind. Drawing heavily on the 'corrugated iron' school of architecture, with cleverly integrated breeze block and tea-chest influences, this area is home to over ten thousand Egyptians and makes Brazilian shanty towns (or student bedsits) seem salubrious.

## The Egyptian Museum

This contains lots of Egyptian artefacts but then so does the British Museum which is nearer and has better floors for sliding on.

## Nile Water Bus

There are only two requirements for travelling south down the Nile to Old Cairo; lack of any real sense of smell and the ability to hold your breath for 40 minutes.

## The Giza Pyramids

You'll find these to the SW of Cairo on the west bank of the Nile, and tourists are allowed to climb up inside the burial chamber of the largest one, the Pyramid of Cheops. Unless you have a penchant for the strong musky smell of four-thousand-year-old bodies – or can't be bothered to buy new razorblades – it's not worth the trip (not only that, there's no lift).

It is possible to obtain special permission to ascend to the very top but gaining a view over Cairo slums, several pools of stagnant water and a skyline broken by fires from burning tyres is not really worth the arduous climb.

## The Sphinx

Seeing the Sphinx is like having sex for the very first time – it's definitely not all it's cracked up to be. And cracked up is the right phrase – half-man, half-lion. All crumbling. The only 'riddle' associated with this statue is the question 'Why did I traipse all this way just to see this?'

## Memphis

This town is fifteen miles south of Cairo, but don't make the journey under the misapprehension that it's something to do with Elvis. The only king you'll find here is a statue of Rameses II.

## Alexandria

Once home to the oldest and largest collection of writings in the whole world, the original library was burned to the ground in AD 642. The subsequent replacement does not live up to expectations and visitors are likely to be disappointed. Among its 70,000 volumes there is not a single Mills & Boon, James Herbert or Delia Smith. Not only that, but it is singularly lacking in 'true crime', books about the SAS or the X-files. (The news-stand at the airport is far better.)

## Luxor

If your respiratory system lasts, you can follow the Nile southwards until you reach Luxor. This is built on the site of the ancient city of Thebes and is close to the Valley of the Kings (not to be confused with the Valley of the Queens, which is the gay area). There's so many ancient tombs and temples here, that the feeling you'll get is not awe and wonder, but one of *deja vu* – they all look exactly the same as any others in Egypt.

### DID YOU KNOW?
*Egypt smells.*

### DID YOU KNOW?
*Egypt is the easiest place in the world to pass your driving test.*
*All you have to do is drive between two sticks –*
*or give your examiner a packet of fags.*

### DID YOU KNOW?
*Every Egyptian you meet will have claimed to have fought*
*with Monty at El Alamein.*
*(If it's true, they probably started it.)*

# EIRE

It's said that there's no concept of *mañana* in Ireland – the Irish don't have a word to describe that degree of urgency. This is true. As a race, the Irish are so laid-back they make the Mexicans look like Germans. Eire is a country where everything happens at its own pace – where tourists can expect wake-up calls missed by 48 hours and breakfast-in-bed to turn up at 3pm.

The real reason the Irish are so laid-back is squarely down to a combination of heavy drinking and the fact that it takes them forever to comprehend any instructions they've been given. To the outsider, this delay in actually carrying out tasks makes them look like they're philosophising about everything. This is wrong – and alcoholism and gross stupidity should never, ever be mistaken for thoughtful contemplation.

If visitors can put up with a race that takes an hour and a half to watch *60 Minute Theatre* or have to ask who wrote Beethoven's Ninth Symphony, then there are a number of sights of limited appeal:

### The Blarney Stone
The town of Blarney is about six miles from Cork, and most famous for the castle which houses the Blarney Stone. The Irish believe that kissing the Blarney Stone will make them charming and eloquent. Since no Irishman is either, this proves the stone is just a slab of rock and completely ineffectual. In addition, since kissing the stone entails being held upside down by the shins with your head bent back you're more likely to gain a neckache and a mouth infection from the sputum of the previous person than any ability to be articulate.

### Trinity College, Dublin
Established in 1591, the university courses in 'Bricklaying', 'Drilling holes' and 'Tarmacking Front Drives For Cash, Guvnor' are held in high esteem worldwide. Since the 1912 Home Rule Bill, the university has offered degrees in 'Ambushing' and 'Evading road blocks'.

### Limerick
This city near Shannon Airport is where the five-line stanza of the same name orginated. The famous Poets' School (adjacent to the Customs House) is where all aspiring poets go to develop their skills in rhyme, rhythm, cadence and metre. The city also hosts the annual World Limerick Championship, of which the 1996 winner was:

*With piggie eyes and skin that's white*
*The folks from Ireland aren't bright*
*The ones from Killarney*
*Claim they've got the 'Blarney'*
*When all they are talking is 'shite'*

## Museum of the Potato Famine, Kilkenny

Only a race like the Irish could have problems with potatoes, the easiest of all vegetables to cultivate and requiring no special skills apart from the ability to dig a shallow hole and then go and do something else for the next four months.

Despite the fact that the deadly Colorado beetle was 4,000 miles away, the Irish potato crop somehow failed between 1845–48. Between these years, potatoes were in such short supply that those rich enough to have invested in them made a killing, while those poor enough to subsist on them, died.

This museum is dedicated to the famine and is naturally of limited interest to anyone. If it's raining and you do happen to go inside you'll see exhibits like an engraving of the last potato being dug out of a Kilkenny Bog (5 June 1845), a monument entitled 'Carbohydrate' made entirely from potato skins and a multi-media exhibition all about shovels.

## Leprechauns

Literally, 'little people', the Irish claim that these elf-like creatures can be seen all round the country, making shoes and sipping mountain dew in the moonlight. They also claim that leprechauns can show visitors where to find a crock of gold. There is a crock involved all right – but it does not contain gold.

## Bogs

Eire has the highest number of peat bogs in the world and Alcock and Brown crashed in one while making the first transatlantic flight. That's the only interesting thing about bogs.

## Food and Drink

No-one visits Ireland for the food, which is often described as 'simple' or 'hearty' – synonyms for 'meat and potatoes'. This is the Irish staple diet and makes holidaymakers yearn for the days of the potato famine, if only to force the Irish to change their menu.

When it comes to drink, stouts such as Guinness, Murphy's or Beamish are the expected accompaniment with every meal. The first time visitor, however, should be aware that a 'four course meal' is actually 'meat and potatoes and three pints of Guinness, Irish stouts are an acquired taste and visitors should prepare themselves by drinking oil from a freshly drained engine or creosote to acclimatise themselves to the flavour before partaking.

## Artists

Eire prides itself on the high number of writers and artists to have been born there and uses this fact to rebuff allegations of Irish 'stupidity', quoting artists like George Bernard Shaw, Oscar Wilde, Samuel Beckett, James Joyce and William Yeats as proof.

Unfortunately this might have been true up to fifty years ago, but today's crop, including Frank Carson, the Pogues, Sinead O'Connor, Feargal Sharkey, Patrick Kealty and Jimmy Cricket, fail miserably to live up to their heritage.

---

# EL SALVADOR

El Salvador has been an independent republic for nearly 180 years, during which time it has had 200 changes of government. Its rich political vocabulary has given the rest of the world some now well-known words and phrases including 'electoral irregularities', 'insurrection', 'power-seizures' and 'death squads'.

But if the people of El Salvador are forever arguing among themselves, they are also perpetually arguing with their neighbours in Central America. Since it's the smallest of these countries, El Salvador has always felt insecure and has continually prepared itself for invasion. To compensate for its lack of size (and political stability) there has long been a tradition of insulting neighbouring countries in an effort to stimulate a feeling of (misplaced) national importance. If you're travelling through El Salvador, some or all of the following jokes will guarantee a warm welcome from the locals:

**Q:** What happened to the Guatemalan who got a job sweeping leaves?

**A:** He fell out of the tree

**Q:** What has an IQ of 186?

**A:** Managua

**Q:** Why do Nicaraguans smell?

**A:** So blind people can hate them as well

**Q:** What do you call a handsome, intelligent man in Honduras?

**A:** A tourist

**Q:** What's the difference between Belize and yogourt?

**A:** Yoghurt has culture

**Q:** What do you call twenty Costa Ricans at the bottom of the Panama Canal?

**A:** A start

Political unrest since 1990 has resulted in sporadic civil war ever since, including tourists being kidnapped by both pro and anti-government factions. If you are kidnapped, the worst that can happen is that you'll be tortured to within an inch of your life, then decapitated, with your head left rolling about the street like tumbleweed – a warning to opponents of whatever regime happens to be in power that day. If you're really unlucky, you'll be kept alive a bit longer and will have to endure countless cups of coffee, the country's main export. Like El Salvadorian politics, this too will leave a bitter taste in your mouth.

## SIGHTSEEING

### 'El Governmento Perpertuoso' statue

Located in the town of San Vincente, this 20-foot high bronze monument was erected in 1963 in commemoration of the first (and only) government to survive more than 365 days in office. (All that remains today is the 10-foot plinth, the actual statue being kidnapped and never returned.)

A cut-out and keep guide for kidnap victims in El Salvador

✔ The key to staying alive is to co-operate at all times with your captors. After all, if well-respected Jesuit priests have been murdered in cold blood by the military, the same soldiers will have even less qualms about disposing of a lippy backpacker or two

✘ Don't claim you're related to someone important in the hope that your captors will be too scared to keep you. Claiming you're the son/daughter of an arms dealer, a senior diplomat, the Secretary General of the UN or a millionaire who likes devoting money to political causes will often have the opposite effect

✘ Don't insult el Presidente, the US Government, the Salvadorian military or the FMLN guerillas. It's likely that you won't know which side your captors are on. (Even if you do, they don't)

✘ Likewise, don't insult the national football team

✘ Don't carry anything that could be construed as vaguely communist. This might include a T-shirt with Che Guevara on it, a copy of *Das Kapital,* your collection of Nicaraguan postage stamps or last Wednesday's *Guardian*

✔ A kind word to your kidnapper will accomplish far more than the liberal use of the word 'dago'

# ETHIOPIA

Ethiopia grew out of the joining of the empires of Solomon and the Queen of Sheba – but for all this historic grandeur it's now an impoverished arid dump of a third world kharzi. It might be situated in the Horn of Africa but there's nothing remotely sexy about it.

Proof of its reputation as a hovel is that it's one of the few countries in Africa never to be colonised (not even by the Germans who were never that fussy). Ethiopia's main growth areas have traditionally been flies and starvation, neither of which attracted a large overseas market, apart from parts of Biafra and Bangladesh.

Successive Ethiopian governments since the Second World War have misjudged the importance of their country and – under the mistaken belief that it might be worth invading – have stockpiled weapons to prevent this happening, with a devastating effect on the economy:

---

## 1977

| | | |
|---|---|---|
| TOTAL EXPORTS: | £48.00 | *(12 carved giraffes and a clay pot with a broken handle)* |
| TOTAL IMPORTS: | £332,482,983.00 | *(26 Tu162 tanks, 15 Mig 21 aircraft, 56 SS20 missiles, new radar installation and a training video)* |

**£332,482,935.00** BALANCE OF TRADE DEFICIT

---

## 1987

| | | |
|---|---|---|
| TOTAL EXPORTS: | £28.37 | *(5 carved lions and a raffia fruit basket with a broken handle)* |
| TOTAL IMPORTS: | £457,622,382.00 | *(530 SAM missiles, 12 Mig 23 aircraft, 119 150mm self-propelled guns and a new runway)* |

**£457,622,353.63** BALANCE OF TRADE DEFICIT

## The People

With so much spent on arms, the Ethiopian Government has no money left to spend on food or health care, resulting in the lowest life expectancy in the whole world. Ethiopian men and women can both hope to live well into their mid-thirties, and many Western companies trying to exploit the Ethiopian economy for commercial gain have come unstuck.

## PRODUCTS IT'S NOT WISE TO IMPORT

Zimmer frames
Denture cleaner
Alzheimers disease medicine
Copper rheumatic bracelets
Incontinence trousers
Sholleys
James Last albums
Plastic rainhoods
Honda cars
Stair lifts

## PRODUCTS YOU'LL MAKE A KILLING WITH

Fly spray
Fly swatters
Fly electrocuters
Fly-bite medicine
Distended tummy medicine

### Falashas

Long thought to be the 'lost tribe' of Israel, there is a very small Jewish religious community known as the Falashas in the north-west of Ethiopia. Although looking like most other Ethiopians, Falashas can be recognised by their distinct pattern of speech:

You call this a drought? I'll tell you about a drought!

Oy! Am I thirsty!

Oy! Am I hungry!

Western aid? Smeshtern aid!

Flies? Of course they're flies, you schmendrick!

Ethiopians claim that the ancient Ark of the Covenant was brought to the city of Axum in the first century AD and that it's still there, currently locked-up in the church of St Mary Zion. Unfortunately, only the 'Official

Guardian' is allowed to see it, so this story needs be taken with a pinch of salt (if they had any salt in Ethiopia).

## FOOD AND DRINK

There isn't any. (Tourists are advised that strip searches at Addis Ababa airport are not undertaken to detect drugs - they're just an excuse to see if there's anything edible left in your colon.)

## ENTERTAINMENT

The best thing about Ethiopia is that due to the famines, Comic Relief celebrities are perpetually making documentaries or filming appeals. This means that at any weekend, if you go to any open-mike night at the local comedy club you'll more than likely see a bill containing Lenny Henry, Ben Elton, Jenny Eclair, Victoria Wood and Mark Thomas – and all for an entry fee equivalent to 2p.

# FIJI

Have you ever met anyone who's just come back from Fiji?

*Precisely. – **Be warned.***

The islands have remained remarkably unchanged since Captain Cook first visited them in 1774. The sparkling sandy beaches still look out over splendid coral atolls. The sun still burns down out of a vividly blue Pacific sky. And the natives still want to eat you.

A warm welcome awaits you at Fiji's main airport at Suva, where grass skirted islanders perform the traditional ceremony of greeting, which involves smacking their lips and chanting 'Yum!' Next comes the ceremonial 'weighing' of guests, when tourists are put onto huge bamboo scales and things are muttered behind their backs. Visitors should join in the spirit of the occasion, but never turn their backs on anyone carrying a large meat tenderiser.

You will also be asked to join in a general knowledge quiz game and be asked twenty questions. If you get more than ten right, you will see the crowd heave a disappointed sigh and then slope off home rubbing their stomachs and kicking at the ground. This is because Fijians are fully aware that eating brains gives them the equivalent of CJD. They make it a rule, therefore, only to eat stupid people.

Fijians have become extremely adept at promoting their islands to the stupid, culminating in their triumphant and bloody hosting of the First International Space Precinct Fan Club Convention in 1994.

They have also stepped up their efforts to attract the overweight and succulent. Fiji has now bid (unsuccessfully) on no less than seven separate occasions to host the world Sumo championships and if you wonder where Les Dawson's Roly-Polies have gone – ask the manager who sent them on their sell-out Fijian tour of 1992.

The visit by the then Duchess of York also ended in near-disaster in 1993. She was only saved by a quick-thinking aid who advised her that being asked to stand in a cooking pot with an apple in her mouth was not a traditional way of saluting royalty. Attempts have been made to lure her back to the island on numerous occasions since, as she fits the criteria of the perfect visitor so closely. The offer of free holidays, coupled with all the sticky buns she could eat and the promise of being invited to a native toe-sucking contest have failed to bring her back so far, but Fijians keep trying.

If you want to avoid being eaten while on your holiday, wear spectacles. Fijians take this as a sign of brains. You can also read algebra textbooks on the beaches, or consider purchasing an Albert Einstein disguise kit from a novelty shop prior to departure. As a last resort, you can also smear yourself from head to toe in 'Utterly Butterly' as no-one in their right mind would eat that.

Avoid the beaches, especially when the sun as at its highest, as the smell of cooking flesh can attract the wrong sort. Late afternoon, when the population has already fed, is the best time to hit the beach. At night, you can sleep safely and soundly by digging a pit and covering yourself over with palm leaves.

## SIMPLE SAFETY PRECAUTIONS

\# Do not accept an islander's invitation to 'come home for dinner'

\# Never let anyone baste you

\# If you hire a car on the island, never give a lift to anyone carrying a chainsaw and wearing a bib

\# Do not enter a native 'self-service' restaurant

\# If someone tries to lure you away with a Harold Robbins paperback, do not follow him

\# Never admit that you watch *Catchphrase* or *Schofield's TV Gold*

# FRANCE

France is only 22 miles away from us at its closest but, in terms of attitude and affability, Great Britain and France could be on opposite sides of the world (or in different solar systems). Opponents of the Channel Tunnel cite the fact that it might enable rabies to enter Britain. They are overlooking something far more virulent and terrible – it is already letting French people in.

As a race, the French are one of the most impudent, offhand and downright insulting people in the world, and many New York cab drivers visit the Universite d'Insolence in Paris (situated just off Rue de Remarke) for job training. This attitude is common to all major cities and will be encountered within minutes of arriving in Paris:

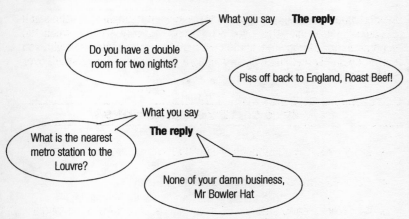

Even in rural France, the people are no better. Most visitors interpret the Gallic shrug practised by peasants as an affectionate gesture of indifference. It means no such thing. It's their way of saying, 'Fuck off'.

To survive in France it's important to be able to use the following two invaluable phrases:

J'en ai marre de toi!   I've just about had enough of you!

Va te faire foutre   Go fuck yourself

There is little else you are ever likely to want to say to anyone French.

## Misconceptions about France

The French see themselves as being the world's best lovers and chefs. However, this is just propaganda desperately perpetrated to hide their ineptitude in both areas.

## Why French men are lousy lovers:

❏ They spend so much time in the bathroom admiring themselves in the mirror that by the time they're ready, an erection the size of a French loaf has taken on the consistency of a croissant

❏ They hate getting sweaty since the perspiration will mingle with the Givenchy Pour Homme they are wearing and spoil it

❏ They are so busy worrying about getting emissions over their £650 Gaultier suit that they can't be spontaneous.

---

## 10 REASONS WHY THE FRENCH CUISINE IS AMONG THE WORST IN THE WORLD:

---

1.    Fraises de veau (veal testicles)
2.    Cuisses de grenouilles (frogs' legs)
3.    Pieds de porc (pig trotters)
4.    Rognons des venaison (venison kidneys)
5.    Tripes de mouton (mutton tripe)
6.    Congre (conger eel)
7.    Torte des escargots (snail flan)
8.    Tortue au miel (turtle with honey)
9.    Rognons blancs des lapins (rabbit's testicles)
10.   Cheval perigourdin (roast horse)

## SIGHTSEEING IN FRANCE

### Calais/Boulogne
Good for hypermarkets selling 275 ml cans of Stella Artois at 40p a go.

### Paris
The French claim their capital is chic, glamorous, exciting, stimulating, magnificent and charming. The reality is that it's dirty, crowded, shabby, dilapidated, noisy and smelly. And full of Frenchies.

## Cannes

This millionaires' playground has lost some of its cachet now that it hosts hundreds of conferences and trade shows each year. While the annual film festival is the most exclusive, visitors are more likely to brush shoulders with members of the 'Institute of Heating, Ventilating and Plumbing' or the 'Prefabricated Concrete Producers Association' than they are starlets.

## St Tropez

Topless bathing is *de rigueur* and that's the only reason you need for visiting.

## Provence

This place is so dull it's difficult to spend a month here, let alone a year.

## Dordogne

This is the DIY centre of France; the place where British families are conned into buying decrepit and condemned old barns and farmhouses and where they attempt to convert them into something habitable. The tranquillity and solitude of this region is therefore perpetually broken by the sounds of electric drills and circular saws, and swearing matches with slothful French plumbers for whom an appointment at midday Monday means 7.00pm Wednesday – and you'll end up paying an emergency call-out charge for that!

## BATTLES

The British have won more battles against the French than any other country – even the Germans. Tourists should ensure their French hosts show them around the following towns:

- ❑ Crecy
- ❑ Agincourt
- ❑ Oudenarde
- ❑ Waterloo *(OK, it's in Belgium, not France, but you could still make a day trip of it)*

### DID YOU KNOW?
*The 'French kiss' is so called because it carries lots of germs.*

### DID YOU KNOW?
*The 'French letter' is so-called because everybody hates them.*

# G

## THE GAMBIA

Inconsequential. Drab. Dreary. Unexciting. A mind-numblingly boring squat-toilet of a country. All of these adjectives apply to The Gambia, a West African country so dull that its founders couldn't even be arsed to think up an imaginative name for the country and just named it after the river which passes through it.

The country is officially called 'The Gambia' in a frankly desperate attempt to make this dump sound rather more important than it actually is, and to pretend to differentiate it from an imaginary other place called just plain old 'Gambia').

It's so dull that perhaps the single most interesting thing about The Gambia is that it has the world's funniest name for an airport – Yundum – and that's not very funny. There's also a town called Kuntaur, which is marginally mirthful – and sounds a bit like a very evil (and rude) opponent of the Power Rangers.

The ancestors of Alex Haley, author of *Roots*, originated in The Gambia, and the birthplace of Kunta Kinte is Juffure on the north bank of the Gambia river. Once you visit Juffore, you'll suddenly see what a happy story *Roots* really is.

The Gambia relies heavily on tourists for its economy. Tourists and peanuts. And if the tourists have an unusually huge penchant for peanuts, well, it's like all the Gambian Christmases have come at once. Today, The Gambia has become the best known West African package holiday destination for adventurous travellers looking for winter sun but who are bored with Florida, Spain or the Canary Islands. This is a mistake. Lanzarote in the midst of freak blizzards and temperatures only experienced by Scott of the Antarctic is preferable to The Gambia any time of year.

But let them speak for themselves...

# The Gambian Tourist Commission says:

'Hi. Big Number 1 welcome to Number 1 West African most interesting country! Yowza!

You hear rumours that The Gambia is boring? No sir!

## The Gambia guaranteed twice as exciting as dirty-dirty Chad!

Dirty lying monkeys in Chad! Straight-talking big fellas in The Gambia!

## Our great nation jolly explodes full of excitement day and night round the clock! You visit us and you be amazed at multiplicity of action! Bam! Pow!

We have roads, long and straight. Some smooth. Others not. But they join A and B. Marvellous!

## We have great river full of wet brown water. Splendid! – only in The Gambia. Why settle for common old blue type?

We have peanut crop plenty big. You visit peanut processing factory on day trip excursion. Best peanut processing factory in all North West Africa. 100% guaranteed! Remember camera to stop disappointment! Fine!

## Action stations! We have nightclub. Beautiful people dance and smile to hot sounds of Bobby Crush. Glorious!

We have roads, long and straight. Some smooth. Others not. But they join A and B. Marvellous!

## We have sun. 93 million miles away but hot. And very, very yellow. All day we have it. Wonderful!

So what you wait for in rainy country? You book holiday of lifetime to interesting The Gambia tickety boo!'

# GAZA AND THE WEST BANK

In the days of the *intifada*, Gaza and the West Bank used to be a dangerous place to visit. Today, with the Palestinians given a degree of autono-
my and having their own police force in place, the area is a *really* dangerous place to visit.

Gaza itself has nothing to recommend it. Absolutely nothing, unless
you are making a study of rubble for your PhD or something. There are
no sights, nothing of historic or religious significance and the town is
periodically rocked by large explosions as some arsehole in a tower block
gets his red wire and his blue wire confused.

The West Bank is more interesting and more popular with tourists who
don't have a death wish. Many people who visit the West Bank do so
because they wish to walk in the footsteps of Jesus. This is still literally
possible to do, provided you know what sort of sandals He wore, because
the Palestinians haven't cleaned the streets in two thousand years.
Nazareth in the West Bank is worth visiting, if only to come away thinking 'If I was the Son of God, there's no way I'd end up in a shit tip like
this.' Bethlehem is a depressing mixture of squalor and commercialism
where you can buy souvenir crowns of thorns and a hologram of Jesus
that winks down at you from the Cross. Overall, the value of the West
Bank is in making you realise that Israel is actually quite nice in comparison.

If you do decide to visit the West Bank, be prepared for a very different way of life. First time visitors will no doubt be shocked by the sight
of young Arab men holding hands openly in the streets and souks. This
does not mean that they are gay. It just means that they fancy each other
and are sleeping together.

Travel by bus. These smell and sometimes catch fire or plunge into
ravines, but are safer than the alternative. Whatever you do, never hitch-
hike and never accept a lift in a car from anyone. Accepting a lift from
another man is tantamount, in Palestinian eyes, to saying 'I want your
penis inside me imshi, imshi'. In fact the Arab slang for 'hitchhiking is 'al
el meschra', literally 'to bite the strap'.

Despite these warnings, you will find that Palestinians are a friendly
people who will often invite you to their homes to take tea. This is not
always because they want to hold you hostage or drug you and steal your
wrist watch. Sometimes they want to tell you about how oppressed they
are, which is just as bad.

## THINGS NOT TO DO FOR YOUR OWN SAFETY

- Wave a bank note in the air
- Call anyone with a gun a 'Kus-a-Merch'
- Hum 'Hava Negila'
- Say rather loudly, 'I think I'll build my settlement here'
- Pull down your trousers and bend over in front of a Mosque
- Pull down your trousers and bend over anywhere else
- Visit

## ON THE PULL

It is not worth going 'on the pull'. All Palestinian women look like Yasser Arafat in a dress. Indeed, that is precisely who they might be, as the PLO originally started out as a cross-dressers' self-help group. You have been warned.

# GERMANY

The biggest problem with Germany — apart from the fact that it still exists at all — is that the population has never recovered from losing the war. To paraphrase Oscar Wilde, 'To lose one war may be regarded as a misfortune; to lose both looks like carelessness'.

Even today, German thirtysomethings refuse to acknowledge what their fathers did between 1939–45, and when pressed, will cough, go red and say things like:

*'He was out shopping'*

**'He was at the library'**

*'He was looking for Atlantis'*

**'He was in a coma'**

*'I will only give his name, rank and serial number'*

The British Tourist Association recently undertook a survey to see just why people visited Germany and the results were as follows:

| | |
|---|---|
| I want to meet genial, good-natured locals | 0% |
| I'm taking part in a foreign exchange programme organised by my school | 24% |
| I'm taking part in a foreign exchange programme organised by the British National Party | 45% |
| I'm a Leeds United fan and I want revenge for that match against Bayern Munich | 11% |
| I want to see just what damage that 1,000lb bomb really did to Dresden Cathedral | 20% |

As far as sightseeing goes, the names of German towns and cities will be as familiar to all fans of war films as they are to ex-Lancaster bomber pilots.

### Düsseldorf

Germany's richest city means that it's also the most expensive (and a prime source for jokes about costing a bomb). The Altstadt is known as 'the longest bar in Europe' and it's here that you can enjoy a Himmler Wallbanger, a Tequila Krupps, a U-Boat on the rocks or any one of the hundreds of cocktails with coincidental names. The traditional toast is 'Heil Hitler', which according to the locals just means, 'good health'.

### Cologne

The fourth largest city in Germany and famous for its breweries and the annual spring carnival. The locals claim this carnival has its roots in the eleventh century and is supposed to represent fertility rites – although what fertility has got to do with thousands of young men goosestepping in unison and singing 'A new age is dawning; purity shall overcome!' is not clear.

### Hamburg

This city was burned to the ground in 1943 and the cause, according to residents, was a 'flaming meteor from the Andromeda galaxy' – as opposed to the real reason, 18 squadrons of B-17s dropping 200,000 tons of incendiaries. Still, the city has since been re-built and is most famous for the Reeperbahn. Unfortunately, this centre for prostitution has not escaped the German obsession with efficiency, and the issuing of these strict guidelines was designed to increase the throughput of prostitutes' clients, making their businesses more economically viable:

# Reeperbahn Rules and Regulations

Payment is strictly in advance and no refunds are available for impotence or premature ejaculation

✖✗✖✗✖

Condoms must be worn; the lower lip of the condom being no less than 90mm from the tip of the penis at all times

✗✖✗✖✗✖✗

No penis must be inserted within the vagina for more than 3 minutes 25 seconds

✖✗✖✗✖

If breast fondling takes place, users are reminded that this is a zero-rated sexual act and exempt from VAT. Please record the percentage of time spent in the manipulation of the breast and claim a deduction against your total vatable liability

✗✖✗

Pelvic thrusts shall take place at a rate of two every five seconds rising to a maximum of four every five seconds immediately before climax

✗✖✗✖✗✖✗

Noises directly associated with the sexual act should be kept below 45 dB in consideration of others in adjoining rooms designated as licensed sexual pleasure areas

✖✗✖✗✖

You shall ejaculate between 5 cc and 12.5 cc of seminal fluid of which no more than 22% (in volume) shall be semen

✖✗✖✗✖✗✖✗✖

Ejaculation shall be followed by immediate withdrawal

✖✗✖✗✖

Receipts for tax purposes will be made available on request. Prices are exempt of VAT for visiting EC nationals. Please submit a form 2/300 'Use of a Whore' for refund at your point of exit from the country

## Bonn

The German capital and birthplace of Ludwig van Beethoven. Each year since his death in 1827, his life has been celebrated by the 'Musikafest'. More recently, the traditional recitals and open air concerts have been replaced by the burning down of hostels used by migrant workers, which, locals claim, are just a modern interpretation of the event and in the exact same spirit.

## Frankfurt

The financial centre of Germany and also home to the country's largest art museum on Domstrasse. This gallery houses some of the best examples of plundered European art in the world.

## Stuttgart

Home of the German motor industry and *the* place to go if you want to see Turkish workers being persecuted.

## Munich

The capital of Bavaria and site of the largest cemetery in southern Germany. This is an interesting place for the tourist to visit because the graves themselves are intriguing.

Examining graves of anyone dying between 1939 and 1945 shows that the causes of death were very similar, reflecting once again the German inability to come to terms with losing the war:

| | |
|---|---|
| 'Tripped and fell down the stairs' | (37%) |
| 'Struck by lightning' | (23%) |
| 'Contracted salmonella poisoning and never recovered' | (19%) |
| 'Electrocuted in a freak hedge-trimming incident' | (18%) |
| 'Gored by bull' | (3%) |

## Berlin

Destruction must be in the German psyche because they even demolished one of the greatest post-war monuments – the Berlin Wall. The only other monument of note in Berlin is a destroyed concrete bunker just outside of the city which is mobbed by thousands of young Germans who lay wreaths in its ruins with messages proclaiming 'We pledge to carry on your divine mission A.H!' Locals claim this bunker is a 'fine example of 1930s reinforced concrete well worth a visit' and the A.H. referred to is none other than Anita Harris, the 'British Cher whose song and dance artistry has inspired a generation'.

## Dresden

Up until 13 February 1945 this was acknowledged as the most beautiful city in Germany. After that date it became better known as Europe's biggest crater. Don't go here if your surname is 'Harris' (unless your first name is Anita).

## Black Forest & Environs

One of the few places in Germany to be called after a cake (except for Battenburg, near Potsdam, Eclairburg near Bremen and Meringuesheim, near Munster), the Black Forest traditionally celebrates its links with the world of fondants and fancies by persecuting anyone different.

The principal town of the Black Forest region is Baden-Baden. Originally called Baden-Baden-Baden, the place name was shortened to Baden-Baden when Baden was completely destroyed in a daylight bombing raid.

## BEER FESTIVALS

No overview of Germany would be complete without a word about the many beer festivals held each year. Forty per cent of the world's breweries are in Germany, and the British are naturally drawn to these huge events, where they soon become so drunk they can forget which country they're in.

## WINES

There is only one German wine – Liebfraumilch. This is the cheap syrupy wine you drink at the very end of a party because all the good stuff's gone. Remarkable for its ability to taste cheap and unpleasant, even when you are heavily innebriated, Liebfraumilch is usually served at parties in an already used plastic cup with a dog end floating in it.

Liebfraumilch is not a 'natural' wine, but was refined by Nazi scientists during the closing months of the war, and designated the V-4 'Vomischenschaften'.

# GIBRALTAR

Not so much a country as an ugly lump of rock, Gibraltar is the European equivalent of Malta and you'll find it under most guidebooks under 'places to visit when you've left it too late to book somewhere good'.

The ancients are said to have built one of the Pillars of Hercules in Gibraltar and one in North Africa. They viewed Gibraltar as the end of the world and most tourists today would tend to agree.

Known affectionately by the locals as 'Gib' (and not so affectionately by everyone else as 'that tedious little polyp on the end of Dagoland) Gibraltar is a peninsula connected to mainland Spain, which actually belongs to Britain. This fact irritates the Spanish no end, which helps to justify its existence.

Even better, when a referendum was held in 1967 to ask the local population if they wanted Spanish rule the voting was 12,140 against - and 44 for...(and 31 of those put the cross in the wrong box by accident). President Franco took this rebuff personally and in 1968 he closed the border, cut off all telephone links and stopped the ferry from operating - effectively isolating Gibraltar entirely from Spain for fifteen years. The locals were delighted.

Tourists wanting to forget all about Britain when they go on holiday are likely to be disappointed when they visit Gibraltar. The police look the same, so do the pillar boxes, so does the currency and so do the High Street stores. The only real difference is that the shops are a little behind the times and stock produce which has long since gone out of fashion back in the UK. It's not uncommon for newsagents to still be selling Spangles, Amazin' Raisin, Super Mousse and Aztec chocolate bars, Cresta orangeade and sherbet dib-dabs. These are worth purchasing for the nostalgia value rather than the taste, as they have long since putrified and now all taste like McDonald's Fillet O Fish.

## Barbary Apes

These are the only wild monkeys in Europe and are supposed to have reached Gibraltar via a secret tunnel all the way from North Africa. This is unlikely since apes are not known for their dexterity with a shovel.

Other sources claim the apes were brought there by the Moors in the fourteenth century – probably as concubines – and that the creatures today are partial descendants of the original Arabs.

Legend has it that when the apes leave Gibraltar, the British will lose the island. This is highly improbable since no-one, not even an ape, is likely ever to defect to Spain.

### The Locals
Gibraltar's location means it's been a melting pot for Spanish, British and North African cultures. Corresponding intermarriage has resulted in a breed of local who's lazy, surly and unhygienic, and therefore ideal for crossing the border, gaining employment in a Spanish hotel and sleeping with your girlfriend.

### The Royal Navy
There's a substantial Royal Navy presence on Gibraltar due to its strategic position in the Mediterranean. The Turkish navy is also often in port, usually coinciding with the precise time when the Barbary apes are in heat. (Many Barbary apes now enjoy dual Gibraltese-Turkish nationality, as the ship's captain is empowered to perform wedding ceremonies. The bride usually wears white, to help tell the couple apart.)

# GREECE AND THE GREEK ISLANDS

One of the great mysteries of human development on earth is how Greek civilisation went from exploring the mysteries of reality and existence to flogging dodgy kebabs out of the back of a van.

One popular – although probably untrue – explanation is that all the greatest minds in ancient Greece were visiting the doomed continent of Atlantis when it sank. As to why they had gathered there, opinion varies. Some say it was a cheese fondue party of magnificent proportions. Others that a pro-celebrity philosophy competition was being staged and that Plato was devastating his partner's argument and proving that reality was entirely unsubstantial when he got hit by a 45-mile-high tidal wave. Others say that the philosophers had gathered to judge the annual 'Mr Young Atlantean Adonis' contest and that the sea god Poseidon was displeased because the one he fancied came third.

Whatever happened, Greece rapidly went from being the highest seat of learning to a country teetering on the edge of the Third World. Truly stupid dancing replaced Pythagorean discourse, and plate-smashing in grubby tavernas displaced building architectural splendours as the favourite pastime of the Greeks.

Today, Greece and its hotchpotch of 1,425 islands are a popular holiday destination for those who think they are too good for Spain. The Greeks welcome the tourists and their money (especially if kept in a wallet in the back pocket of their trousers) and do everything they can to rob you blind during your stay. Many holidaymakers have had their holidays ruined because of theft. Many have returned after a day on the beach to find their hotel rooms gone. Others have their entire holiday stolen, or lose treasured memories. (It is rumoured that 1948 was briefly appropriated by a gang in Athens, before police recovered it in a lock-up.) Never trust a Greek.

Still, anyone who hates the Turks can't be all bad.

## THE ISLANDS AT A GLANCE

### SARONIC ISLES

**AIYINA** - All right if you like goats (book ahead in high season as most hotels fill up with Syrian sex tour parties)

**MONI** - Not worth wiping your arse with

**POROS** - Two exquisitely dull islands for the price of one

**IDRHA** - The so-called 'Greek St. Tropez'. An odd label, as it doesn't have any beaches and reeks of spoiling fish

**SPETSAI** - You can walk around Spetsai in a day – but it's not worth it

### THE CYCLADES (WESTERN)

**ANDROS** - A good place to get your bottom pinched (women should take care too)

**TINOS** - Spiritual home of the tummy bug

**MIKINOS** - Popular gay resort with unofficial nudist beaches. What more reasons do you need to give it a big miss?

**SIROS** - A rock in the middle of the water. Fine if you're a basking seal, but most holidaymakers require something more

## THE CYCLADES (NORTHERN)

**SIFNOS** - named after the Greek God of unprotected sex. An unappealing name hides an unappealing island

**SERIPHOS** - Unpopular holiday destination since the word got out

**KITHNOS** - Popular with the Greeks. Unpopular with those of us who expect toilet paper in our hotel rooms

**MILOS** - Popular holiday destination for those who choose to spend their annual two-week vacation in a slate quarry

## THE CYCLADES (SOUTHERN)

**PAROS** - The pride of Paros is the 'Church of One Hundred Doors' – which should tip you off as to how exciting a place this is

**ANDIPAROS** - People come here to see a cave apparently (if you like dank smelly holes, Birmingham is a lot more convenient for British travellers)

**NAXOS** - Scenic but smelly

**IOS** - The party island. Smells of Rum & Coke and vomit from March to September

**SIKINOS** - So called, because sea breezes bring the smell across from neighbouring Ios

**SANTORINI** - Dirty-looking island remnant of a huge volcano. Mule-beating is the official form of entertainment among locals

## IONIAN ISLES

**ZAKINTHOS** - Avoided by those in the know

**KEFALLINIA** - Ugly isn't the word, but it's close enough...

**ITHAKI** - Voted 'most pointless island' six years running. Capital is called Stavros

**LEFKAS** - The chief feature is the Lefkada gramophone museum. Party on dude...

## DODECANESE

**CARPATHOS** - Underdeveloped because tourists choose to avoid it. Home of the 'Miss Karpathos' beauty pageant which is usually won by a man (if photos are any guide)

**SIMI** - natives are called Symians. Otherwise of no interest

**KOS** - A fun island, mixing the cosmopolitan sophistication of Majorca with the smell of a major fish-gutting plant

**KALIMNOS** - Wonderful if you like diving for attractively-coloured sponges. Tedious if you're not mental

**PATMOS** - The biblical Book of Revelations was written here. Cheerful place

## NORTH SPORADES & SPORADES

**SAMOS** - too close to Turkey for comfort

**CHIOS** - Site of many Turkish massacres. Visitors now discouraged

**LESBOS** - Come on, what do you think? In summer, the place throngs with women trying to get a suntan in dungarees and screaming as their nose studs get really hot and start to burn their nostrils

**LIMNOS** - Hardly worth mentioning

**THASOS** - Even the Greeks have forgotten it's there

**SKIATHOS** - Pretty scenery, pretty beaches, pretty boring

**DAVROS** - Not a Greek island, but the first leader of the Daleks

**SKOPELOS** - An increasingly popular destination for those who actually believe what the tour brochure tells them

## CORFU

If you choose Corfu, count your blessings (they'll steal anything here).

## CRETE

The people who come from Crete are called Cretans. The people who go there are called cretins

## MAKING FRIENDS

TRY

Do you want to hear a joke? These three Turks go into this bar...

## NEVER SAY

Hello. Are you Turkish?

Hello. Is your wife Turkish?

I thought only Turks pinched other men's bottoms

Those are great tits on your daughter, sir. You must be very proud

---

### DID YOU KNOW?

*HRH Prince Philip is Greek – which is why you have to count the ash-trays after a royal visit.*

### DID YOU KNOW?

*There's a lot of truth in the old phrase 'beware of Greeks bearing gifts'. This is because they're inevitably stolen and the police can do you for receiving.*

## HOME OF THE OLYMPICS

Greece founded the ancient Olympic Games and came up with many of the original events we know today – based on their love of theft rather than fair play. Both pole vaulting and the high jump started out as celebrating the favourite techniques of Greek cat-burglars. Discus throwing was originally an accepted way of getting rid of the evidence, while hurdling represented escaping from pursuing magistrates across back garden fences.

# HAITI

Many nations have been built on the sacrifices of their people. Haiti has just taken that notion a little too far...

The visitor will soon discover this Caribbean island has its own form of magic and charm. Unfortunately this is black magic and the charm, no matter how powerful, can't make your holiday go any quicker. Probably the most loathsome country in the world, with the possible exception of Wales, only the foolhardiest traveller would think to venture there. It is dangerous. The American armed incursion may have helped to quell the worst atrocities of voodoo, but the tourist is now at a far greater risk of a friendly fire incident, so things have definitely not improved.

A veneer of stability now covers the island, but not far beneath lies a land riddled with black magic under the shadow of former dictator 'Papa Doc'. For years, Papa Doc ruled the island by fear, along with other members of the evil Duvalier clan, including 'Grandma Locum' and 'Cousin G.P.' Even distant relatives, such as 'Great Uncle Osteopath' and the much-feared 'Auntie-by-marriage Chiropractor' were given whole districts to rule (as feudal fiefdoms) with an iron fist.

Haiti (which in Creole means 'let's hope it sinks') is still very much run by voodoo, which is an odd mixture of Catholicism and mental illness. Human sacrifice is still practised. On the summer solstice, the chief priests still thank the Gods for their prosperity by ritually slaying 'the chosen of the loa' (i.e. all those who can't run away fast enough). People with violent epilepsy are believed to be 'blessed by spirits' and are given all the important jobs like driving the island's buses, and complete raving lunatics are promoted to positions of great power – rather like the EC.

It is all too easy to look down upon a country that believes in sacrificing its people to ensure prosperity, but when you think how many people Norman Lamont and Kenneth Clarke have sacrificed in their day, perhaps this is not as unusual as we might think.

The island would desperately like to attract more tourists but this seems highly unlikely, at least in the short term, because the head of the tourist board is possessed by the demon Pazzuzu. It's considered a compliment to welcome you to the island by putting a top hat and a live rattlesnake in your bed, and any entertainment staged by your hotel will inevitably revolve around the ritual slaughter of a goat.

Every single item of food on the island is poisonous to normal people, and medical facilities are extremely primitive. The treatment for everything involves having your head smeared with goat dung and being bitten by a viper. This is only 50 per cent more effective than homeopathy, and your best bet is to wait to seek proper medical attention at home. Worse than this, many parts of the island are exceedingly dangerous for visitors. In country areas, a white man's soul is particularly valued (they obviously haven't come across many white people). In Port-au-Prince, the capital, the opposite is true. White men are not believed to possess a soul. The reason for this belief is not known for sure, but it is thought to date back to the time when a white American tourist left a Waylon Jennings tape behind in his hotel room. Rural areas are also plagued by zombies. These are not really the resurrected dead, but shambling mindless hulks in the grip of a powerful mind-numbing drug. In Britain, we know it as Prozac.

To add to its troubles, Haiti is also one of the poorest nations in the world. It has no industry, no commerce, no gold and no mineral deposits. This is why the nation's currency and means of exchange is based on the only commodity found in abundance on the island – goat dung. The official currency of Haiti – the pellet – is only usable on the island and you are unlikely to be able to get some through your local bank or travel agent before your holiday. Instead, you will have to rely on the 'dung changers' who hang around the airport (if you can't find them, look for the cloud of flies). One British pound sterling buys approximately a tonne and a half of pellets (subject to fluctuation), but with some hard bargaining you may be able to take away considerably less than this. You are advised not to keep the currency in your wallet, as it smells, and you should change as little currency at a time as possible. On leaving Haiti, throw any remaining Haitian currency away as you won't be allowed to bring it on board the aircraft.

Most shops on the island will only take pellets. Haggling is approved of, but Haitian shopkeepers get confused by tourists who attempt to keep driving the price up in an effort to get rid of their pellets. As to what souvenirs to bring home, your choice is rather limited because most Haitian shops only cater for fellow Haitians and their voodoo practices. Hollowed-out monkey skulls will be confiscated by HM Customs and live boa constrictors are subject to extended periods of quarantine. If you go shopping in Port-au-Prince, avoid Friday which is payday, as the town smells extra bad. Take time to browse at the voodoo shops, like 'Firstborns of Port-au-Prince' and 'The Dead Body Shop'. Note the sign saying, 'If it possesses you, you've bought it'. This rule is strictly adhered to.

You can purchase curses in 'The Curse Shop' which is sort of a malevolent version of Interflora, and have them despatched around the world with a personal message. You can also purchase love-charms made out of iguana diarrhoea which are guaranteed to make you irresistible to anyone with no sense of smell, good luck charms to ensure you don't lose your return airline ticket and bloody-good-luck charms which cause your tour operator to go bust and mean that you have to leave the island on the next available flight.

# HAWAII

The British, under Captain James Cook, brought three things to Hawaii when they first landed in 1778: TB, alcoholism and VD. Since then, most British holidaymakers have been happy enough just to continue these last two traditions.

Hawaii actually consists of eight main islands that share two similar characteristics – they're all of volcanic origin and they all have stupid names. To confuse tourists, the largest island, Hawaii, is also the name given to the whole lot.

**HAWAII, MAUI, KAUAI**: OK if you like volcanic ash and lava fields

**MOLOKAI:** as above but also the site of an active leper colony (this has caused the tourist trade to drop off)

**NIIHAU:** Privately owned island; if you try to land here the inhabitants will greet you with 'Aloha' (approximate translation: 'piss off')

**KAHOOLAWE:** EXIT organise package holidays to this unpopulated island – it's used by the US navy for bombing practice

**LANAI:** Site of the world's largest pineapple plantation (see notes below)

**OAHU:** This is where the action is and features Honolulu, Waikiki beach and the most famous tourist attraction of all, Pearl Harbour. Every year, hundreds of thousands of American tourists visit the memorial to the sailors who died on board the USS Arizona. If you can insult just a few dozen before being deported or thrown in jail then your trip has been worthwhile.

---

## HOW TO UPSET VISITORS TO PEARL HARBOUR

---

❏ Point at the sky and yell, 'Oh my God! Zeros at two o'clock high!'

❏ Run around with your arms outstretched, making aircraft noises and screaming 'Tora! Tora! Tora!'

❏ Wear a T-shirt that proclaims 'Kawasaki. From the people who brought you Pearl Harbour'

❏ Strut around with slitty eyes doing your best impression of Admiral Yamamoto

❏ Tell a certain joke with the punchline, 'because they're both full of dead semen'

❏ Wear a naval uniform and a skeleton mask and walk, zombie-like, moaning that you're here to avenge your death - and anyone with a Toyota in the car park is in deep shit

❏ Stand facing the USS *Arizona* and say, 'Quiet everyone! I think I can hear tapping...'

❏ Read everyone a poem you've composed that uses the rhymes 'Mitsubishi Zeros' and 'American naval queeros'.

### Waikiki Beach

If the only surfing you've done is visiting the porn sites on the Internet and you think that 'point break' is a snooker score, or a 'wipe out' is what you need after a serious Biryani, then keep away from here. This beach is for top surfers only, surfers skilled in all the latest aspects of their sport, like knowing which after sun is best – Coppertone or Hawaiian Tropic – how many smears of zinc cream are most effective to prevent nasal discolouration and whether Pantene Pro-V or Vidal Sassoon makes the best conditioner.

## Pineapples

Hawaii's prosperity was founded on the back of the pineapple industry, and many archaic laws are still in place which date back to the late eighteenth century. These have not been repealed and unbelievably, even today, it's still illegal on Hawaii to:

- ❏ 'Carry more than three pineapples about your person'
- ❏ 'Hold a public dance within an area bordered by pineapple trees'
- ❏ 'Cut a pineapple between sunset and sunrise on the second Sunday of each month'
- ❏ 'Enter the house of a church warden with a pineapple on your head'
- ❏ 'Show disrespect to the fruit'
- ❏ 'Become betrothed to one'

There are over 270 laws pertaining to pineapples on the Hawaiian statute books, and many of these formed the bases of plots for the first season of *Hawaii 5–0* ever made (e.g. 'To Catch A Pineapple', first broadcast 7 May 1968; 'A Pineapple For Steve McGarett', first broadcast 21 May 1968 and 'The Great Pineapple Caper', first broadcast 2 June 1968). Although also set in Hawaii, *Magnum P.I.* has avoided playing 'the pineapple card' to date and has given all tropical fruits equal prominence in its episodes.

## The Guinness Museum Of Pineapple Records

If you want to see the largest, smallest, heaviest, lightest, yellowest, oldest, smoothest or sweetest pineapples in the whole world, this museum on Kukui Street in downtown Honolulu is definitely worth a visit. If you have a life, don't bother.

## The Hawaiian Alphabet

If you're wondering why all the place names in Hawaii look the same it's because the Hawaiian alphabet only contains twelve letters: a,e,i,o,u and h,k,l,m,n,p,w. Unfortunately for graffiti artists, it looks like it was devised to prevent any form of profanity. Only using these letters means that the nearest you'd get to spray painting the word 'wanker' is 'wanke' – which is better than 'bollocks', where you'd only be able to write 'ollok'. (The 'F' word, while possible, would be phonetically rather than linguistically correct).

# HONDURAS

Don't contemplate coming here if you're scared of alligators, snakes, big spiders and scorpions – this tin pot Central American republic has them all in abundance. As if that's not bad enough, part of the north shoreline is named 'The Mosquito Coast' and there's no prizes for guessing why.

Because of this, the Honduras tourist industry is minimal and the economy relies solely on exporting its banana crop, making it the original banana republic. So important are bananas to the Hondurans that the supply of this fruit has made it the cocaine of Central America, and Medellin-style cartels have sprung up to control the harvesting and processing.

## The Banana Wars

Competition between the banana growers is fierce and 'Squash-Bys' are common. These involve rival cartels turning up at a banana plantation, pulling the bananas off trees and jumping up and down on them before driving off at high speed. Tourists have been known to get caught up in Squash-Bys and several have slipped over on skins they failed to see.

In the past, Western tourists have also fallen prey to approaches from gangs to help smuggle bananas out of the country, to get round the quotas imposed by the Honduran government. The area encompassing the north-west of Honduras, Belize and East Guatemala is known as the 'Yellow Triangle' and it's here that most smuggling takes place. It often begins as a friendly chat with a stranger over a banana milkshake but soon the talk turns to the money that can be made banana smuggling. You're told that it's easy, that government officers are too busy chasing the gang leaders to be bothered with one or two individuals. Gullible tourists agree, and soon they've got up to forty bananas taped to their body or within their stomachs in condoms.

Although there's easy money to be made, don't do it. If caught, banana smuggling carries a mandatory life sentence in Honduras, and there have been many cases of the condoms splitting, causing bananas to dissolve in the stomach leading to an overdose of roughage and potassium, and diarrhoea for a week. Honduran customs officials at the airport are also equipped with the very latest detection devices, including specially trained 'sniffer monkeys'.

The growing strength of the banana cartels looks set to continue and the more powerful ones are beginning to expand their operations to include cocoa bean extortion and sugar cane racketeering.

## Religion

Bananas play such a large part in the life of Hondurans that a religion and a whole series of superstitions have arisen based around them. Although most people are Catholics, 'The Cult of The Banana' currently has an estimated 250,000 members with a headquarters in the capital Tegucigalpa. The leader of the cult is an ex-TV evangelist who came to Honduras to avoid a prison sentence for tax fraud in the USA. Since establishing the cult in 1986 his followers consist mainly of disaffected youth who have to renounce all their worldly goods in favour of banana worship. Features of the cult include free love using bananas and praying to a great golden banana idol which, according to followers, has the power to grant your wishes, as long as they're banana-related.

Tourists are especially vulnerable to brainwashing from the cult since they are away from home and their families. If approached by one of the cult's acolytes it's important to remember to get bananas in perspective. They are good for a tasty ice-cream dessert; they cannot fill a spiritual void.

## Mayan Ruins

If you survive being bitten or stung by the wildlife, or getting caught up with organised crime or organised religion, then you might want to consider visiting the Mayan ruins at Copan, near the Guatemalan border. Although lauded by many, this once great Mayan city is not that marvellous. The so-called pyramids are not even a pyramid shape – they're flat on top and one statue of someone in a feathered cloak looks pretty much like any other. An altar is an altar wherever you go, and as for telling a story by writing hieroglyphics all over a huge flight of stairs, well you'll probably trip over some archaeologist who's on his hands and knees trying to read them.

No-one knows why this Mayan city was suddenly abandoned in AD 1200, but with a bunch of kings with names like 'Waterlily Jaguar VII', 'Smoke Monkey' or '18 Rabbit', the writing must have been on the wall (or on the steps).

# HUNGARY

Where would you go for a sex holiday? Thailand? Amsterdam? The Philippines?

Perhaps you should consider Hungary. Since the break up of the Eastern Bloc, Hungarians have been puzzling over just what they can offer the West. The answer they have come up with is their women. Cheers, guys.

Facilities in the new red-light districts are basic, to say the least, and most of the action is centred in the capital Budapest. Having next to no sex industry before the fall of communism, the Hungarians have quickly adapted their one form of night life – the Tejivo or 'Stand-up Milk Bar' – to meet the need of the hordes of sex tourists now descending on the capital.

Budapest has swiftly earned itself the nickname of 'The Bangkok of Eastern Europe' – and there is certainly no other place in the world where you can watch a live sex show and enjoy a cool glass of strawberry Nesquik.

---

## BUDAPEST DAIRIES PROUD TO PRESENT TO YOU... MUCH WELCOME TO BUDAPEST! SHAG CENTRE OF EASTERN EUROPE

### Hey British Big Boy!

We open Hungarian number one capital for sex holidays scene and our women open their legs for foreign men looking for shag shag! Many big bosoms and sexy flaps await you. You get big horn thinking of prime Hungarian pussy, we bet! But no worry! No Sir. Many girls to go round in Budapest – the Bangkok of Central Europe!

You have hot time – but not worry! Milk soon cool you down in twelve delicious flavourings while you do-do with Milk Maidens ! You suck on straw – they suck on you!

Plenty bonk bonk all day and all night! Our girls gobbly-gobbly all time for naughty UK spunk monkeys. Yes sir! Plenty places to sex – and milk – and all for low, low coinage! You think you in heaven – but you only in Budapest!

---

Just look at exciting fuck places in glorious capital city. Watch out. You go stiffness just reading them!

### Carnaby Street Milk Bar

Eighty Go-Go girls – plenty with own teeth. Most not on period – guaranteed! You buy them milk drink and go to room for fuckity fuck fuck. Low money all you need. Star attraction is Big Bertha. You do it. She wipe!

### Milko A Go-Go Disco

Dance nights away to hip groove sounds of Gibson Brothers and David Gates – but if you think that exciting, you wait for weekend! Saturday is party party! Bee Gees night drives high class Budapest women in sexy frenzy and wet in knickers! You pull easy-peasy!

### Madame Sin's House Of Sexy Fuck and Horlicks

Budapest's most famous expresso whore complex. Two thousand girls with pussy wetness for cock dogs. All girls checked by Ministry of Health and Fisheries for clap disease and scabby, but all clean. Certificates prove no lies here! You go home with dickie normal colour! Girls love all sexy action – anything they do! Even bottom passages much OK by them (triple thick shake on tap so no soreness worries!)

### Top Magyar Escort Agency

You arrive in Budapest on own. No need for hand shandy and spunking alone in sad hotel room or railway station. Our sexy escort girls will show you city delights like State Turnip Processing Plant and the Janos Kadar Memorial Pig-Iron Smelting Works! Then they go back to hotel place and licky-dickie all night!

### Café Bonk Milk Bar and Grill

Topless hostesses parade heavy bosoms to you with best Hungarian goulash! You eat meal then you eat pussy for all-in inclusive meal cost! Must be bargain of the year. Is like eating at Ritz (except for pussy).

### Rokosi Street

Budapest's red-light boulevard of genital satisfaction! Watch out Hamburg or Amsterdam. Hungarian girls hot for fucky action too!

But cheaper! One English pound coin will buy night of sex so big you think that spunk bag empty but Magyar girls prove you wrong, mister! Luncheon vouchers and Shell tokens also!

## Most Pleasure Peep-a-Rama

If you no need fuck but want wanky cum then this place for you! Watch Budapest women play with rude areas while you put oculars to them. You play with dickie and get much happiness!

Executive luxury single booths also sometimes available.

## London-Soho Striptease Club

Wow! Ovaltine flows like champagne while beauty womens dance sexy to Smokie or Racey and take off all clothes in horny striptease action! Twenty girls every night – most under 45. Finale is nude-ness girls walking in audience and you stuff monies up to show thank-yous (coins OK).

*So, British big boys! After reading, you much horny in pants. We bet you spunky down trousers now! Yes? Easy to go Hungary for shag. Just arrive travel agent in High Street location anywhere and say 'Me thirsty for great milk drink and want fucky at Budapest. Quickly!' They fix up you faster Jack Robinson! See you early! Cheers, men!*

### DID YOU KNOW?

*Despite the song title, 'The Blue Danube', the river itself is actually a sort of greyish-brown and smells like hamster litter.*

### DID YOU KNOW?

*Despite their geographical position, Hungarians are not Slavs. They're worse. Today's Hungarians are actually descended from the Magyars, a bunch of tent-dwelling, horse-eating Mongolian lookalikes who travelled west with no more to offer Europe than the recipe for goulash, a soup-cum-stew of no particular taste or culinary merit.*

# ICELAND

Not so much a country as a giant, desolate, volcanic glacier stuck in the inhospitable and bleak North Atlantic. The most famous Icelander is Magnus Magnusson. Ask him why you should visit the land of his birth and he'll scratch his head and say, 'pass'. You can't blame him. Iceland is extortionately expensive (a cupasoup can cost up to £18), there's no railway system, only one major road (that's invariably blocked with snow and/or elk), only a few hours daylight at the best of times and, worst of all, the women all look like Bjork's ugly sisters.

### Food and Drink
You'll willingly pay £18 for a cupasoup when you consider that traditional Icelandic delicacies include 'red pudding' (cows' livers baked with egg and onions), 'blood sausages' (lamb's intestines mixed with flour, wrapped in the stomach lining) and 'ram's testicles and milk' (which, surprisingly enough, are ram's testicles and milk).

If you don't fancy these then there's one main alternative – cod. Like the Swedes and their herring, the Icelandic economy owes a great deal to cod fishing and many Icelandic fishermen will regale you with tales of gallantry and acts of bravery in the cod wars fought with the Royal Navy in the 1970s.

## THE LANDSCAPE

People who visit Iceland say that it is never the same twice.

This is because it is hugely geologically unstable, riven with volcanic eruptions, tectonic upheaval and dramatic glacial shifts. This is what helps to make a visit to Iceland totally unique. In what other country in the world can you go to bed in your hotel room in Reykjavik and wake to find yourself and your bed mysteriously floating on a 50-foot by 50-foot ice flow now providing a major hazard to shipping as you drift west past Greenland? Iceland presently loses several thousand square miles of its landmass every year. If this continues, it is estimated that, by the year 2150, Iceland will be the size of a postage stamp.

Native Icelanders have a saying which roughly translates to, 'Bugger! There goes my back garden'. Icelanders take all this in their stride by consuming vast amounts of alcohol and befuddling themselves.

## WHERE TO GO

Ninety-nine per cent of Iceland is comprised entirely of lavafields, bubbling mud pools, volcanoes and unstable glaciers. This is why 98.9 per cent of the population live in Reykjavik.

### Reykjavik

Reykjavik is the only city in the world that bans dogs. This is good news if you hate dogs or bad news if you're a professional dog walker, owner of a poodle parlour – or blind. The Icelandic blind have tried adapting to guide-seals and guide-puffins – with predictably tragic results. Local dog lovers try and get round this restriction by keeping dogs in secret, dressing them up in human clothes and training them to walk upright so they can go out in public. By adopting these traits it's amazing how human-like these canines look and this might go some way to explain why no-one has yet tumbled the the real identity of the Icelandic singing star Bjork (AKA Princess).

Reykjavik also holds the distinction of being the only capital city in the world which melts. You are advised to avoid going in summer, when hotel accommodation is sparse and locals are busy desperately tethering outlying suburbs to the city centre with huge chains.

### Sightseeing

If you want to visit the city's cultural centre, it was last sighted at 30 degrees west, 60 degrees north. Anyone finding the city's banking district could be in for a big cod reward.

The 'must see' sight in Reykjavik is the Viking Experience, an interactive museum adjacent to the tourist office (unless the tourist office has slipped its chains again and is drifting through the Orkneys). Expect to take three hours to walk round the whole exhibit, during which time you'll be raped and pillaged in an authentic Viking way before having the opportunity to try your hand at broadsword fighting and (in the summer) being cremated on board a blazing longship.

# INDIA

India. The country where cataracts, religious intolerance and diarrhoea are a way of life. An exotic sub-continent where east meets west – and comes off worse. A nation so poor that nails take the place of mattresses and one of its most illustrious leaders, Mahatma Gandhi had to drink his own urine because he couldn't afford Perrier and it was the nearest thing to it.

The good thing about travelling in India is that Western currencies go a long, long way.

The bad news is that there are millions of dirty beggars fighting with each other to relieve you of it. Indians are proud of this tradition of begging, called 'baksheesh', and how their very persistent use of the word has helped firmly establish it in the West's vocabulary. If you're accosted by anyone demanding 'baksheesh' just shake your head and tell them that Britain, too, has contributed a word to the vocabulary of the East – bollocks.

## TRAVELLING BY TRAIN

India is geared up to travelling by train. You, on the other hand, are not geared up to travelling by Indian train. The trains cover vast distances, but equally take vast amounts of time to do so, during which time many Hindu travellers can expect to pass through several incarnations. Many reach Nirvana before they reach Delhi or Bombay. The problem is that no steam engine was ever designed to pull so many people and barnyard animals packed into each and every one of its carriages.

Travelling by train in India makes the 8.00 am Basildon to Liverpool Street commuter service seem like the Orient Express. Where else (apart from anywhere else in the Third World) would you have to share your carriage with eighty smelly locals (rightly called 'the untouchables'), an incontinent donkey, sixty chickens, three pot-bellied pigs, eighteen pot-bellied women and a bag of manure which splits 300 yards out of Lahore? Second and third class accommodation are far worse.

Executive-style first class, along with second and third class tickets are all reasonably priced compared with British train fares. But then, tickets on Concorde are also reasonably priced compared to British train fares. If you're travelling on a really tight budget, there are a number of 'bargain offers' on sale at Indian railway termini.

❑ For ten rupees you can lash yourself to the outside of a first-class compartment until you succumb to heat exposure and scalding steam burns.

❑ For six rupees you can travel on the roof as far as the nearest tunnel.

❑ For four rupees you can travel as far as you like, provided you can keep hold of the door handle and dangle off the side of the train.

❑ For two rupees you can run alongside the train until you get out of breath.

❑ For one rupee you can wave at the train as it leaves the platform.

## TRAVELLING BY CAR

*DON'T. Indian drivers ignore the following:*

- **red lights**
- green lights
- **indicating**
- right of way
- **pedestrian crossings**
- give way signs
- **stop signs**
- any other form of road sign

- lane discipline – speed limits
- **the slightest display of courtesy**
- oncoming traffic
- **multiple punctures**
- the need to keep their vehicles in a roadworthy condition
- **any other driver**

## OTHER ALTERNATIVES

### CYCLE RICKSHAWS
Part bicycle, part carriage, all slow

### AUTO RICKSHAWS
Part motor scooter, part carriage, all unstable

## SIGHTSEEING

### Taj Mahal

Situated in the city of Agra, south of Delhi, this marble shrine to Mumtaz Mahal looks just like the Brighton Pavilion, which they undoubtedly copied. The Brighton one is the best, and also has the advantage of not being infested with cobras. Unless you're into marble and inscriptions from the Koran you'll be bored and even frustrated; after the arched gateways and pointed domes you'll be disappointed to discover that, despite all appearances and pretences, there's absolutely no Indian restaurant contained within it.

### Bhopal

The capital of the Madhya Pradesh region of India but more famous as being the site of the world's worst industrial accident courtesy of Union Carbide and a poisonous gas leak in 1984. If you do visit Bhopal try to avoid saying any of the following:

❑ 'Can you smell anything?'

❑ 'This place stinks of methal icosynate!'

### Golden Temple at Amritsar

Every Sikh attempts to make a pilgrimage to this spiritual centre of their faith. Non-Sikh visitors are allowed in but, quite frankly, like Mecca or Jerusalem, once you've been to one spiritual centre of the world you've been to them all (not only that, but there's a good likelihood of someone swiping your shoes when you leave them outside).

### Bombay

Home to 'Bollywood', centre of the Indian film industry and the city responsible for films that make Ed Wood's look like cinematic classics. Films where every hero looks like an Indian Hugh Grant and every villain looks like an Indian Saddam Hussein. Bollywood turns out comedy, drama, adventure, tragedy, farce, horror, romance, musical and religious epics – all in one single two-hour film. Indians think it's value for money. Westerners think it's shite. Who's to say who's right?

# IRAN

Harbour no illusions – you will not find yourself welcome in Iran. Tourists are routinely spat upon or stoned – and that's in the Tehran tourist office. Outside in the streets, people can get positively hostile. Iranian women are the worst, shrieking and spitting after you. Luckily, as they wear the veil, the spit will not reach you and ends up plastered all over the insides of their headgear where it congeals on their moustaches.

Since the revolution, fundamentalism has taken hold in every part of Iranian society, provoking a strong hatred for all outsiders. In country areas in particular, infidel foreigners are regarded as unclean devils and anyone who gazes upon one must stone himself to death – a method of suicide that can require a great deal of patience. In such a climate of religious zealotry, Iran must be one of the purest countries on earth, mustn't it?

In fact, the truth is very different from what you might expect. Iran today is a seething mass of sexual deviation.

The problem is the Burqa or 'veil', that all-encompassing black bin-liner-cum-body-stocking-cum-shroud that all Iranian women are forced to wear.

Tehran, for example, is awash with hard-core pornography. In the most repressed country on earth this might seem strange, but the fact is that most Iranians have never seen a woman and so have no idea what it is they're looking at and see no reason to ban it.

The veil is also a convenient cover for the country's estimated 100,000 transvestites. No-one is aware of their 'sin'; they walk openly in the streets with no fear of detection.

Even amongst heterosexual couples, the bedroom is a hotbed of perversion in the average Iranian household, because the Iranian man rarely if ever has any idea which way up his wife is on the bed and takes pot luck.

Wife-swapping has also reached epidemic proportions in the years since the veil was imposed. Men park their wives outside the mosques, and then accidentally pick the wrong one up on the way home again. Since women are forbidden to talk – and are certainly not allowed to contradict a man – they must say nothing and go along with it. Even if the woman was not wearing her traditional veil, the Iranian husband would not know he had the wrong woman. An Iranian bridegroom never sees his wife before the wedding, or after for that matter, and so is totally in the dark about who he is married to. It is no coincidence that the word for wedding in Farsi also means 'lucky dip'.

Fundamentalism also gives the illusion that Iranians are humourless. This is another misconception. Whoever said that Iranians have no sense of humour has obviously never visited the country. Iranians delight in practical jokes. One popular joke is to dress a goat up in a woman's veil, get a friend to have relations with it and then stone him to death for practising abominations. It never fails to get a big laugh.

After almost two decades of sealing itself off from the outside world, Iran is slowly starting to realise that it needs valuable foreign currency and is taking the first tentative steps towards establishing a fledgling tourist industry, opening up holiday camps in remote desert regions well away from the Iranians themselves. These camps serve two functions – to bring in revenue from tourists and to train representatives of the world's leading terrorist organisations. Entertainments on offer include a nightly cabaret, supervised children's activities and instruction on how to assemble a pipe bomb. All rides are included in the price, as is use of the AK-47s. Particularly entertaining are the suicide bomber training sessions on Wednesdays, when devoted young Islamic radicals kill themselves in preparation for an assault on Israel. Non-terrorists are fairly safe in these holiday camps provided they don't possess an American passport, and most hostage-taking episodes end in eventual freedom.

Finally, you should be aware that a number of fatwahs or holy death sentences are in effect inside Iran. Best not to get involved. In addition to the fatwah against author Salman Rushdie, there are also less well-known fatwahs in progress. There is a fatwah against Salmon (for sounding like Salman), the pop group Rush (for sounding a bit like Rushdie) and Pinky and Perky for being 'unclean beasts of the trotter'. One of the strangest fatwahs has been declared against penguins. All penguins are to be killed on sight, because the mullahs have heard that they were responsible for publishing *Satanic Verses*. Thankfully, there are few penguins in Iran, so casualties are light, but it is best never to wear a dinner jacket in public or to pretend to be Jack Dee, who is wanted as a collaborator.

## IRAN

## THINGS YOU DON'T OFTEN SEE THERE

- ❏ Miss wet T-shirt contests
- ❏ Lapdancing bars
- ❏ Fashion shows
- ❏ Mosh pits
- ❏ Oasis tour dates
- ❏ Stand-up comedians
- ❏ Trendy mullahs
- ❏ Book-signing sessions by Salman Rushdie
- ❏ Book-signing sessions
- ❏ Books
- ❏ Poor men with both their hands

## IRAN

## THINGS YOU DO OFTEN SEE THERE

- ❏ People whipping themselves with knotted clumps of barbed wire for seemingly no reason
- ❏ Men taking a goat home to meet their parents – and ask their blessing for the forthcoming marriage
- ❏ American flags being torched
- ❏ People foaming at the mouth (let's be honest – it takes some doing to be that emotional about Bill Clinton)

# IRAQ

The region now occupied by Iraq was once occupied by the Assyrians, the Sumerians, the Mesopotamians and the Babylonians. This area used to be home to the world's greatest civilisations; now it's home to the world's greatest fuckhead.

These days, the majority of visitors to Iraq are those who happen to be in Kuwait or Saudi and accidentally stray across their borders. In cases like these, it takes more than a return airfare to get back home – usually nothing less than the direct intervention of the United Nations or strategic bombing by coalition forces will repatriate you.

However, if you do consciously make the decision to visit Iraq it's important to note that due to continuing UN sanctions, everything is in short supply. Tourists should therefore ensure they take with them essentials like a portable generator, a water purification unit, back-up desalination plant, every single food item imaginable and lots of medical supplies.

## Medical Care

Chaotic, dirty, overcrowded, smelly and full of so many sick-looking people you have to literally step over them. No, it's not one of Baghdad's street markets but a description of a typical Iraqi hospital. Since 1990 all government funding has gone towards the theatre of war rather than the operating theatre with the result that the most sophisticated hospital in the country is equipped with only some dirty bandages, a box of plasters with Mr Men on them, a used dressing and a blunt bread knife. Desperate doctors are reduced to trying to kiss things better.

## SIGHTSEEING

Tourism has never been a big industry in Iraq and only the Gulf War helped its fortunes. At the height of the fighting, occupancy rates in Baghdad hotels averaged 95 per cent, mainly due to CNN news crews.

However, since the end of the war, Iraq has tried to capitalise on its arms build-up once more, and many new tourist attractions and landmarks have suddenly opened for holidaymakers:

## The Basra Aqua Park

(This looks suspiciously like a Scud missile factory with a child's paddling pool and slide out the back.)

## Aladdin World

(The story of Aladdin is recreated in what looks like a bunker full of biological warheads and an old oil lamp. Closed when the wind blows from the East.)

## Euphrates Crazy Golf

(A hangar containing among other things, a six-hole crazy golf course and some missiles with skulls and crossbones painted on them.)

## Baghdad Shopping City

(A few hand-carts selling mouldy fruit in a corner of what very much resembles a command and control centre.)

## Ali Baba Multiplex

(A Betamax VCR with a 'Postman Pat' tape, attached to a portable TV is set among countless cylinders labelled 'mustard gas'. This is a popular attraction with local Iraqis. When electricity is restored, this will prove more popular still.)

## The al Furat Game Reserve

(This must be the only zoo built within 20-foot thick bomb-proof walls. Next to a large door with the sign 'Danger! Radiation' are cages containing a few lizards, a meerkat, a starved looking rat and two missing UN peacekeepers.)

## The Tigris Shooting Gallery

(A day-trip to the Kurdish settlements in a helicopter gun ship.)

### DID YOU KNOW?
*Wow! Since the Gulf War there are now 350 Iraqi women for every Iraqi man – and chances are he lost his genitals in Basra.*

# ISRAEL

Fancy getting away from it all for a fortnight? Then try Tel Aviv – because it has nothing.

To be blunt, Tel Aviv is dull. **It is dull.** You will note that the Palestinians never ask for Tel Aviv back. They are not that stupid.

Sightseeing in Tel Aviv can take up a considerable amount of time as it is extremely hard to find anything worth seeing, and you may have to walk for hours to find something even remotely disappointing. When the sun goes down, your choice of nightlife is either to be ripped-off for the price of a tiny cup of coffee in Dizengoff Street, or sit in your hotel room and count the minutes until your flight home.

When exploring Tel Aviv, note the mixture of the mildly bizarre and the seriously tedious, brought together with aplomb. Note the Seafari, the only seafood restaurant with a revolving illuminated gorilla as its emblem. Note all the dishevelled adobe buildings and tangles of telephone lines and wonder how this fits with the brochure's description of Tel Aviv as 'sophisticated and cosmopolitan'. Note that you're booked to spend another thirteen days, fifteen hours and twenty-six minutes in this dump.

Jerusalem – and the Old City in particular – is far more interesting. Here you can eat pizza by the slice where Jesus once walked, or play falafel roulette by purchasing from any of the dirty-looking Arab vendors thronging the narrow alleyways.

The Jerusalem market – or souk – is world famous for being not quite as good as you thought it might be. Traders, mostly Christian Arabs, pride themselves on displaying items of complete uselessness or low artistic merit. Haggling is the order of the day here and, after half an hour's hard bargaining, you can often pick up items for just twice what they're really worth.

Goatskin coats are a particular bargain if you're nasally challenged and don't mind being followed everywhere by aroused Syrians. You can also buy freshly squeezed orange juice that tastes every bit as good as week-old Kia-Ora and stock up on items that you will be trying to get rid of at car boot sales for years to come.

Jesus is big business in Jerusalem. For example, there is also a dismaying plethora of restaurants all claiming to be where He ate his last supper. No-one knows which, if any, is genuine. You can at least cut down the odds as it is unlikely He had a curry or a Big Mac.

While in Jerusalem, do visit The Dome of the Rock, the third holiest shrine in Islam, which is inlaid with gold and smells of tear gas. The view over the city from the Mount of Olives is also worth taking in, although the area is congested with camels named after characters in *Melrose Place* to intrigue gullible Americans.

While visiting Jerusalem or Tel Aviv, do not worry overmuch about suicide car bombers. They are easy to spot and avoid because the drivers all poodle along at 20 miles an hour being especially careful not to accidentally detonate themselves. Genuine Israeli drivers never drive at less than 90 miles an hour and happily collide with everything in sight. Suicide bombers also do not have 50 watts per channel of cheesy Phil Collins tracks blasting out of their cars, preferring instead to spend their last moments in silent contemplation rather than pumping the gas pedal in time to the drum beats on Sussudio.

Last – and probably least – there is Eilat, Israel's answer to the French Riviera. Israelis claim that Eilat is where the sun spends its winter vacation. This is a lie. The sun stays at least 93 million miles away from Eilat. You would do well to follow its example.

An obvious forgery

# HOTEL EILAT
## GUEST REGISTRATION FORM

NAME: *The Sun*

ADDRESS: *Solar System*

REASON FOR VISIT: *Winter Break*

ROOM: *407*

AGREED ROOM RATE: *Stellar*

BREAKFAST
[ ✔ ] Continental  [   ] Full buffet

## KIBBUTZIM

One of the most popular ways to see Israel is by staying on a Kibbutz – a collective farm. In exchange for your board and lodging you help the Kibbutzniks with the chores. Sounds fair? A noble socialist communal sharing experience? Bollocks is it. They saw you coming...

| | VOLUNTEERS' WORK ROTA | KIBBUTZNIKS'S WORK ROTA |
|---|---|---|
| Mon. am | Muck out chicken shed | Watch TV |
| pm | Shift manure heap | Have a cold drink |
| Tues. am | Weed fields | Lie in |
| pm | Pick pears | Sit on backside |
| Wed. am | Crate chickens for market | Read the paper |
| pm | Clean toilets | Shout at volunteers |
| Thur. am | Dredge irrigation ditches | Eat some chocolate |
| pm | Lick out septic tank | Scratch fat buttocks idly |
| Fri. am | Do Kibbutzniks's shopping | Doze in comfy chair |
| pm | Clean Kibbutzniks's house | Listen to music |
| Sat. am | Plough field with sharp stick | Shabbat |
| pm | Rebuild cowshed | Shabbat |
| Sun. am | Check under buildings for vipers | Watch a video |
| pm | Muck out the goat pen | Go swimming |

**DID YOU KNOW?**

*There are no swear words in Hebrew. (This causes Israeli Tourette's sufferers no end of problems.)*

# ITALY

Corruption is rife in Italy. It starts in the government and permeates down through every level of society. Tourists first experience this corruption immediately after landing when Italian airport staff demand 60,000 lire to make sure your suitcase doesn't 'accidentally' come undone when it's loaded on to the carousel. But then what else would you expect from a country in which even the Tower of Pisa is bent?

## Italian Men

The Italians are proud of the fact that they gave the word 'macho' to the rest of the world. Even self-portraits of Galileo and Leonardo da Vinci have that 'Come on – if you think you're hard enough' type of expression. This macho tag is completely misplaced, however, when you consider that Verdi was gay, Puccini wore womens' underwear, Titian skipped everywhere he went and Michelangelo's David has a manhood so small as to be almost irrelevant. Even Shakespeare's great Italian play was originally titled 'Romeo and Tybalt'. And that's before you think about *The Two Gentlemen of Verona*.

Perhaps because they cannot live up to their macho ideals, Italians remain one of the most volatile races in the whole world and are just as likely to pick a fight as give you directions to St Peter's Basilica. The Italians are quick to pick up on body language, and a momentary wrong stance or gesture is all it takes to create an international incident...

---

## A GUIDE TO BODY LANGUAGE

You do this: **Point at a monument**

What you can expect: A slap round the face

---

You do this: **Look lost**

What you can expect: Being spat on with a cry of 'Bastardo!'

---

You do this: **Stare at a map**

What you can expect: A kick in the shins

---

You do this: **Say 'scuse...'**

What you can expect: Having your arm bent up right behind your back

---

You do this: **Queue**

What you can expect: Being taken to an empty warehouse and severely beaten with a hammer

## The Mafia

Visitors to the south of Italy and Sicily are warned that although its power has been reduced considerably by recent governments, the Mafia are still a force to be reckoned with.

Today, their influence is felt most in the traditional Italian ice cream industry. At the time of writing, Don Carlo Cascio controls Tutti Frutti with his two main adversaries Don Vito Cesare and Don Luciano Gambini controlling lemon sorbet and Rocky Road respectively. The three largest Mafia families who, between them, controlled 95 per cent of the chocolate, strawberry and vanilla flavours in the 1920s, signed a pact in Naples in 1932, at the same time launching a new flavour, Neopolitan. Since the 'Chocolate Mint Chip' gang wars of the early 1980s, the streets of Salerno and Palermo have been relatively quiet, apart from ice cream vans playing the theme from *The Godfather*.

## Crime

Petty crime in Italian streets is quite common, usually perpetrated by gangs riding Vespas. If you're a woman, two things are likely to be pinched in this way, your handbag and your bottom.

---

## SIGHTSEEING

---

## Vatican City

The centre of the Roman Catholic Church and the home of the Pope. It is possible for tourists to have an audience with the Pope although this is not as enjoyable as 'An Audience With Freddie Starr' or 'An Audience With Bob Monkhouse'. On Easter Day the Pope stands on his balcony and talks crap (which is similar to 'An Audience With Jimmy Tarbuck').

## Venice

The Romans gave the world the concept of an efficient drainage system but must have lost the plans when they designed this city-cum-open-cesspool. Venice is not the most romantic city in the world but it is the stinkiest. Don't fool for the romance of the gondola – the gondolier has that long pole to help push you through water that is semi-viscous with human waste.

## Pisa

The only city in the world where subsidence has become a tourist attraction.

### The Colosseum
The world's most famous roundabout.

### Pompeii
A dead city. The Hemel Hempstead of ancient Rome.

### Trevi Fountain
In the good old days, throwing three coins in this fouintain would assure you a wish. Nowadays, with inflation, you must deposit at least 10,000 lire. After a major modernisation scheme, the fountain now accepts Amex, Visa and traveller's cheques.

### Florence
The only Italian city named after a character from *The Magic Roundabout* (except for Zebedee, near Genoa). A wonderful experience if you like renaissance art treasures. But let's be honest. You don't, do you?

---

# IVORY COAST

Aptly named, this West African republic (also known rather pretentiously as 'Côte d'Ivoire') is, of course, home to the kingdom of Barbar the elephant and his family who reside in the capital, Celesteville. Barbar is the King of the Elephant People and a wise monarch to boot. As with all monarchs, he is a blood relative of the Windsor – Saxe-Coburgs and a third cousin of HRH Prince Charles, to whom he bears more than a passing family resemblance.

The Ivory Coast is very much a country made by elephants for elephants, and is perhaps not the best destination for tourists who find the sight and smell of elephant dung littering the streets offensive, or who have a pathological dislike of big ears.

When he's not on an overseas goodwill visit, Barbar is very visible and tourists can catch sight of him and Queen Celeste in the capital most days, as he meets and greets his subjects. Tours around the palace with Zephir the monkey take place daily on the hour from 10am. Opposite the palace is the Royal Park where Barbar's children, Pom, Arthur, Alexander and Flora play, accompanied by The Old Lady.

Although friendly towards visitors, Barbar is very wary of ivory poachers.

His dear departed mother was shot by poachers, an event which has left deep scars. (He still attends a victims' support group with Bambi to this day.) He is therefore all too aware of the threat poachers pose and the danger of one or more of his feet ending up as exotic wastepaper baskets. Therefore, all tourists' luggage is thoroughly searched on arrival at Barbar International Airport to check for elephant guns, ammunition or giant hacksaws.

The Ivory Coast is the world's largest producer of dung, and the world's leading importer of sticky buns. Most of the population are engaged in heavy manual labour, such as uprooting trees and barging things out of the way. However, they certainly know how to mix work with play, and you can often find them balancing on large gaily coloured beach balls or standing on two legs and trumpeting loudly.

Service in the Ivory Coast's hotels is basic. You will have to carry your own bags up to your room, for example, because elephants can't climb stairs.

Avoid the Ivory Coast's nightspots, as elephant discos can be hazardous affairs, especially during line dancing or punk revival evenings.

It is difficult to get to know the inhabitants of Celesteville, as they only speak trunk. This is a difficult language to master, unless you have a six-foot nose which you can swivel through 360 degrees.

Being a nation run entirely by elephants, this country has no official standing in the United Nations assembly, but delegates are allowed in when they need someone to reach up and change the light bulbs or for the annual UN vs non-affiliated nations tug-o'-war match.

# JAMAICA

Sandy beaches, rum cocktails, reggae bands, unspoiled palm forests –
Jamaica is all this and much, much less.

The sweep of luxury beach-front hotels, gleaming swimming pools and
opulent nightlife is just a facade. If you want to see the real Jamaica, try
looking down the toilet before you flush it.

The true Jamaica is a dump. If it was any good at all, do you think thousands of Jamaicans would have left it to work on London Transport? It
boasts the highest unemployment rate in the world, and a level of squalor
and deprivation in its numerous shanty towns that would be a scandal if
anyone actually cared.

Kingston has no industry at all, and yet the entire city appears to be
wreathed in perpetual industrial smog. This is not smog. It is a cloud of
marijuana smoke. This makes it very difficult to sightsee without giggling,
taking off all your clothes and then falling over. Many visitors who come
back from Jamaica describe Kingston as 'really, really beautiful.
Spiritual. Sort of...there.' They have experienced it in an altered state
entirely, and their description should not be trusted.

Rich tourists are an insult to the poverty-stricken islanders, and are
about as popular as wash'n'go salesmen amongst the native Ras Tafari
community. Be sensitive. For example, while out in Kingston at night, do
not go around punching yourself repeatedly in the face. Do you want to
put another Jamaican out of a job? Do not misplace your traveller's
cheques, or you cannot be robbed of them.

June sees the biggest reggae festival, when bands who all sound alike
play what seems to be the same song for an entire weekend. Go along
and mingle with the crowds if you have no ear for music and nothing to

live for. An integral part of the reggae scene is the use of marijuana. This helps the music to sound better, but not enough.

Avoid visiting Jamaica during election year. The Jamaicans are truly passionate about their politics and things can very easily get overheated. Every Jamaican has one vote – and six bullets – to use during the campaign. The vote must be cast for the party of his or her choice. The ammunition can be split between politicians, rival supporters and young children out attending the chickens.

This system has much to recommend it as politicians are assassinated with delightful regularity and those who survive are those smart enough to hide in a deep hole and keep absolutely silent and still until the campaign is over, making them among the brightest elected members of a legislative body anywhere in the world.

Once parliament has been elected, most political issues are hammered out by committee in reasoned debate, and then settled by a frantic exchange of gunfire. The capital, Kingston, is the official home of the Jamaican parliament, although the day-to-day running of the country is usually conducted from the intensive care ward of the local Kingston General Hospital.

**DID YOU KNOW?**
*The longest Jamaican political speech on record is
'Mi fella Jam – BANG!'*

## STRANGE BUT TRUE
In Jamaica, the unemployment exchanges are bigger than the hotels.

---

# JAPAN

Almost 95 per cent of the Japanese islands are wild and mountainous, which means that the Japanese are squeezed into the few habitable areas afforded them. Prices of land in Tokyo, for example, are the highest on earth, and few can afford even enough land to stand up in. Almost all homes are rented, and the average Tokyo apartment sleeping a family of four is now the size of a Morris Minor and shrinking every year. The streets are just as packed, and plans are now underway to introduce a system of sitting on people's shoulders to double the effective use of space – the world's first commuter 'body pooling' scheme.

The Japanese have adapted well to their lack of space. They are one of the runtiest peoples on the planet, and have laboured long and hard in the field of miniaturisation, making technology smaller and smaller to fit their shrinking living space. Even their trees are small, like the dwarf Bonsai, and chocolate-covered ants are a popular delicacy. Hell, even their poems are small. Haiku are the smallest poems on earth.

Land is at such a premium that it is regularly smuggled into the country with the connivance of the Japanese Government. The Yakuza – or Japanese Mafia – control the smuggling operation, bringing land in by the acre hidden in concealed holds on board supertankers. Slices of Mongolian tundra, perhaps cut with Korean peninsula, are considered low risk because it is unlikely to be missed. The most valuable land is prime Scottish golf course, which can sell for a million yen a square inch.

Naturally, taking land out of the country is expressly forbidden, and you may well be searched on departure for possession of a hillock or coastal outcrop. Penalties are severe.

Few westerners ever visit Japan. Those who do describe the Japanese people they meet as quiet, withdrawn and reserved. This is often mistaken for politeness. It is not. It is barely concealed contempt. The Japanese hate everybody and think that everyone is inferior to them. They even have a saying to describe their views on gaigin or foreign visitors: 'A dog thinks it's a member of the family but, to the family, it's just a dog'.

Quite why a nation famous for karaoke, Godzilla movies and shops openly selling used schoolgirl panties should think itself racially and morally superior is a puzzle. But then, Adolf Hitler probably thought he was a pretty tasty bloke...

A further mystery about the Japanese psyche is their almost religious need to humiliate and injure themselves, preferably live on television and preferably in a stunt involving a locked phone box full of writhing vipers. Even killing themselves has long been an art form, with Hari Kiri, Kamikaze and working 22-hour days all considered honourable, rather than bloody stupid.

If you visit Japan, don't bother trying to figure them out. Just ignore them if you can, do whatever you have to do, bow a bit and then get out. Don't even bother going anywhere. It will only perplex you further. Sumo, for instance. What is that all about? Two hugely flabby virtually naked men groping each other? If that's your bag, you can see it around the back of the House of Commons most weeknights at considerably less expense.

You might also be interested to know that, until quite recently, Sumo wrestlers also participated in flatulence contests. Quite how such events were judged – or why they were even tolerated – is unknown.

Don't bother going to the geisha bars. They are not the least bit bawdy. Instead, they are full of elderly women in white fright masks who anoint you with exotic lotions and then make you tea. This might provide the Japanese with all the sexual excitement they can stand, but it is unlikely to arouse many westerners.

The only other form of nightlife in Tokyo is the dreaded Karaoke bar, where hassled Japanese executives go to make complete pricks of themselves. A bottle of Scotch in these places can cost over £100, but it is worth it to blot out the sound of some Sony middle manager doing 'Gleen Gleen Glass of Home' ten times in a row.

## TRAVEL TIP
Go for a ride on the crowded Tokyo–Kyoto bullet train, if only to find out what a people who eat nothing but raw fish smell like close up.

## MANNERS
If you see someone about to commit suicide, do not interfere. You may be invited to join him and refusal often offends.

## SAFETY TIP
Do not go to a fancy dress party in Japan disguised as a dolphin.

### DRINKS

Don't bother joining in with a traditional tea ceremony. It takes hours while they sod around, and the tea gets cold.

# JORDAN

### Exports
*Glossy 10x8s of Queen Noor.*
*Pistachios.*

### Imports
*Everything else.*

Be honest. As reigning monarchs go, there's not many that you'd want to shag nowadays. Once upon a time, the Queen of Sheba had a reputation as a right royal raver, Cleopatra could, according to the statesman Pliny, 'suck a golf ball through a hose pipe' and Catherine the Great of Russia would do it with anything wearing trousers (or a saddle). Nowadays, however, bonkable monarchs are noticably thin on the ground – until you get to Jordan that is.

Jordan's Queen Noor is probably the most shaggable monarch in the world, combining a regal demeanour with a great pair of tits.

Queen Noor is the best reason for visiting Jordan.

*Unfortunately, as well as Queen Noor being the best reason to visit Jordan, it's actually the only reason to do so – unless your life revolves around carpets.*

### Carpets
The Jordanians are crazy about carpets. The city of Al-'Aqabah near the border with Israel alone boasts 5,000 families involved in the carpet business. This might be good for potential buyers but it makes for very predictable and extremely boring conversations.

## MAKING FRIENDS IN AL-'AQABAH

### TRY SAYING:

---

'Nice weather for weaving'
'How's your loom?'
'Call that a pile?!'
'So I said to the carpet buyer...'
'How are you off for beige wool?'

---

### DON'T SAY:

---

'Have you got any linoleum?'
'Where are all those five-year-olds going this early in the morning?'
'I'm looking for a good shag'

---

## The Bedouins

Anywhere else in the world you'd call them 'homeless' or 'dossers'. However, in the south of Jordan this bunch of scruffy itinerants has attained the romantic status of 'nomads'. The Bedouins are renowned for their hospitality towards tourists, but have strange rules of etiquette. For starters (and the main course, and dessert) this involves the use of their left hand:

---

## A HANDY GUIDE TO BEDOUIN ETIQUETTE

Rule:     Guests must approach a Bedouin tent from behind

Reason:  Bedouins prefer to be approached from behind

• • • • • • • • • • • • • • • • • • • • • • • • • • • • • • • • • • • • • • •

Rule:     Guests may only stay for three and one-third days.
          (There is a Bedouin saying that 'the serpent is more
          acceptable than the guest who overstays his visit')

Reason:  Soreness.

● ● ● ● ● ● ● ● ● ● ● ● ● ● ● ● ● ● ● ● ● ● ● ● ● ● ● ● ● ● ● ● ● ● ● ● ● ● ● ● ● ● ● ● ● ●

Rule:     If invited to share a meal with a Bedouin, you must eat
          with your fingers – but only use the right hand.

Reason:  Using the left hand is considered very bad manners;
          the left hand is only used for putting your shoes on,
          cleaning your feet, wiping your backside and for use
          while thinking of Queen Noor

● ● ● ● ● ● ● ● ● ● ● ● ● ● ● ● ● ● ● ● ● ● ● ● ● ● ● ● ● ● ● ● ● ● ● ● ● ● ● ● ● ● ● ● ● ●

Rule:     If someone passes something to you, make sure you
          accept it in your right hand

Reason:  Grasping it between clenched buttocks is unhygienic,
          not to say giving the wrong signals to your hosts

● ● ● ● ● ● ● ● ● ● ● ● ● ● ● ● ● ● ● ● ● ● ● ● ● ● ● ● ● ● ● ● ● ● ● ● ● ● ● ● ● ● ● ● ● ●

Rule:     Don't point the soles of your shoes at your host

Reason:  You might have trodden in camel dung and it will
          probably be more tempting than the food on offer

● ● ● ● ● ● ● ● ● ● ● ● ● ● ● ● ● ● ● ● ● ● ● ● ● ● ● ● ● ● ● ● ● ● ● ● ● ● ● ● ● ● ● ● ● ●

## KENYA

No trip to Kenya would be complete without a visit to the Masai Mara game reserve, home of the Masai tribe. Nomadic herdsmen fiercely proud of their traditional ways, the Masai celebrate their ethnic identity by jumping up and down as high as they can.

The origins of this peculiar ritual, which sees the Masai pin their arms by their sides, place their heels together and then leap skyward, is not known. Some suggest that this was how these cattle herdsmen once turned their milk into butter. Many believe it is a symbolic attempt to reach 'Masai Heaven'. Others believe it has something to do with all the red ants in the area.

Whatever the truth, Masai tribal dances are quite something to see. Some young Masai can manage as many as one hundred jumps before they get bored and sit down, and today the whole thing is a highly popular tourist attraction.

Long ago, however, Masai dancing was the source of numerous conflicts with neighbouring tribes who could not match the Masai's leaping prowess and whose sideways hopping or circular skipping dance rituals seemed poor by comparison. When the British arrived in 1844, they considered jumping up and down to be an unspeakable heathen blasphemy and banned the practice. Instead, the Imperial British East Africa Company made every effort to convert the Masai to their own foxtrot. Dancing teachers were brought over from England to help in the conversion, setting up dancing schools in the bush to 'educate' the heathen young.

'Whatever steps our Lord did at the wedding at Canaan, it was damn certain He didn't jump up and down with His heels together and His privates flapping' one zealous dancing teacher was quoted as saying in the mid-nineteenth century, summing up the prevailing mood of the time.

Throughout the repression, the Masai kept doing their traditional dance whenever they thought they were out of sight, but frequently gave themselves away by bouncing up from behind a tall shrub in plain sight of the British authorities, who clamped down on them with a stern talking to. Many Masai even had fingers wagged at them in some of the most brutal acts of repression ever perpetrated by the British Empire.

Inevitably, resentment grew into out-and-out conflict. 'Dance Mutinies' were commonplace, and colonials were forced to flee before fiercely bouncing rioters. (Luckily, as the Masai bounce up and down on the spot, the whites always outran their pursuers.) News reached the ears of Queen Victoria, herself a staunch supporter of ballroom dancing, and General Gordon was despatched to bring order. This he did by rounding up the Masai and cruelly confining them to bungalows with low ceilings.

After decades of despotic British rule, many Masai forgot how to jump. Bouncing up and down became a lost art, whispered of by the tribal elders as proof of a golden age of Masai culture and learning. Secret attempts were made to rediscover the technique, and many Masai fell over in the process. The toll in grazed knees and bruised elbows was truly terrible and is one of the most shameful periods in African history (except for the time when cross-dressing swept the continent).

It wasn't until World War One that the Masai resumed jumping. Far from being a 'heathen blasphemy', the British authorities now considered the Masai practice to be extremely useful and actively trained them to jump once more. Masai warriors were inducted into the British Army and shipped overseas to serve in the trenches. They were valued lookouts, being able to spring up above the trench parapet, view the German lines and then bob down again. Many Masai won medals for their bravery - usually posthumously – as the Germans brought in champion clay pigeon shooters to thin their ranks. Two Masai won Victoria Crosses for jumping under fire at Ypres, and a third won the DSO for bouncing at Mons.

When peace came, the British quickly forgot all about the contribution Masai dancing had made to the war effort and banned it again (45 minutes after the armistice). Surviving veterans felt used, especially those who had lost an ear while jumping for the B.E.F. and had consequently lost all sense of balance. There was to be no war pension for those invalided out with jumping disabilities.

Now the Masai began to jump in earnest once more, reasserting their heritage. This brought them into conflict with the large number of Indians who had been brought into the country to construct the Mombasa-Uganda railway. Indian dance baffled the Masai, who thought there was not nearly enough jumping in it. Resentment simmered throughout the Second World War and flared up into bloody warfare in the early 1950s when, threatened by the new jitterbug, the Mau Mau rebellion swept the country and led to eventual independence.

# KOREA, NORTH

A tourist must be very determined to get to visit the Democratic People's Republic of Korea. Visas are not easy to come by and you will need every vaccination known to man. Authorities will insist you carry paperwork for your inoculations. They will also insist you have your head examined.

North Korea is poverty-striken and close to economic collapse, as you would expect from any country which spends 96 per cent of its gross national product on tanks. Tanks are the only reason to visit the country and tank-number collecting the chief hobby of North Korean children. If you collect tank numbers, bring along an extra notebook or two! Also bring along a bulletproof vest, because the penalty for spying is death by firing squad. There goes that reason to visit then...

If you are unfortunate enough to visit North Korea, you will find yourself staying at the Kim Il Sung Hotel on Kim Il Sung Street. This is because all the hotels are called the Kim Il Sung Hotel – and all the streets are called Kim Il Sung Street. The locals don't seem to mind very much about this potentially confusing situation, because if they venture outside they get run over by Kim Il Sung tank battalion.

In fact, everything in North Korea is called Kim Il Sung. This is because the country is in the grip of what sociologists call 'the cult of the personality'. Kim Il Sung led the country from independence in 1948 until his recent death and, as with all communist men of the people, enshrined himself as a god. Now everything bears his name, without exception. You drink Kim Il Sung rice beer, you eat Kim Il Sung rice curry (when there's any food in the country) and you do a huge Kim Il Sung into the Kim Il Sung afterwards. The most popular name (the only name) in North Korea is Kim Il Sung, for both boys and girls. It is also the most popular – and only – name for pets, livestock, buildings, plants and tank battalions.

This causes no end of confusion for western tourists. The phrase 'Kim Il Sung' is both a greeting and a swear word. It also means over four hundred other things but at least if you master the phrase, you will be fluent in North Korean and as able to make yourself as misunderstood as any native!

All museums, art galleries and cultural centres are called both 'Kim Il Sung' and devoted to Kim Il Sung. Visit the Kim Il Sung museum to see the largest preserved collection of a leader's underpants in the world. It is open from Kim Il Sung to Kim Il Sung, opening at 8 Kim Il Sung and closing at 4 Kim Il Sung (Kim Il Sung Street). The Kim Il Sung dance the-atre specialises in dances about Kim Il Sung and is unique in producing works combining both dancers and tanks in routines. They are often spectacular, sometimes bloody, but never less than totally baffling.

## THE NATIONAL ANTHEM

The national anthem is played every fifteen minutes in the capital P'yongyang (Kim Il Sung City), and foreigners are expected to show respect by throwing themselves to the floor and beating the pavement in grief while singing the catchy lyrics:

O dear is the name of our beloved general

O glorious is the name, General Kim Il Sung

Kim Il Sung. Kim Il Sung. Kim Il Sung. Kim Il Sung. Kim Il Sung.

Kim Il Sung. Kim Il Sung. Kim Il Sung. Kim Il Sung.

Kim Il Sung. Kim Il Sung. Kim Il Sung. Kim Il Sung. Kim Il Sung.

Kim Il Sung. Kim Il Sung. Kim Il Sung. Kim Il Sung.

Kim Il Sung. Kim Il Sung. Kim Il Sung. Kim Il Sung. Kim Il Sung.

Kim Il Sung. Kim Il Sung. Kim Il Sung. Kim Il Sung. Kim Il Sung.

(Repeat until you lose your voice)

# KOREA, SOUTH

Seoul, the capital of South Korea, is one of the most modern cities on earth. None of the buildings is more than twelve months old. This is not because the country is wealthy and prosperous. It's because nothing built in Korea ever lasts for more than a year.

The hugely corrupt government traditionally turns a blind eye to building regulations, allowing contractors to erect multi-storey buildings out of the flimsiest and cheapest materials available. Balsa, styrofoam chips and UHU glue-sticks are the building materials of choice, with reconstituted eggshells used for more important structures like stairwells and fire escapes. When the buildings collapse with horrific loss of life, as they inevitably do, the same contractor wins the contract to rebuild the property all over again – and so on. The phrase 'making a killing' springs to mind.

Seoul is therefore an exceptionally difficult city for the tourist to find his way around in. Buildings – and indeed whole streets – fall down with such alarming regularity that street maps are hopelessly out of date before they are even published. Clouds of billowing dust make navigating by sight equally difficult, and you should never ask a policeman for directions because you will be arrested under suspicion of being a just-arrived North Korean infiltrator. This goes double if you're wearing a wetsuit. If you intend to go anywhere while on holiday, check that it is still standing by phoning ahead before you set out – unless of course, the telephone exchange has collapsed again. Better still, book an organised coach tour which will point out to you where any buildings of importance used to stand.

Originally called Ars-Seoul (literally, 'Seat of the King'), the city changed its name in 1937 to avoid making World Atlases rude. There is little worth seeing here. Tourists are advised to check out the bustling city parks, thronging with Koreans sheltering well away from the buildings. You may also want to check out the Seoul Funland Amusement Park, which is totally unique in that all the rides stand perfectly still. This is an incredible novelty to the average Korean, who is used to floors constantly tipping, buckling and pitching under him. Westerners may find it a tad dull.

If your hotel is still standing when you arrive, observe a few sensible precautions. Stay around the edge of your hotel room. Do not go out into the centre where the support is at its weakest. If you absolutely must venture into the centre of the room, lie flat on your stomach to spread your weight, as if crawling across thin ice. Do not bring heavy luggage. Do not test your bedsprings by sitting down on your bed.

Because of the fragility of its buildings, Korea has introduced a number of laws which are always strictly enforced. No exceptions are made for foreigners. If you want to stay out of jail, do not lean on a building. Do not jump up and down, even on a ground floor. Never exhale against a supporting wall and never knock on a door. Other laws prohibit the popping of crisp packets, putting up shelves and more than two people occupying the same room at the same time.

Westerners are not a popular sight, as they tend to be taller and heavier than Koreans, and therefore more likely to bring a building down. Expect to be barred from many shopping malls and other buildings on the grounds of public safety. If you are allowed in, do not be put off by the intimidating sight of all the Koreans hugging the walls and inching their way to the exits on tiptoe.

*If you must visit South Korea, try going out into the countryside. It's as boring as hell, but at least the buildings are smaller.*

All in all, there are probably much better ways to spend your annual vacation than being pinned under tonnes of masonry and forced to drink your own urine to survive. However, it still beats a fortnight in Malaga.

## SHOPPING AND EATING OUT

While out shopping for souvenirs, if you come across a store full of cute little puppies do not be tempted in. Many tourists have had their holidays ruined by losing their hearts to a mischievous little scamp, pointing it out to the vendor and then standing paralysed with horror as the pup is unceremoniously beheaded and offered up with the Korean phrase meaning 'do you want it with or without giblets, honoured sir?'

Dog is a Korean delicacy. If you like dogs (in the non-culinary sense) then this may well not be the holiday destination for you. If, on the other hand, you think they're all smelly, butt-sniffing bastards who deserve all they get, Korea opens up a whole new world of gastronomic possibilities, from cordon blue chien right through to Fast Food Fido . Throughout Seoul, for less than a fiver, you can eat well at Pug-U-Like, McDognalds, Waggy

Snaks or Lurcher King. For more up-market meals try Chows, Scooby-Doos or The Basted Basset on Ha-Nong Street.

## TIPS

# Before retiring to bed each evening, liberally smear yourself with aniseed so that rescue dogs can find you easily
# If you weigh more than 11 stone, or have a bad cough, insist on a ground floor hotel room
# Don't be tempted to venture out onto your hotel balcony. It is attached with Pritt
# Do not flush the toilet in your room. Toilet flushing is the second most common cause of building disasters in Seoul, after leaning on things
# Never visit the country from November to March, when winds can exceed five miles an hour

## SPECIAL ADVICE FOR STUDENTS

Students are most definitely not welcome in South Korea. The local student population takes some of the hardest drugs in the world and is consequently out of touch with all reality. This is why they regularly stage bloody riots in the hope of uniting their country with one of the poorest, most vicious dictatorships on earth.

Visiting students may find themselves referred to psychiatric clinics.

# KUWAIT

Kuwait is such a popular destination that some half a million Iraqis visited it in 1990 alone. Many of them decided to stay for a while, and many took back a few souvenirs other than bath-towels and shower caps (which no Iraqi has any use for anyway).

At The Central Museum (Arabian Gulf Street), you can see where one of the greatest collections of Islamic art used to be, while at the Tariq Mahuji Museum in the Jabriya district, you can spend several hours exploring the vast collection of empty display cases. At the Rhijef Palace, you can look under the collection of exotic matresses where the emir used to stash his collection of stroke mags, unsurpassed outside the

Vatican. (These magazines were instrumental in shortening the land war, as they kept the elite Iraqi Republican Guard busy in their billets until it was too late.)

The Iraqis have stolen everything of interest in Kuwait and taken it back to their own museums in Baghdad. This is not a good reason to visit Baghdad instead of Kuwait. Even five years on, there are still shortages in Kuwait. The entire country's stock of toilet paper was stolen by the Iraqis, for example, partly because they had never seen any before, partly because it was far more valuable than Iraqi banknotes and partly because the Republican Guard requisitioned it. There is also a shortage of night clubs and restaurants, but this is more due to the fact that the Kuwaitis are a boring bunch than to anything else.

Despite the devastation caused by the Iraqis and the destruction of almost all its oil wells, Kuwait has regained much of its former wealth by a serious of ingenious insurance frauds. On request, you will be shown where the emir kept his personal collection of 200,000 26-inch Sony Trinitron TV sets with Fastext (serial numbers unfortunately not recorded), and the National Warehouse of Hi-Fi Separates – all of which, needless to say, have supposedly been cleared out by the Iraqis.

After seeing the famous and lofty Kuwaiti Towers, used by western businessmen as a base of operations and by the Iraqis as a practice target even they could hit, the other major attraction in Kuwait City is the Souk. The Souk is easy to find, provided you don't have a heavy cold, and is packed with things you will later wonder why you bought. Do haggle, to ensure that you don't waste quite as much money as you might do otherwise.

Otherwise, there is nothing else in the country.

## RELIGIOUS TABOOS

Being more relaxed about their religion, Kuwaitis are harder to offend than most Arab peoples. But do try.

## MAKING MONEY FAST

In a jam? Need extra money? In an emergency, go to the back door of the Palace, knock four times and tell them 'George sent me'. They will then give you a large suitcase full of cash, no questions asked.

# LUXEMBOURG

Calling this country 'The Grand Duchy of Luxembourg' is like saying 'The Glorious Kingdom of Bangladesh', 'The Magnificent State of Ghana' or 'The Shit-Hot Nation of Chad'.

Luxembourg is a tiny, nonentity of a place which, through an accident of European history, became an actual country and not a province or a colony. Its main claim to fame is that it's the most expensive place in Europe to live, and the only thing 'grand' about it is that's precisely what three nights B & B accommodation will cost you. Because of its high cost of living, Luxembourg only allows tourists with sufficient financial means to visit. As well as validating passports or international driving licences, border guards also check tourists' bank balances, pension funds, credit ratings, investment portfolios and whether they have negative equity on their properties or any county court judgements pending.

Luxembourg is not only the smallest European country (Lichtenstein doesn't count, resembling more a cartographic error than a sovereign state), it's also the smallest member of NATO. The country is proud of its armed forces although their contribution to the safety of Western Europe must be viewed as 'meagre' at best, and 'laughable' at all other times.

On the first Sunday of every month, the Luxembourg Army parades through the imaginatively named capital, Luxembourg City. All twelve soldiers usually take part, and are watched by their proud mums and dads. Tourists who blink will miss it. Sometimes they bring the army minibus and rifle. Sometimes they don't. During November, the armed forces take part in the Armistice Commemorations, remembering all those Luxembourgers who gave their lives in two world wars. Their names are read out before a moment of silence is asked for the fallen. The entire ceremony lasts 2.3 seconds.

## SIGHTSEEING

Guidebooks are very kind to Luxembourg, describing its landmarks and sights as 'low key' or 'selective'. The reality is that apart from the armed forces parade, the only other sights in Luxembourg are a castle that belonged to King Wenceslas and a radio station (which didn't).

### King Wenceslas

One of the original rulers of Luxembourg, Wenceslas lived in the south, near Esch-sur-Alzette where his castle still stands. Although the King himself was only famous for 'looking out' on the Feast of Stephen, he did in fact also sneak a furtive glance during the Feast of Bartholomew, have a gander during the Feast of St Francis and indulge in a crafty peak during Lammastide.

### Radio Luxembourg

Luxembourg only has one radio station and this is it. No matter when you tune in, these are the five things you'll hear:

**5 things** you're guaranteed to hear on Radio Luxembourg, no matter when you tune in

❑ The number one song in Finland

❑ The number two song in Denmark

❑ Adverts for tampons in Flemish

❑ DJs that make Capital Radio presenters sound like members of MENSA

❑ Some old shite from Bjork

The current rulers, Grand Duke Jean and the Grand-Duchess Josephine (who sound like an elderly lesbian couple, but aren't) were married in the grounds of the radio station. Although the wedding service was magnificent, the reception was terrible.

Apart from King Wenceslas, the only famous Luxembourger is Jacques Sante, the ex-prime minister who's now president of the EU. He was born in the southern town of Remich and his house is a popular stop for tourists, particularly the British, who take the opportunity to relieve themselves in the front garden and through the letterbox with cries of 'come out, you wanker – and we'll have you!'

## MADAGASCAR

Famous for being tricky to spell correctly, Madagascar is an unknown quantity to most people. Few know where to find it on the map, and even fewer try. It is nestled off the coast of East Africa, in the Indian Ocean, and is largely forgotten by everyone except for tour companies, specialising in exotic holidays, whose clientele have now rumbled how crap Cuba and the Maldives are.

*For almost a decade, Madagascar has been 'the next in-spot'. It is still waiting. Obviously the charm of its most famous wild animal, the hairy-eared Lemur, has failed to pull in the punters.*

Some visitors say that they have been put off of Madagascar because of the natives' obsession with death. All Madagascans want to die, because it is only when they join their venerated ancestors in 'The Valley of the Dead' that they get any love or respect. Each year, many kill themselves in search of 'promotion', usually by jumping in front of tourist buses. Don't sit at the front, and don't offer the bus driver your hankerchief. After death and interment, ex-Madagascans are dug up every so often and told what great blokes they were by friends and family gathered around in a big circle and ceremonially pinching their noses. Shamen or witch doctors allow the relatives to speak directly to the dead. This is big business. Do not ask a Shamen to speak with one of your departed loved ones, as the messages are usually disappointing and consist mainly of the 'he says to make sure you look after the pigs and see that the goat is milked' variety.

Do not bother buying souvenirs. The market stallholders will not respect you unless you are dead. Forget dining out also. The service is awful and when you complain and ask to see the manager, as you will inevitably have to do, he will be exhumed and wheeled in on a gurney. No-one who is alive holds any position of importance on the entire island. All elected officials must, by law, have been dead for at least ten years before holding office. This has made the Madagascan delegation at the United Nations exceptionally unpopular, especially with the Luxembourg and Malawi delegates, who have to sit next to them. (In 1987, Luxembourg considered changing its name to Aardvark Land, just to be moved.)

Also, do not buy good luck charms from the Shamen. 'Good luck' to a Madagascan means dying horribly. Instead, buy a 'bad luck' charm which is guaranteed to keep you alive even if you drop your trousers inside the holiest of Islamic shrines. It may also protect you from the local food which is best kindly described as 'fucking rancid', the local Romeos who fit much the same description, and the local vanilla beer which would make even the most hardened wino puke.

Avoid going to Madagascar in summer. Avoid it in autumn, winter and spring too.

### DID YOU KNOW?

*Madagascans call God 'The Fragrant One', so avoid splashing on the Brut if you don't want to be worshipped! Or maybe not...*

# MALAWI

Malawi, apart from sounding like a disease of the colon, is one of the less developed African nations and, for the tourist, such abject poverty brings many problems. The first is apparent when you try to call home and discover there are only 4,000 phones in the country. Now that might sound like a lot but when you consider there are 6 million Malawians, that means there's just one phone for every 1,500 people. Queues at public call boxes can stretch several miles, and it's no fun waiting days getting to the front only to discover that a) you don't have the right change, b) it's been vandalised or, c) at least 600 people in front of you were just using it as an urinal.

Being a predominantly agricultural country limits Malawi's potential for visitors. Unless you're heavily into parched, overgrazed savannah and bloated cattle dying in their thousands, prepare to be disappointed in the sightseeing stakes. Most of the problems facing Malawi agriculture are due to its climate; the Malawi calendar is divided into three main periods:

May-August: the dry season

September-December: another dry season

January-April: a season that's also dry

When it comes to wildlife, compared with other African countries Malawi offers a pretty drab choice for would-be safari goers. Forget giraffes, lions, rhinos and zebras – the most exotic beasts in Malawi are boars, guinea hens, geese, snipe and the flying lemur. (Malawi guides are renowned for regaling tourists with tales of how they survived a stampeding snipe, or the discovery of the legendary flying lemur's graveyard.) Humour (and pity) them.

## Entertainment

If you thought the situation with telephones was bad, then with TVs it's almost impossible. There's one television for every 3,333 Malawians so the chances of being able to watch what you want, at the time you want, is virtually nil. In Britain, viewing is interrupted by commercials every fifteen minutes. In Malawi, viewing is interrupted by fighting over the remote control every five seconds. As if that isn't bad enough, having to change the batteries in the remote controls once every half-hour, and straining to peer over the heads of 3,332 other people in the room can make the whole TV experience in Malawi quite frustrating. What's even more frustrating, there is no TV station actually broadcasting there.

## Lake Malawi

This imaginatively named lake takes up a full two-thirds of Malawi and borders Tanzania and Mozambique. It also makes the waters off Canvey Island look positively spa-like.

Imagine rounding up the hundred dirtiest, crustiest, scabbiest, flakiest down-and-outs sleeping rough on Victoria embankment and giving them a bath without changing the water each time. Imagine taking that bath water, throwing in a decomposing horse carcass, some waste from a nearby septic tank and several bottles of Dr Pepper, then letting the whole lot stand in the sun for a month. Imagine what that water would look and smell like and you've got Lake Malawi in microcosm.

Don't even think about swimming there. Don't even think about not thinking about swimming there. It's the place where 200 million mosquitoes go on holiday, and what's more, they all bring a friend. If the crocodiles or poisonous water snakes don't kill you, any one of 115 different virulent diseases will. One whiff of the lake is enough to give you cholera and malaria and even a splash of its festering waters will give you 'river blindness' – not to mention hepatitis A, B, C, D, E, F and G. In fact, Lake Malawi is so disease-ridden that even reading about it is likely to give you typhoid.

Sorry.

# MALDIVES

A chain of islands some 1,000 strong, the Maldives got their name from mal, French for 'sick' or 'bad', and dive, which is English for 'dive'. Not the most promising name for a place, but certainly more honest than 'Great Britain', and every bit as frank as the 'Wankie Game Park' in Zimbabwe.

Brochures describe them as 'unspoilt' or 'unsophisticated', which is travel agent speak for 'Third World' and 'conspicuously lacking in adequate toilets'. The Divehi people who live there are described as 'informal', which means lazy and untrustworthy, while the overall holiday is usually feted as 'relaxing', which means there's nothing to do. (Masturbation is regarded as a serious criminal offence, so there goes the most promising form of activity on the islands.)

As you would expect of an island chain, the emphasis is on watersports (some of which are also illegal), but these are expensive and soon become tedious. You can also go coral diving to inspect the reefs if you're not afraid of 20-foot long Great White Sharks and have an abnormal interest in brightly coloured sponge. If you are lucky, you may be able to join in an impromptu game of volleyball on the beach. These are organised by bored holidaymakers, fortunate enough to have won the hotel 'ball lottery'.

Because the islands have next to no agriculture or industry, almost everything has to be imported, which means prices can be very high. Unsurprisingly, fish is cheap as is coconut, but fish in coconut sauce can become distinctly unappetising after one or two meals. You are certain to become sick of the sight of fish, which will further restrict your diving activities and your nightlife, which also tends to revolve around fish, with natives performing 'The Fish Dance' in cabaret and beating oil drums with fish to traditional ryhthms while stinking the nightclub out. As grass and shrubs are at a premium on many tiny islands in the chain, most traditional Divehi costumes are also made out of fish, further spoiling your stay and wrecking almost any thought of a holiday romance.

Many holidaymakers choose a sailing holiday around the Maldives on a Dhoni or motor sailing yacht, as at least it gets them off the islands.

When booking your holiday, avoid the monsoon and hurricane season between September and July, as many of the smaller islands can become submerged. Even on the bigger islands it is little fun to spend your entire holiday lashed to a palm tree to avoid being swept out to sea.

Package tours to the island by Air Lanka usually involve a stopover in Colombo and a fair to average chance of being killed by Tamil separatists.

# MALTA

No-one makes the pitiful island of Malta their first choice for a holiday, and it's only thanks to overbooking in Majorca or the Costa del Sol that it survives as a holiday destination at all.

Even the island's most famous residents, the Knights of the Order of St John only settled there by default. In the 1500s Charles V of Spain offered them two sites for relocation after they were kicked out of Rhodes – Malta and Tripoli. They visited both places, describing the former as 'merely a rock of soft sandstone… about 12,000 inhabitants, the greatest part of whom were poor and miserable'. Unfortunately, Tripoli had already been taken and Malta was where they ended up.

During the Second World War, the strategic position of Malta in the Mediterranean meant it was subject to almost daily Italian and German air raids. In recognition of Maltese bravery, King George VI awarded the entire country the George Cross. This caused resentment for two reasons. Firstly, King Edward VII had previously awarded New Zealand (the North Island) the more valued Victoria Cross in 1905. And secondly, since Malta only received one single medal to be shared among its

255,000 population, it meant that in the course of the year, each islander could only have the medal for 2.06 minutes before having to pass it on.

---

### OTHER ISLANDS AWARDED MEDALS:

**Corsica** - French Legion of Honour (1933)
**Tenerife**   Distinguished Flying Medal (1952)
**Cuba** - Croix de Guerre (1917)
**Madagascar** - 500 yards hurdles bronze (1944)
**West Samoa** - Norwegian Order of Saint Olav (1928)
**Christmas Island** - Navy & Marine Corps Medal (1944)
**Guam** - Order of the Purple Heart (1945)
**Eire** - The Iron Cross (1939)
**Sumatra** - Cycling Proficiency Medal (1961)

---

## Food and Drink

Throughout its history, Malta has played host to some of the greatest civilisations – the Phoenicians, the Greeks, the Romans, the Arabs – but they all got bored and left. You will do likewise. You'd think that with such cosmopolitan influences, the food and drink served on the island would have been some of the best in the world. Unfortunately 'Maltese Cuisine' is an oxymoron and the island's only appeal in the food department is to people with absolutely no sense of taste (or smell). Even Oliver Twist would have claimed to be 'full up' when confronted with Maltese dishes.

## The National Dish

If you're fond of fluffy animals then stay away from Malta – the national dish is feneka which sounds quite appetising in a Mediterranean kind of way, until you find out it's bunny rabbit. As a meat, rabbit is only eaten when you're desperate and there's nothing else available, coming well down the list after horse, dog and victims of Andean plane crashes.

On Malta, rabbits are specially bred for food and you'll find live bunnies sold at most markets for slaughter. The Maltese cook this versatile meat in many different ways – fried, fricasseed, casseroled, stewed or just plain baked in a pie. Books on Maltese cuisine are few and far between, but you can try 'Floyd on Flopsie' to give you an idea of what to expect.

**Wines**

There's nothing like a good wine to wash rabbit down – unfortunately there is nothing like a good wine on Malta. Kind wine experts describe the local wines as 'an acquired taste'; less charitable ones might go so far as to call them 'disappointing'. Those who don't mince words would say they're a cross between anti-freeze and industrial chemicals used for unblocking drains, with just a hint of cough linctus. The tradition of sampling wines and then spitting them out began right here, as did the phrase 'the acid test'. All Maltese red wines resemble fizzy Mateus Rose. So do the whites. So do the island's unique blues. And greens.

## WHAT TO SEE

Malta is jammed full of churches, chapels and basilicas – and bars showing Roy 'Chubby' Brown videos. The Church architecture might amaze but only Chubby can shock.

# MEXICO

Mexico was once home to some of the most advanced civilisations on the planet, including the Mayans, Olmecs, Toltecs and Zapotecs. Now it is home to the Mexicans, one of the least advanced civilisations on the planet. The Mayans, for example, had sophisticated calendars that could predict the timing of the celestial equinoxes down to the last few seconds. Most Mexicans, you will find, don't know what day it is.

**THE FIRST** thing you will notice about Mexico upon arrival is that it is dirty. *Muy* dirty. This baffles American tourists in particular, who cannot understand how the country got into such a state – because they know Mexicans make such good cleaners back home.

**SECONDLY,** you will notice that everyone looks like 'Manuel' from *Fawlty Towers* and sounds exactly like Speedy Gonzales. Men, women, children – it doesn't make any difference.

**THIRDLY,** everywhere you go, you will find a Mariachi band playing and a festival in progress. It will probably come as no surprise to you to learn that Mariachi is slang for 'no good'. Mexicans love their festivals because it is a chance for them to take a day off. There are 365 festivals in the

Mexican calendar. These include the infamous 'Festival of the Dead'. This is like Halloween, only in Spanish, and combines a ghoulish fascination with the supernatural with the sort of loutish behaviour you can find any Saturday night in Blackpool. Avoid it.

When a festival is in full swing, you will be treated to an unusual sight. Mexicans on their feet. Most of the rest of the time Mexicans may only ever be found slumped in doorways with their sombreros pulled down over their heads. They are a truly lazy people. When shopping for souvenirs, do remember to avoid 'siesta' when the shops are shut. Officially siesta lasts from 12 noon to 2pm, but most Mexicans have unofficially extended these times, so that siesta now lasts from the beginning of March to the end of September.

Although far too bone idle to excel at sports, Mexicans do flock to compete in the massive *Rio Grande Festival de Sport de Mexicanos*, held on the border with the US every year. Look out in particular for the massed trampolining, long jumping, sprint, swimming and pole vaulting events. Curiously, the winners of these events never reappear to claim their medals.

Of equal curiosity value, the official sport of Mexico has no name, but seems to involve seeing how long you can cling on to the axle underneath a moving flatbed truck with all your worldly goods in a plastic bag gripped in your teeth.

Cynics have suggested that this 'sport' has much in common with the nation's official pastime – trying to escape en masse to a better life in America. Despite the claims of certain right-wing American politicians, very few potential illegal immigrants do make it successfully into the States. Most are captured within minutes. A frightening game of cat and mouse with US customs officials, combined with a national diet consisting almost entirely of chillis and beans, does not allow the average Mexican to successfully hide in silence. Another common mistake made by wannabe illegal immigrants is hiding in small clumps of bushes whilst wearing huge gaily coloured sombreros – a dead giveaway.

The sombrero is the symbol of Mexican pride – which says it all really. Mexicans really do love their hats. The Mexican hat dance is not performed for the benefit of tourists. It is done out of necessity. Just as women in Britain dance around their handbags to prevent them being stolen, so Mexicans dance around their hats to prevent a thief making off with them. This is because, for many Mexicans, their hat is the most valuable item they own.

Probably the world's only 'hattist' culture, headwear goes a long way towards conveying whatever status it is possible for a Mexican to have in society. Generally speaking, the bigger and more gaily coloured the sombrero, the more important the Mexican. Mexican TV game shows often revolve around the chance to win hats, and a two-hat man is regarded as 'a hat millionaire'. Being mugged for your hat is not as uncommon as it is sad, so try to avoid wearing ostentatious looking headwear in public.

This said, Mexico is not crawling with criminals. The police force is so corrupt that there are very few opportunities and openings for career criminals.

Politically, the country is in a state of near collapse. Although Mexico pays lip service to democracy, elections are often decided by who wears the largest hat. This may be why the country is riddled with poverty and the authorities can find no economic answer.

If you do want to visit Mexico for some reason, it is better to do it sooner rather than later – because the entire country is gradually disappearing. The solution to Mexico's woes which the politicians have come up with is radical – and long-lasting. Each night, by presidential order, specially trained units of the Mexican army sneak out and move the border with America a few more inches south while no-one is looking. By 2116 the whole of Mexico will be in America and people who go looking for the country won't be able to find it any more. This will break few hearts.

## ACAPULCO – THE TRUTH

If you can afford to go to Acapulco, you can afford to go someplace better, because Acapulco has all the creepy 'sophistication' that you might find in a cheap early-1970s aftershave commercial. The only good thing about the beaches and hotel pools here is that there are no indigenous Mexicans in sight. This is because any Mexican who can swim has long since gone off to run a hubcap-stealing racket in Los Angeles.

## IMPORTS AND EXPORTS

**CHIEF EXPORT:** Mexicans
**CHIEF IMPORT:** Mexicans returned by US border patrols

## DID YOU KNOW?

*Mexican jumping beans do not actually jump. They are called 'jumping beans' because they are jumping with insects and bacteria..*

### EATING OUT

Lovers of Mexican food are in for a shock. Authentic Mexican food tastes nothing like the so-called Mexican meals you get back home. Only in Mexico can you get proper Mexican food, because only in Mexico is it made with that special something extra – dirt. You will find authentic tortillas taste of mud, while genuine refried bean tacos should be liberally speckled with tapeworm eggs. Look out for authentic chicken fajitas, which are hot, spicy and very very gravelly. Tostardos are another unique taste experience, especially if you've never eaten sand basted in human sweat.

## CUSTOMS TIPS

When leaving Mexico for America, be sure to check your hire car and luggage for any hidden Mexicans. Smuggling a Mexican into any civilised country is a serious offence. You will be asked at the airport on departure and arrival at your destination if you have any Mexicans to declare. You may also find yourself subjected to a body search, as several Mexicans have recently been discovered hidden in body cavities.

# MONGOLIA

Think of Mongolia and the image conjured up is one of the mighty warrior Genghis Khan and his Golden Horde of proud Tartar warriors thundering across the Gobi Desert in search of new lands to conquer.

By the thirteenth century, Mongolia had conquered half the world. Today most of the country doesn't even have running water. How the mighty have fallen.

Nowadays Mongolia is a country with very little to offer the tourist, and very little to offer Mongolians (more Mongolians live outside the country, in China or Russia, than actually in Mongolia).

## *What today's Mongolia can offer the tourist:*

- ❑ Shops that specialise in empty shelves
- ❑ Temperatures that range from the surface of Mercury in summer to the far side of Neptune in winter
- ❑ The most ridiculous sounding currency in the entire world – the togrog (which consists of 100 mongos)
- ❑ A town called 'Moron' (670 km from the capital Ulaanbaatar)
- ❑ Hospital facilities so primitive that the nearest casualty department is in Tokyo
- ❑ An indigenous population who all look like Chinese who have spent too long under a sun bed
- ❑ No obvious differences between sexes
- ❑ Few physical differences between sexes
- ❑ Accommodation that consists primarily of large tents (called 'Gers'), which have no running water and a stove that burns Yak dung as fuel, which smells so bad that most Mongols prefer to spend the winter months sitting outside in the snow
- ❑ A phone system marginally more efficient than two cans and a length of twine
- ❑ The chance to contract diarrhoea, rabies, tetanus and bubonic plague simultaneously
- ❑ Unfinished metal goods

Perhaps Mongolia's most famous claim to fame is that it offers tourists positively the worst, most disgusting and nauseating cuisine in the entire world. A cuisine so revolting that even Ethiopians would rather go without; a cuisine so foul that when it was demonstrated on *Masterchef*, the BBC pulled the entire show and agreed a substantial out-of-court settlement with Lloyd Grossman.

What is this cuisine? Well, since there are ten times as many sheep as there are Mongolians, it's not surprising that the national dish is boiled, greasy mutton. Boiled greasy mutton cooked on a yak dung fire. This slow cooking method is what gives Mongolian boiled greasy mutton its uniquely distinct taste – that is, the taste of yak shit.

Just as Russia has its beluga caviar and France its pâté de foie gras, Mongolia values mutton fat as a true delicacy and indeed, a confectionery. Gift boxes of mutton fat misshapes are a common gift between lovers, and Mongolian sweetshops should be given a wide berth. Mongolians don't stop at eating excess mutton fat. It's also used by women as a moisturising cream, a soap substitute and a douche. Not surprisingly, cunnilingus is not popular in Mongolia.

Nothing short of imbibing a liquid oven cleaner will take the taste of the mutton fat away and clear the palette. However, even this might be preferable to the drinks that are likely to accompany your meal – a salty tea that tastes like the water left in the sink after washing up, or a local drink with the viscosity and taste of fermented horse sweat.

For the discerning gourmet, there are a few alternative dishes, such as Yak cheese pancakes and fried Yak milk curds. However, in the absence of vegetable oil, these are all cooked in congealed mutton lard, so you're back where you started.

---

## THE WORST SELLING (MONGOLIAN-BASED) COOKBOOKS OF ALL TIME

Delia's Gobi Desert Dessert

Let's Cook Mongolian!

Mongolian for Two or Twenty

Floyd With His Head In A Bucket

Ready, Steady, Vomit

Rhodes on The Toilet

---

## WHERE TO GO AND WHAT TO SEE

*Don't bother.*

Public transport is erratic, signposts non-existent, maps are as rare as an appetising meal and no-one, absolutely no-one, speaks English. If you do happen to find something of vague interest, the chances are that it'll be broken down or shut or both.

# MOROCCO

Some towns in the world have contributed a definite something to the world. Manila in the Philippines has given us envelopes, Bombay has given us duck and Philadelphia has given us cream cheese. Unfortunately, Morocco's towns just don't compare:

**AGADIR:** Gave us the song by Black Lace

**MARRAKESH AND TANGIERS:** Gave us boy brothels where Joe Orton used to hang out (physically as well as geographically)

**FEZ:** Gave us stupid red hats with tassels

**CASABLANCA:** Didn't give us a genuine 'Rick's American Bar' and so disappoints thousands of visiting film buffs annually

Apart from these uninspiring towns, Morocco is dominated by its mosques and an orthodox Muslim religion. Tourists should note that these people have no sense of humour and are unlikely to see the funny side of a joke about 'Sunni and Cher', or one that relies on a misinterpretation of the word 'Shi'ite' for its humour.

## MOSQUE CRAWLING

If you want to visit a Moroccan mosque (say, for instance, the boy brothel in Tangiers is closed for refurbishment and you're at a loose end – or wished you were) it's essential to show respect for the Islamic religion and win the trust of its devotees.

Remember that a mosque is a place of worship and a sanctuary, not the location for an impromptu farting or spitting competition, or a good place to supplement your shoe collection. Being dressed in accordance with Islamic requirements is the first prerequisite for entry:

### Acceptable clothing to gain entrance to a mosque

✔ Modest clothing which covers your arms and legs.

### Unacceptable clothing to gain entrance to a mosque

✖ Skirt so short that it reveals split-crotch panties worn underneath
✖ Skirt so short that it reveals absolutely no panties worn underneath
(Both the above are true for men AND women)

✖ Teddy Sheringham replica Spurs football shirt
✖ A gorilla fancy-dress outfit
✖ Lycra cycling shorts so tight that they reveal your religion
✖ Peephole bikini
✖ Any form of footwear
✖ A Jean-Paul Gautier pointy bra and basque
✖ Anything with the Star of David embroidered on it
✖ Pearly King or Queen outfit (these are offensive to everyone, not just Muslims)

## SHOPPING

Marrakesh is famous for its weekly market, the Medina, one of the largest bazaars in the world. Tourists can spend the whole day wandering around the hundreds of narrow side streets which offer a cornucopia of bargains, including:

❑ Dried fruit and sticky sweetmeats so manky that anything found round the rim of a kitchen swing-bin would be more appetising. (Ensure that the weight you are sold does not include the flies)

❑ Copper pots and pans that look as though they've all been thrown out of a fifth floor window. Picked up, thrown out again. Used as a make-shift ball in a local five-a-side tournament and then hit with a big mallet

❑ Silver religious icons which would disgrace a darts team trophy cabinet, let alone a major faith

❑ Spices so pungent that they'll clear a blocked sinus at fifty paces

❑ Ceramic tiles so nasty that lining your bathroom wall with Jacob's cream crackers would be more aesthetically pleasing

❑ Wicker baskets that look as though they've been woven by teams of myopic Parkinson's disease sufferers

❑ Brass candlesticks which wobble (and would most likely catch fire and melt if ever used)

❑ Brass animals so misshappen that they might be an elephant, a tiger or a crocodile (then again, they might be a camel)

❑ Fish which went on the turn three days ago

❑ Caged, scrawny chickens just waiting to have their heads chopped off

❑ Uncaged, scrawny chickens who just have

❑ Letter openers shaped like scimitars which bend when faced with anything tougher than Manila

❑ Clay vases which leak

**SAVING MONEY**

The Moroccan Tourist Council constantly promotes the wonder of haggling at the country's many bazaars – that it's a way of life and how, by skilful bargaining, you can make huge savings.

One useful tip to make even greater savings is not to buy any of the worthless junk on offer. When was the last time you really needed a wooden camel with one leg longer than the others anyway?

# MYANMAR

The repressive nation formerly known as Burma, Myanmar is one of the least westernised countries and most brutal military dictatorships in the world. Many tour companies refuse to include Myanmar in their brochures on ideological grounds. This is to be commended. After all, how could civilised human beings condone a country which denies its citizens even the most basic right to Coca-Cola, McDonald's and *The Simpsons*?

Tourists must realise that every penny they contribute to the Myanmar economy is likely to be used by the government to buy electric shock batons, leg irons, hypodermic syringes and jackboot polish.

The vicious bastards given the responsibility for supressing the Myanmar people are called SLORC. Although this sounds like something to be hunted in an Edward Lear poem, or else a splinter group of THRUSH in *The Man From UNCLE*, SLORC is actually the Military State Law and Order Restoration Council, who established martial law in 1988.

### Eating
Politics aside, Myanmar is bordered by China, India, Bangladesh and Thailand, making it well served for takeaways. The downside is that the rampant inflation means that a bowl of rice can go up by 380 per cent between the time you order it and when it's ready.

*Stupid facts about Myanmar*

## FACT!
It has the most ridiculous looking alphabet in the world. This consists of 44 different interlocking circles making it the only language inspired by the Olympic symbol.

## FACT!
According to traditional Myanmar astrology there are 8 days of the week – the eighth day being called 'Yahu' (now we know what the Beatles were referring to).

## FACT!
A Myanmar can change his/her name as many times as they like in their life and will do so if they think this will change their fortune, or if SLORC are after them. For example, the 1962 coup was successful because the rebel general changed his name to General U Win to inspire his troops (he thought no-one would follow a leader called General Snowball's Chance In Hell).

## WHAT TO SEE AND DO

The best thing about visiting foreign countries is the chance to observe and ridicule local customs and traditions. The Amazonian Indians with big wooden discs in their lips that make them all look like a race of Mick Jaggers are well worth having a crack at – but by far the best geeks to abuse are in Myanmar. These are the Padaung 'Giraffe Necked Women' of the oddly named 'Karen' tribe, who add a new copper or brass ring around their neck every year since puberty. This results in a neck 10" long which, while ideal for remakes of *Deep Throat*, causes persistent trouble going through airport metal detectors.

As far as landmarks go, there's not much to see in Myanmar apart from monasteries and pagodas and, quite frankly, if you've seen one shrine to Buddha you've seen them all. Myanmar only has two cities, Yangon (the southern capital formerly known as Rangoon) and Mandalay (the regional centre formerly known as Mandalay), in the centre.

### Yangon
If you feel you really must visit one Pagoda, make it the famous Shwedagon Pagoda just west of the Royal Lake. This 100 m high temple

features nearly 9,000 solid gold slabs on the outside and the spire is encrusted with 5,000 diamonds (if you do visit, don't forget a chisel).

## The Royal Palace

This is situated in Mandalay, but don't get excited. The tourist guides all describe it as a royal palace but it was actually burned to the ground during the war and is now just a scorchmark on some scrubland.

# NEPAL

Nestled high in the Himalayas between China and India, Nepal has succeeded in combining the worst elements of both countries, with altitude sickness thrown in for good measure.

When you arrive, you must understand that all Nepalese assume that you've come here to climb. As soon as you reach your hotel and hand the porter your cases, he'll beckon you to follow and – if you're not very careful – the next thing you know you'll be halfway up Everest. If you haven't come here to climb, the Nepalese are almost completely at a loss as to what to do with you. Try to climb something just to make them happy. They will be almost childishly grateful for it.

Nepal is most definitely not the place to go for a cycling holiday, as *everywhere* is uphill. Cycling is further complicated by the idea the Nepalese have that the bicycle is actually a western breed of cow and you will receive many baffling offers to milk it for you. Let them do it. It's their problem.

If you decide to ignore this advice and set off to explore by bike, you will find that the only places to stop for refreshments are roadside stalls selling hot Bovril drinks and Oxo stock. These are made with freshly melted snow which is then boiled. All very well, but traditionally Sherpas melt the snow by urinating on it. Aware that western customers find this off-putting to the point of physical violence, more forward-looking Sherpas have now taken to melting the snow by cramming it down their underpants and grimacing for 90 seconds – which is marginally better. Still want to go cycling?

If you have come to Nepal to climb and have a strict budget, don't buy the first Sherpa guide you see. It pays to shop around. Sherpa hire stores accept Visa and American Express, and offer you a wide choice of Sherpas including end of season bargains, slight seconds, shop-soiled models and ones that have simply gone out of fashion. Sherpas can be hired by the day, by the week or just to make your dinner, and some top of the range models come complete with stereo cassette. A safety tip – never pick the runt of the litter just because you feel sorry for him. He will invariably become exhausted and disorientated and then plunge down a glacier taking your tent and supplies with him.

Of course, you can hire a mule to carry your provisions instead of a Sherpa. They smell better, but tend to kick and cost more.

While climbing, remember that plunging onto your face from a height of 13,000 feet is likely to kill you, so observe simple safety precautions like changing your mind altogether.

If you get homesick, try looking up the British contingent in Kathmandu. These are ancient hippies who travelled overland to get here in the 1960s and got so stoned that they couldn't even find the correct plane of existence, let alone the right plane back home. So they have stayed and grown old here. Many are in their sixties or even seventies now, and Kathmandu can boast the only Darby and Joan club that plays The Doors. Many still run around naked except for beads and face paints, so you have to be very homesick to want to look them up.

# THE NETHERLANDS

Potential visitors to the Netherlands are likely to be put off first and fore-most by the language, which sounds like an effeminate German pretend-ing to be Welsh.

If you can put up with this during your visit then you'll find a country with a liberal attitude towards all aspects of life and a people who are so easygoing, it's almost impossible to wind them up. Even driving a com-bine harvester through prized tulip fields, calling their country 'Holland' and not 'the Netherlands', sawing through the crossbar of every bicycle you find or saying that their beloved Queen Beatrix has a face like an arse will only engender a cheery smile and a hearty slap on the back.

Most people associate the Netherlands with windmills, tulips and cheese but the reality is that it's much more famous for sex, drugs and euthana-sia...

## Sex

Holland is known the world over for its open attitude towards sex, and the authorities are keen to teach sex education at a very early age (all Dutch five-year-olds know the the story about the boy with his finger in the dyke).

Visitors to Amsterdam's famous red-light district are warned that any sex act with a prostitute is likely to be interrupted, not by the police but by a school party of ten-year-olds on an educational trip. If this should happen, just ignore them, their cameras and their childish pointing and giggling. Try to hold still while they complete their project book.

## Drugs

The country is so liberal in its attitude towards drugs that it's actually a criminal offence NOT to bring any into the country with you. Police naturally suspect any tourists who are clean-shaven with smart clothes and respectable, well-paid jobs.

Tourists arriving at Schiphol airport are subject to random searches and any found not to be carrying drugs are taken behind screens where they will have a plastic bag of cannabis resin shoved up their rectum, or else be forced to swallow twenty condoms containing cocaine before being sent on their way with a smile.

## Euthanasia

The Netherlands is the only country in the world where mercy killing is not just legal, it's a way of life (or death). Elderly tourists – or those just looking unwell – are advised to be on their guard at all times against over-zealous doctors and well-meaning Dutch passers-by. When a Dutchman asks, 'how are you?' always tell him you are 100 per cent fit and well and have just passed a stringent medical thank you very kindly and offer to show them your last stools as proof. Never cough, blow your nose or complain of sore feet in public.

When visiting a Dutch civic facility, never leave through the door marked 'Exit', as mercy killing bureaux are attached to all buildings as a public service.

## GETTING ABOUT

If the Netherlands was a person, then it would be Kate Moss – seriously dull and totally flat. The flat countryside makes it perfect for getting about by bicycle

Unfortunately, the popularity of cycling in the Netherlands means that everyone goes around wearing skintight Lycra cycling shorts – good news for men whose genitals resemble Linford Christie's – but bad news for men whose genitals resemble Agatha Christie's.

## Haarlem

Many visitors here can't understand how they can walk through this area at night without being shot, stabbed, raped, mugged or all four simultaneously. The reason is simple: they're not in Harlem in Manhattan, but in a city of the same name in the Netherlands, about 30 minutes from Amsterdam.

---

## HOW TO TELL YOU'RE IN HAARLEM AND NOT HARLEM

The coolest footwear is clogs, not a $190 pair of Nikes

Youths on the street corners play a hand-wound hurdy-gurdy, not a 150-watt Muthafucka of a sound system

The skyline is broken by windmills, not cars on fire

The town's filled with paintings by Frans Hals, not pointless squiggles from an aerosol

You can buy 38 types of soft cheese, not 68 types of hard drugs

The most popular fast food is chips covered in mayonnaise, not chili dogs

Van Gogh is revered more than Snoop Doggy Dog

The average family has more than one parent

The locals are welcoming

---

## *TULIPS*
*There is nothing worth saying about tulips.*

# NEW ZEALAND

New Zealand is an affable, backwater country which plods along at its own pace – not the sort of place where you'd expect to find an intense hatred of another culture such as is rarely seen outside of the Persian Gulf, let alone in the South Pacific. It's a country which, because of its relative isolation, usually welcomes international visitors warmly – just as long as they're not French.

Although the French are universally despised, New Zealand has more reason than most to hate them. First, French secret agents sank the Greenpeace boat *Rainbow Warrior* in Auckland in 1985. A few years later they annoyed them slightly more – by conducting underwater atomic testing at nearby Moruroa Atoll in French Polynesia.

This has led the New Zealand Government to prohibit entry by anyone French – or anyone they think might be French.

The following questionnaire has to be completed by all visitors on arrival and any 'yes' answer will result in instant deportation:

## NEW ZEALAND DEPT OF IMMIGRATION

**Part A**

Are you French?                                                  [  ] yes    [  ] no

If you answer 'yes' go home
If you answer 'no', go to Part B

**Part B**

Is your nickname 'Frenchy'?                                      [  ] yes    [  ] no

Do you have a stripey jumper at home?                           [  ] yes    [  ] no

Or a beret?                                                      [  ] yes    [  ] no

Do you have a stupid pencil moustache?                          [  ] yes    [  ] no

Do you like horse meat?                                         [  ] yes    [  ] no

Do you have a total disregard for the speed limit?             [  ] yes    [  ] no

Do you have a total disregard for personal hygiene?            [  ] yes    [  ] no

Do you smoke unfiltered cigarettes that smell as
much as you do?                                                 [  ] yes    [  ] no

| | |
|---|---|
| Do you like going to the toilet in the middle of the street in a little tin hut? | [ ] yes  [ ] no |
| When you're uncertain about something do you shrug your shoulders? | [ ] yes  [ ] no |
| Are you pompous, arrogant and supercilious (or any or all of them)? | [ ] yes  [ ] no |
| Do you think that Jerry Lewis is funny? | [ ] yes  [ ] no |
| Do you think that Jacques Tati is funny? | [ ] yes  [ ] no |
| Do you think that destroying the *Rainbow Warrior* in Auckland Harbour is funny? | [ ] yes  [ ] no |

If you're not French and you're allowed entry, the first thing you'll notice about New Zealand is how similar it is to Australia. Both countries are rugged wilderness, sparsely populated by an extremely ugly indigenous people.

### The People

When it comes to chronicling their own history, the native Maori are as bad as the Aborigines. They believe that the god Maui was fishing one day and slung his hook (made from the jawbone of his grandmother – who was also a sorcerer) over the side of his canoe. Eventually something caught on the hook and he reeled it in – it wasn't a large fish as he'd thought, but was actually the North Island of New Zealand. If you believe that, then you'll also believe that the Maui's canoe later became the South Island. Right.

Apart from talking crap the Maoris have a reputation for giving guests a warm welcome. The ritual consists of donning a grass skirt, poking their tongue out, putting their hands on their hips and doing a stomp like the dance to Mud's 'Tiger Feet'. Rather than appearing charming and 'ethnic', this just makes the Maoris look like a bunch of thugs – as does having more tattoos on their faces than the entire membership of the British National Party combined.

### The Animals

On the animal front, New Zealand has both its good and bad points. The good news is that it's one of the very few countries in the world without snakes. The bad news is that it's one of the very few countries with 70 million sheep. While this may not seem to be a bad aspect for tourists, it is if: a) you're allergic to wool or b) you're trying to abstain from ovine sex.

## New Zealand and the Arts

Like nearby Australia, New Zealand is often viewed as a cultural waste-land. However, the preponderance of sheep – and the economy's dependency on them – has meant the animal has achieved importance in all aspects of New Zealand culture, expecially in the arts, where painting styles have included 'Lamb Renaissance', 'Baa-Baa-Baroque', 'Ram Rococo', 'Cewebism' and 'Ovine Expressionism'.

Britain's Tate Gallery recently loaned the Wellington National Art Collection Damien Hurst's 'Sheep Suspended In Formaldehyde' and people queued for six blocks just to see it. This work subsequently inspired a whole 'Suspended Sheep' art movement, the finest examples of which are on show at the Auckland National Gallery and include 'Ram Suspended In Meths', 'Lamb Suspended In Paraffin', 'Baa-Baa Suspended In That Blue Stuff Used To Clean Silver' and 'Museum Governor Suspended For Buying This Crap'.

Theatre: New Zealand has a burgeoning interest in the performing arts, and long-running shows in Christchurch have included 'One Man And His Dog On Ice', 'The Shari Lewis Summer Spectacular' and a freely adapted version of *Silence of the Lambs* (in which it is a mute lamb – and not Hannibal Lector – who helps agent Starling track down the serial killer).

## HOLIDAYS

### June 7th: Alan Shearer's Birthday
(New Zealanders know he's got nothing to do with sheep
but he just sounds like he might)

### July 21st: Kiwi Fruit Day
(Children go from house to house dressed as Kiwi fruits, knocking on the doors
and saying 'Trick or Kiwi!'. This is not their equivalent of 'trick or treating' as Kiwi fruit
could never be described as a treat)

### 1st August: Lammastide

### August 12th: Bo-Peep Day
(This is a day of national mourning for the sheep which were lost)

# NIGERIA

*Visiting Nigeria is a once in a lifetime experience.
Once you've done it, you'll never do it again.*

The official currency of Nigeria is the bribe (100 bribes = one government official.) It is not necessary to sort out bribes before you go. Immigration officials, customs men and heavily armed soldiers will be more than willing to help you at the airport on arrival. The bribe is almost universally accepted by taxi drivers, hoteliers, tourist officials, police, gaolers and anyone with a gun. They will also accept Amex and Visa cards, but don't ever expect to see them again.

Having sorted out your bribes at the airport, and having set off for town in a taxi, you will note one interesting Nigerian architectural feat almost immediately. The road that they started building from the airport to Lagos doesn't meet the one they started from Lagos out to the airport. In fact, they miss each other by almost a half mile and sort of peter out in the scrub. This is because of the ancient Nigerian tradition of 'Gross Incompetence'. Nigerians tell visitors that they are a superstitious people, and that acting competently in any endeavour is seen as bad luck. Therefore, the 'Dark Gods of the Mountain' smile upon those who make mistakes. This is not true. Most Nigerians are Christians – and are simply incapable of getting anything right, ever. But they do love to tell tall stories...

Nigeria's culture is rich in stories of people who make big mistakes, and who then bribe their way out of trouble and emerge triumphant. Many of these stories, complete with artefacts, are on display at the 'Black Eisteddfod' at the Nigerian Cultural Centre in Lagos, an ambitious complex of display halls and tourist accommodation which has everything except electricity (accidentally left out of the building plans).

The capital Lagos has all the visual appeal of a cat's bottom and boasts many similar odours. Go to the port, where you will see the unusual site of rats jumping off the quayside rather than off the boats. This is the phenomenon known as 'rats leaving a sinking country'. Nigeria is Africa's largest producer of rats and, before oil was discovered, much of its economy was rat-based. Now, Nigeria is one of the world's leading producers of oil but, in a staggering display of incompetence, has actually managed to become much poorer since oil was found. Only Great Britain can match this feat on the world stage, so it is no wonder that many Nigerians come to Britain and regard it as their second home.

Despite being Africa's largest rubber producer, Nigeria still has a chronic overpopulation problem. This may have something to do with the Nigerians' love of cock-ups. Or maybe not.

**ETIQUETTE**

The correct way to address the Nigerian Prime Minister is, 'here's twenty dollars, pal. You didn't see anything, OK?'

# NORWAY

When it comes to Scandinavia as a tourist attraction, Norway comes a poor third. Sweden, awash with adult bookshops is clear favourite, Finland comes off next best since it contains Lapland, home of Father Christmas, while Norway has, well, nothing in particular.

*The artist Edvard Munch was Norwegian and the subtitle to* The Scream *could have been 'Living in Norway' – so dull is the place.*

It's no coincidence that Norway's other most famous inhabitants were explorers who couldn't wait to leave. Thor Heyerdahl was so bored he built a home-made balsawood raft and explored the South Pacific in 1947. He came home but got so bored once more that he decided to sail across the Atlantic on one made of papyrus in 1970. Before him, Roald Amundsen left his comfortable home in a leafy suburb of Oslo to go to the South Pole; he'd considered going to the North Pole but decided it wasn't nearly far enough away from Norway. And as for the Vikings – well, a race leaving its home and sailing 3,000 miles across uncharted seas must say something about the country they're deserting.

## The Fjords
Say Norway and two things immediately come to mind – the group 'Aha' and Fjords. Coincidentally, both share the same characteristics, being cold, uninteresting and barren (one creatively and the other geographically).

---
## INTERESTING FACTS ABOUT THE FJORDS
---

1. It is the only word in the English language where a 'j' follows a consonant
('Bjork' doesn't count since she's a singer, not a proper noun – and not
even a proper singer, come to think of it)

2. That's it.

---

## Expense

For a country so dull it's difficult to see how Norway justifies its position
as the most expensive country in Europe and home to some of the most
expensive beers in the whole world. The prices are so high (£10+ for a
pint) that buying a round is unheard of, and drinkers tend to make the
one pint last all night (by regurgitating it every half-hour or so). Since the
nights often last for six months, this has put many landlords out of business.

## Eating

With a staple diet of elk or reindeer steaks, Norway is not the ideal destination for vegetarians (or those who have more than a passing belief in
Father Christmas).

---
## SIGHTSEEING
---

## Oslo

It won't surprise you to learn that as far as Scandinavian cities go, the
Norwegian capital Oslo is the least visited. It's so dreary that in the seventeenth century, the city council tried to improve its fortunes by actually moving its location and changing its name to Christiana in an
attempt to sound like a sultry temptress and attract more visitors. Three
hundred years later they were looking for something else to enliven the
city – so they changed its name back again. Needless to say, neither of
these moves had any effect whatsoever.

Museums tend, on the whole, to be deadly dull, and Oslo is home to perhaps the world's dullest. The jewel in the crown of mundane museums is
the Norwegian Folk Museum in Museumsveien on the Bygdøy Peninsula,
the main attraction of which is a large display of reconstructed farms
from Norway's deeply fascinating agricultural past and a comprehensive

collection of hand-beaten Norwegian silverware. Save your £5 entry fee (you'll need it for half a pint of beer).

Nearby is the Norwegian Museum of the Sea, home to a thrilling collection of sextants, astrolabes and other navigational tools significant to aficionados of Norwegian naval history – but to no-one else. It is understood that at the time of writing, the museum is constructing a special 'Hall of the Polar Icebreakers' and when completed, will probably be well worth a miss.

If that's too racy for you, then on the city limits you'll find the Holmenkollen Ski Museum, with displays of skis throughout history. Visitors will be hard pressed to notice any difference in any of the exhibits.

## Bergen

Norway's second largest city and second only to Oslo in terms of places of interest (which means very little). However, don't be conned into visiting the Rasmus Meyer's Collection on Rasmus Meyer's Alle. This is a collection of Norwegian art and not, repeat NOT, the Norwegian spelling of Russ Meyer. If you visit the museum hoping to see a series of stills from *UltraVixens* or *Beyond the Valley of the Dolls* you'll be disappointed.

## Hammerfest

Not a three-day convention for ironmongery fans, but the most northern city in the world (and the first to be lit by electric street lamps). As a town, Hammerfest is extremely unlucky, being accidentally burned to the ground in 1891, and then rebuilt only to be destroyed once more by retreating Germans in WW2, before being rebuilt again. Why they bothered no-one knows.

Sites of interest to tourists include the Findus fish processing plant and the Royal and Ancient Polar Bear Society. This sounds grand but it's not – it's a collection of stuffed, manky specimens in the basement of the town hall. Many of the polar bears on display are ancient, but none of them is royal. Why – and how — these stuffed bears chose to form their own society is not known. Temporary membership is available to non-ursines.

Other places of interest (and the term is used lightly) within Norway:

## Lillehammer

So boring it was chosen as the home of the 1994 Winter Olympics.

## Narvik
Spiritual home of whaling. Twinned with Kyoto.

## Spitzbergen
Spiritual home of nothingness.

## Stavanger
Nothing of note.

## Kongsberg
Nor here.

## Trondheim
As above.

# THE SULTANATE OF OMAN

Oman is ruled by an absolute monarchy in the person of Sultan Qaboos Bin Said. Sultan Qaboos is also the Prime Minister, Foreign Minister, Minister for State, Minister of Defence, Chancellor of the Exchequer and Head of the Opposition. Being an absolute ruler has caused the Sultan no end of difficulty because as head of the opposition he recently decided he had no choice but to call for his own removal.

The bitter exchange of words that followed between the Sultan and himself rapidly escalated into threats and ultimatums and then exploded into open warfare. Troops loyal to the Sultan fought it out with pro-Sultan forces, as attempts were made by force to oust the Sultan and replace him with the Sultan. Passionate crowds surged through the towns and villages, chanting 'Up with the Sultan! Down with the Sultan!', burning effigies of their hated enemy and waving pictures of their glorious leader, and vice versa.

At one point, troops actually invaded the Sultan's palace, bodily threw him out and then escorted him back in again to wild cheering by the assembled crowds. The Sultan was kicked out twice more as the fortunes of war ebbed and flowed. At this point, Oman's old ally Britain unwisely chose to get involved. Britain sent a detatchment of the SAS in to kidnap the Sultan and then bust him loose again. Although top secret, a vivid account of the action is given in Sgt Andy McNab's two books, 'The One That I Couldn't Understand' and 'Immediate Confusion'.

In recent years, an uneasy truce has been maintained between the warring pro-Sultan factions. In 1993 President Clinton invited the Sultan to come and meet himself and explore a dialogue for peace at Camp David. It was a triumph for the US State Department, as Sultan Qaboos allowed himself to be photographed shaking hands with himself on the White House Lawn, with Clinton standing behind him making 'looney' signs.

Resolving the problem has proved rather more difficult. Some form of power sharing agreement now seems likely.

Visitors to Oman will be dismayed. That's what comes of choosing your holiday destination by throwing a dart at the map of the world. Be honest. That's how you chose Oman. No-one visits here for any other reason.

The Omanis don't need tourists, because of their oil wealth. Uniquely, traders in the Muscat Souk don't like haggling. Say, 'I'll give you fifty' and the response will be a curt, 'piss off!' This takes all the fun out of the market, which was precious little fun to begin with. Nightlife is almost non-existent, except for one disco bar in a Muscat hotel which has a 'Smurfs Go Pop' LP and isn't afraid to use it. Most tourists make their own amusement, such as sitting on their hotel bed cracking their knuckles or catching up on their toenail cutting.

One last piece of advice – avoid visiting during Ramadan when people have to forego their morning coffee and so are particularly ratty all day.

### DID YOU KNOW?

*When an Omani asks you if you would like a date, he is not asking to go out with you (if he was, he'd put his right hand down your trousers, close his eyes and pout). He is actually offering you a date fruit. Oman produces 50,000 tonnes of dates a year and Omanis are intensely proud of this.*

### DID YOU KNOW?

*Because Oman is the world leader in date production, constipation is almost unheard of in the country. So is tasty food.*

# PAKISTAN

Pakistan used to have the second horniest world leader in Benazir Bhutto but, as a country, it's the council estate of the Indian sub-continent; it's got the worst neighbours in the whole world, everyone's on the scrounge, three-quarters of the people are illiterate, dangerous dogs run loose – and it stinks.

When it comes to its neighbours, the countries that border Pakistan are some of the most deplorable, foul and disgusting places on the planet. As if Iran, Afghanistan, China and India weren't bad enough, Pakistan also has to contend with three former Soviet republics – which happen to be the three most wretched of the bunch – Tajikistan, Uzbekistan and Turkmenistan.

Unless you count abject poverty as a tourist attraction, Pakistan offers very little for the visitor. As one of the poorest countries in the world it's difficult to walk down any of its pitiful streets without tripping over a beggar. While this might be considered a petty inconvenience most of the time, what makes it more annoying for tourists is that they're always whingeing about something – whether it's about having no job, no home or no eyesight.

After a while this becomes very tedious, and taunting beggars often becomes the main source of entertainment for bored tourists.

---

### TAUNTING BEGGARS FOR FUN –
### A GUIDE FOR TOURISTS

---

❏ Throw them commemorative football coins ( Esso FA Cup Centenary set coins have the exact feel and weight of a 2 rupee coin)

❏ Torment them with your salary statement (this only works if they don't have cataracts in both eyes)

❏ Torment them with your Giro, as social security is unknown here

❏ Torment them with a £2 postal order from your granny

❏ Ask if they take traveller's cheques… or if they have change for a $100 bill

❏ Offer them 10,000 Rupees – if they can sing 'Raindrops Keep Falling On My Head', and get all the words right

❏ Tell them that they're scroungers and they should get off their backsides and get a job (OK, so it's difficult to get off your backside if you're born without legs but that's their problem)

❏ Tell them that if they wanted to make something of their pitiful lives they'd be selling The Baluchistan Big Issue

If beggars aren't bad enough, what's worse for the tourist is that Pakistan is a country of cheats. They can't help it. The 'Cheat Gene' is part of Pakistani DNA and its effect goes far beyond the cricket World Cup. The unwary visitor can often find, during a simple shopping transaction, that he's been cheated out of his change, one of his kidneys and even his right to British citizenship. In one instance, a holidaymaker buying a Kashmir sweater found himself cheated out of ten years of his life. On another occasion a tourist bought a leather belt in Lahore and found herself cheated out of her first-born son.

## THE SIGHTS

Unlike neighbouring India, which does have a handful of tourist traps (even if they do include Bhopal and some dreary markets), Pakistan only claims two sights of interest – and one of these is a barefaced lie.

### Mount Everest
Tourists are advised not to be fooled by the offer of expeditions up the world's highest mountain – this is just another blatant example of Pakistani cheating. The mountain you'll see near the Pakistan/China border is actually K2 and signs saying 'K2' have been crossed out and

replaced with 'Mount Everest', which is much more famous and doesn't sound like a distant relative of K-9. To add to the illusion, natives in the region have taken to impersonating the abominable snowman, or yeti. Few visitors are fooled, as yetis tend to be big and hairy and white rather than short and obnoxious and brown. Furthermore, the true yeti is a shy creature and would never stand on the roadside with his hand out saying, 'baksheesh! baksheesh!'

Avoid the Yeti Museum in Nanga Parbat, as this is not in fact a museum at all, but a misleadingly labelled squat toilet.

### The Khyber Pass

The Pakistan Tourist Commission has tried to exploit the enduring success of the film *Carry On Up The Khyber* by creating a series of national monuments and parks in homage to the film's stars:

- ❏ The Sid James Memorial Footbridge
  *(a rope footbridge with the middle planks missing)*
- ❏ Joan Sims National Park
  *(half an acre of sun-dried earth with a dead bush in one corner)*
- ❏ Kenneth Williams Gorge
  *(a particularly steep cliff)*
- ❏ The Hattie Jacques Ravine
  *(a cliff that's not quite as steep)*
- ❏ The Charles Hawtrey Game Reserve
  *(a rock-strewn plateau with a few mountain goats)*
- ❏ The Bernard Bresslaw Botanical Gardens
  *(two juniper bushes and a cactus)*
- ❏ Jim Dale Point
  *(a pile of boulders facing out over the wrong way)*
- ❏ The Barbara Windsor Squat Toilet

# PARAGUAY

International tourism to Paraguay really began in 1945 with an unprecedented number of Germans visiting the country and liking it so much that they decided to stay.

The name Paraguay means 'a place with a great river' although a more appropriate translation might today be 'a place with a great many war criminals'.

There's not much for the tourist to do in Paraguay unless you're looking for ex-Nazis to drug, stuff into a large trunk and deport for trial. The country has a slow pace of life, epitomised by the sunburnt local craftsmen you'll see in the capital of Asunción and the town of Concepción. Under the leafy shade of ban yan trees lining the avenues you'll see them plying their trade in the old Paraguayan arts of tattoo removal, passport forgery and plastic surgery.

The current government, rather than being ashamed of its recent past, has blatantly sought to exploit its past connections with Nazis with the establishment of 'Nazi World', a theme park situated at Ciudad del Este, on the border with Brazil.

---

# NAZI WORLD

# The theme park to last 1,000 years!
# More popular than a
# Nuremberg rally!
# More fun than the Anschluss!

### Himmler Helter Skelter
It's a white knuckle-black shirt ride of your life as you hurtle down this 80-foot high scale model of Heinrich Himmler!

### Bouncy Colditz Castle
Kids, bounce your hearts out in this inflatable prison. You'll have so much fun you won't want to leave (which is good, because you can't!)

### Heavy-Water Chute
Shoot Norwegian saboteurs as you shoot the rapids!

### Hall of Mirrors
You won't believe your eyes when you look as fat as Goering, as short as Goebbels or as thin as Hess!

## Ghost Train

It's fast, furious and very, very frightening. What's more, it always
runs on time!

## Doodlebug Big Dipper

Strap yourself in to this replica V-1 and feel what it's like to pull 3G's as
you hurtle around the track at speeds of up to 120 mph! (Don't worry, German
engineering means it's inherently safe)

## Bumper Armoured Cars

You'll have an 'El of a time driving about the dunes on this
El Alamein simulated desert!

## Fantasy Island

Winning the Battle of Britain! Repelling the invasion of Normandy! Having a
leader with two testicles! All right, so we can all dream...

## The Blitzkrieg Big Wheel

Rotate at lightning speeds without falling off! (It's more secure than
Spandau Prison)

## The Crazy House

A lifesize reconstruction of the Berlin Bunker

## Tunnel of Love

Permanently closed

## U-Boat-ing Pond

Are you man enough to man the torpedoes or will you dive,
dive, dive for cover? See how much merchant shipping you can destroy in
60 seconds! It's full speed ahead for a full five minutes before we shout,
'come in U-87, your time is up!'

## Shooting Gallery

Welcome to Hermann Goering's bathroom...

## Testicle Boxing

Not a ride. Just something that happens to you if the staff think you're
secretly working for Simon Wiesenthal

**PARAGUAYAN TIMES**
BESTSELLERS WEEK ENDING 7 MARCH 1997

1. Mein Kampf *(32nd edition – completely updated)*
   by A Hitler

2. It wasn't me. It was the others by M Borman

3. You Can't Catch Me! Nyahh, nyahh, nyahh! by H Mengele

4. Phew! That was Close by R Hess (the real one)

5. Up Yours, Mossad! by A Hitler

# PERU

What's surprising about Peru is that a nation that is descended from the Incas, one of the most scientifically, culturally and socially advanced civilisations in the world, should end up best known as the birthplace of a bear that likes marmalade sandwiches.

Most South American countries are pointless and Peru is no exception. Inflation runs at several thousand per cent and the government alternates between corrupt civilian administrations and corrupt military dictatorships. Coups and counter-coups happen like clockwork, and fear of terrorism has made tourism a dying industry. Apart from an ancient Inca city or two, wild llamas and the largest flying bird in the world (the Andean condor – in case you actually give a toss), there's nothing here to attract the holiday maker.

### The Language
Spanish is the official language of Peru which is fine if you speak it. If you don't, then the next most common language is Quechua – the original language of the Incas. If you're not descended from the Incas (and let's face it, not many people in the UK are) then you'll certainly have a language problem.

### Clothing
In nearly every civilised culture in the world, a blanket with a hole cut in the middle is just that – a blanket with a hole cut in the middle. In Peru it's called a 'poncho' (literally 'blanket with hole cut in it') and travellers will be accosted by wearisome peasants trying to flog a whole job lot from a hand cart. Do not be tempted in the misguided assumption that wearing a poncho is a fashion statement. It is not. Wearing a poncho will just make you look like the selfsame Peruvian peasant that's just sold you it – or an extra from The Good, The Bad and the Ugly – neither of which carry any credibility once you arrive home.

### Music
Musically, Peru has a lot in common with a lot of the most undesirable places in the world to visit, sharing these countries' unique forms of music which liberals call 'ethnic' but we know better as 'shite'. Just as Burundi has its drums and India has its sitars, Peru has its panpipes, the selfsame instruments featured on those annoying radio commercials for 'Now That's What I Call Panpipe Music Volume 28'. Peruvians claim the

sound of pan pipes is unique. It is, in a way, because it makes every single tune played on them sound identical, whether it's 'Lady In Red' or 'Ace of Spades'.

## SIGHTS OF INTEREST

### Lake Titicaca
The lake with the stupidest-sounding name (unless you count Lake Testes in the Belgian Congo), this body of water is swarming with piranhas. If you've never been in a canoe before this is not the place to start.

### The Nazca Lines
No-one knows what these giant shapes and symbols scratched in the southern coastal desert are for. Few care.

### The Incas
All Peruvians are proud of their ancestors and will bore the pants off any tourist stupid enough to enter into conversation with them. However, if you do find yourself forced to talk to a Peruvian, you can make them feel uncomfortable by raising the following questions:

- If the Incas were so great, how come they didn't invent writing?

- Or the wheel?         - Or money

- Why did they think that the best cure for a headache was drilling a hole in their skull?

- Their greatest gift to modern civilisation was the hammock – hardly an indication of an advanced civilisation, but proof that Incas reached Mexico...

- They believed that observing spiders would foretell the future for them – not very scientific (or effective) was it?

- If they were so great, why didn't they attack and subjugate other rival civilisations (like the Spanish)?

## FLYING IN?

If you're planning to fly into Peru over the Andes, be sure to take a very big packed lunch. How big? Fill your suitcase up to the brim with food and leave your clothes at home. It doesn't matter what kind of food you pack. It is certain to taste better than a South American rugby player. For example, when he left the country and flew over the Andes, Paddington Bear made sure to pack plenty of marmalade sandwiches.

If your plane does crash land in the Andes, tell no-one what you have in your case. Sneak out of the gaping hole in the fuselage late at night under the pretext of 'going for a wazz' and tuck in by yourself. Do not get caught. People who have been forced to resorting to cannibalism for the past six weeks will not react well when they discover you have six dozen packs of mini cheddars in your Samsonite.

# THE PHILIPPINES

The Philippines are not a popular holiday destination with the British. The islands are an odd mixture of the Third World and rampant American consumerism, all of which means you can see people starving to death opposite a McDonald's.

There are few, if any, tourist attractions. However, during your stay, you are sure to meet many interesting people, including several hundred drunken US sailors on shore leave from the USS Enterprise and hollow-eyed women who want you to be their 'bang-bang cocky love honey' for the next twenty minutes, as well as a number of fellow Britons who have emigrated because they're fed up with being beaten up in prison.

With the fall of the Marcos dynasty, unemployment is rife, as the Filipino shoe industry has collapsed almost overnight, driving many shoe workers into prostitution or, worse, into light agriculture. The capital, Manila, is the centre of the sex trade. Here it is cheaper to catch a serious venereal disease than almost anywhere else on earth. Gonorrhoea is best caught in the girly bars and nightclubs. If you want syphilis or herpes, try the massage parlours or streetwalkers.

If you lean more towards leading a long life with full use of your sex organs, the Philippines has much to offer in the way of spectacular nature. Hardly a week goes by without a hurricane, tidal wave, volcanic euption or earthquake to marvel at. The Filipinos normally seem to take these in their stride, but do occasionally offer up the odd human sacrifice to placate the Gods. Virgins are preferred but, at a pinch, anyone who can't run fast enough will do.

Also take especial care to avoid the Ifuago tribe, who still indulge in headhunting to supplement the money brought in from their Burger King franchise. White heads are especially valued, as they can be used as one half of a shrunken-head chess set, a popular souvenir among those who think they're not real.

With one foot in the past and the other in modern day America, Filipinos do not exactly have a treasury of wisdom to draw from. For example, they are still an intensely gullible people who continue to believe that they will actually get paid if they go to work for the Saudis and won't be whipped and locked in a cupboard for days on end with just a dry dog biscuit. Almost half a million Filipinos have set out for a better life as servants to rich Arab families, and many are now trapped in Knightsbridge with no passport, no money and no hymen.

Filipinos have also adopted the Americans' love of guns. They enjoy shooting each other, and there are more gun battles here than anywhere else in the world. That uniquely American phenomenon – drive-by shootings – are on the increase, although usually staged from a passing mule cart or goat-pulled sled. 'Trot-by' shootings sound stupid, but the bullets are real. Be careful.

After shooting people, Filipinos like nothing better than to indulge in a spot of cockfighting. They often win. Our tip – always bet on the man.

# POLAND

What do you say about a country that's so depressing? And so dull? And so depressingly dull? A country where grey isn't just the colour of the streets and skies, it's the national identity. A country where the women all look like men. And the men all look like Pope John Paul II. A country where you open the weekly edition of 'What's On In Warsaw' only to find written large on every page, 'Fuck All'.

Countries as dreary as this tend not to breed great innovators or artists and such is the case with Poland. Apart from the Pope and Lech Walesa, the only three famous Poles throughout recorded time have been Marie Curie (who was so ashamed of her heritage that she pretended she was French), Frédéric Chopin (who was ashamed of his heritage and decided to die, aged just 39) and Ludwik Zamenhof, inventor of Esperanto (who was just mental).

## Food and Drink

For Poles, a meat-free meal is a contradiction in terms. Meat consumption is among the highest in Europe, but so far there has been no evidence that beef causes CJD here – just dreariness. Poles love meat with everything, and breakfast is likely to include frankfurters, a selection of cold meats, a selection of hot meats, a black pudding, some more cold meats and a bread roll – washed down with a beef-extract hot drink.

But if the Poles really like their meat, then they really love their vodka. In Poland, vodka is drunk neat and downed in one go, followed swiftly by a vodka chaser. Poles hold the current world records for 'Highest Number of State Registered Alcoholics In The Northern Hemisphere', 'Inhabitants Most Likely To Die Of Acute Kidney Failure' and the 'Betty Ford Award for Pissed Slavs'.

## Sightseeing

The last major influx of visitors to Poland occurred on 1 September 1939 and it's not surprising to see why. There's very little to see and even less to do. Poland has a national debt that's the envy of most Third World countries, with the result that state funding of the arts or tourist attractions have been virtually non-existent.

## The Arts

The Krakow-based Polish National Theatre has long been admired for its professionalism and its ability to continue performing despite the loss of its grant. However, despite the company's commitment, this severe underfunding has resulted in some of the recent Shakespearean performances on its European tour being less than convincing:

'ONE GENTLEMAN OF VERONA'
'THE MERRY WIFE OF WINDSOR'
'EIGHTH NIGHT'
'ROMEO'
'AS YOU'D SETTLE FOR IT'

## Gdansk

The legendary home of Lech Walesa and the Solidarity movement, this city on the Baltic Sea is home to 'Shipbuilding Land', where visitors are able to enter into a multimedia tour of boiler making and steam riveting. However, in Polish terms, 'multimedia' consists of wearing a Walkman while looking through a ViewMaster. (The ViewMaster slides on offer actually show stills from *Lassie Come Home*, but 10 out of 10 to the impoverished Poles for trying.)

**Bialystok**

A city approx 180 km to the north-east of Warsaw and the birthplace of Ludwik Zamenhof, creator of Esperanto. Ludwik was an eye doctor with no special skill in languages – which made him superbly qualified to invent Esperanto in 1897 (voted 'Language Least Likely To Get Adopted' 1898). Zamenhof, who laboured his entire life under the mistaken idea that different people of the world might want to talk to each other, forged a language that absolutely no-one speaks, except for William Shatner, and who's got anything to say to him?

Besides, everyone knows that the world's official language is English.

# PORTUGAL

Portugal is a country full of surprises; it's surprising how many Britons go there on holiday and it's surprising how many swear they'll never go again.

The most popular destination is the Algarve, which is Portuguese for 'Coastline of Shame'. The Portuguese themselves are deeply embarrassed about visitors seeing their country, and so have made every effort to run bus and train services as inefficiently as possible so that tourists do not get to see very much during their stay. Roads are poorly maintained, and deliberately dull-sounding festivals are staged so that holidaymakers choose not to visit them. In Miranda, for example, locals perform 'The Stick Dance' which is like morris dancing only not as exciting. Visitors consequently stay away in droves.

Should Portugal be so ashamed of itself? Probably not. But, without the shame, there would be no national identity. National self-loathing set in as early as the fourteenth century, when virtually any Portuguese with access to a ship, canoe or upturned bathtub set to sea in search of somewhere better. Vasco de Gama discovered the Western route to India (he was in no hurry), Pedro Cabral discovered Brazil (interestingly, Brazil was originally called Cabralla, but Pedro petitioned to have his name removed when he realised what a hole it was), Magellan sailed the far Pacific and a humble fisherman called Sanchez is said to have discovered America fifteen years before Columbus, when he didn't feel like coming back to port.

One of the most unpopular customs in Portugal, with visitors at least, is the Fadista or 'wailer'. Fadista come to your table when you are eating out and perform the 'Fado', a caterwauling lament of national self-loathing. The most 'popular' Fado contains the chorus:

*Fa La La La*
*Why couldn't I have been born in Spain?*
*The border is only 30 km away from the place of my birth.*
*So near, yet so far.*
*Curse my mother, curse my father.*
*I think I will drown myself after another twenty verses of this.*
*Oh oh oh oh.*
*Sorry if I am spoiling your supper, but I am so sad.*

Other top Fado hits include *'You Don't Know What It's Like To Be Portuguese'*, *'It's All Right For You, You're Going Home Soon'*, *'I Dreamed I Was Italian'* and *'Shoot Me – You'll Be Doing Me A Favour'*.

The Portuguese are also ashamed of the quality of their port wines. Certainly they would never drink them, leaving that to an undiscriminating nation like Great Britain which consumes the vast majority of them. If you order port while dining out in Portugal, it comes with several breath mints, a full cash refund and the restaurant owner's personal apology. Be considerate to your hosts – do not order Portuguese wines or foods when dining out if you wish to avoid causing embarrassment. Also, don't mention Lisbon.

# ROMANIA

An efficient and economical public transport system. A zero crime rate. A modern, effective health system. A temperate climate. Friendly, accommodating locals. A burgeoning economy. Interesting, appetising local dishes. A land flowing with milk and honey. These are all highly desirable aspects of a country which Romania would dearly like to one day achieve. Sad to say, it has far to go.

Instead, the unwary visitor will find one of the poorest countries in Eastern Europe where everything is in short supply – electricity, water, gas, bread and people who don't all look like Stan Ogden. The country is still trying to recover from the Ceausescu regime and the economy is characterised by two features: queues and a 'spiv' mentality.

## Queues

If you're used to trying to get out of the Castle Donnington 'Monsters of Rock' car park (or even waiting to use the portaloos) you'll love Romania. Queueing isn't just an inconvenience, it's a way of life. Romanians have to queue for everything. They even have to queue to join queues – that's how popular the queues are. It's quite common for people to sleep on the pavements outside bakers' for two or three days just to wait for a new sliced bloomer. Queues for bagels can continue for three or four blocks and as for jam doughnuts (or those gingerbread men with chocolate drops for buttons), queues can stretch from the capital Bucharest, in the south-west 150 km right over the border into Bulgaria.

Tom Petty once sang, 'The waiting is the hardest part', and this has since been adopted as the official Romanian national anthem. (This is technically incorrect; the hardest part is actually the centre of a Romanian jam doughnut).

## The Black Market

This thrives due to the severe shortages previously mentioned, and even

a brief stroll down Calea Victoriei or Bulevard N. Balcescu, in the centre
of Bucharest will result in you being accosted every few yards by ferret-
faced men with big overcoats saying, 'Pssst! How are you off for powdered milk?', or 'See this egg, I can get hold of another five if you're interested'. Travellers are warned that while some of the deals might seem
attractive, there is no guarantee that the goods are genuine – tales of
powdered milk being bulked up by talcum powder are commonplace.

## Where to go

Straight back to the airport is the best advice we can give. However, if
you really want to see just how awful Romania is, you only need to visit
one city – its capital, Bucharest.

## Bucharest

Known fifty years ago as the 'Paris of the East', there are still some similarities. For instance, both cities smell of piss and the people are surly.
There the similarities end, and the visitor to Bucharest will find a city
shamefully devoid of any charm, where concrete and breezeblock housing estates form the most inspired architecture on view and where crumbling churches threaten to dislodge falling masonry on anyone coming
near.

Sightseers are also likely to be disappointed since many public buildings were burned to the ground during the 1989 revolution. Visitors to
the university library in the centre of Piata Revolutei will just find a
signed copy of *The Carpet Baggers* by Harold Robbins and two or three
Jack Higgins books with smoke damage. (Why these weren't burned
when they had the chance is not known.) Likewise, the Communist
Central Party Committee headquarters just to the south will probably
only be of interest to tourists with a more than passing interest in scorch
marks and carbonated timbers.

## Transylvania

This region to the west of the country near the Carpathian Mountains
needs no introduction. Apart from that sentence, which is actually an
introduction of sorts...

Anyway, to cater for visitors there are organised 'Dracula' tours which
include Dracula's Castle in the small town of Bran (near Brasov). This
might or might not be the residence of Vlad the Impaler (a man who made
Nicolae Ceausescu look compassionate) but if you were one of the
undead, you'd probably live somewhere like this.

The locals are simple and still very superstitious. They are firm believers in vampirism and are likely to drive a stake through your heart if you

arouse their suspicions (they know that the publicity will be good for the tourist industry). With this in mind, if you DO visit Transylvania, follow these simple safety rules:

a) Never sign the hotel register 'Count Alucard'
   (for a joke, or even if it's your real name)

b) Don't act as though you're repelled by the sign of the cross
   (even if you are Jewish or a Muslim)

c) Act positively towards garlic (e.g. order Chicken Kiev at every meal
   time, then eat it, smacking your lips and saying 'yum, yum',
   (which is Slavic for 'yum yum')

d) Never bite someone's neck and drink their blood – even in jest

e) Never go to a fancy dress party dressed as Batman

f) Be seen to walk around in bright sunlight

---

# RUSSIA

The days when the former Soviet Union was a superpower are long gone, as any visitor to modern day Russia will attest.

No visit to Russia is complete without a stay in Moscow, a city rather like Hull but without the glamour. Your first stop should be the Kremlin in Red Square. If you can, you might like to watch the changing of the guards there. This happens at irregular intervals when their commanding officer springs a surprise inspection and finds them rolling drunk. Red Square is also the central location for all the city's best hotels, where you can stay in one- or even two-star luxury during your visit.

Of course, no visit to Moscow would be complete without a look at the city's legendary supermarkets. They are well worth a visit, if only to witness the pandemonium on Fridays when a new turnip arrives. Only top supermarkets have produce of any kind on their shelves. Most shops are completely empty. This has led to a uniquely Russian manifestation of capitalism. Enterprising shopkeepers, stuck without goods of any kind, have opened up 'Nothing Stores' where you can purchase nothing at all for quite reasonable prices. Expect long queues when the shelves are freshly stacked with nothing on Fridays and Tuesdays. Being used to having nothing, Muscovites seem to enjoy shopping in this way, and you can purchase souvenirs for the folks back home which will neither take up space in your suitcase or weigh you down when travelling (you can also, quite legitimately, go through the 'nothing to declare' channel at customs on the way home).

If you actually want to purchase something be sure to visit the Red Square market, where you can pick up anything from half a turnip to an empty Ovaltine can. You can barter for more exotic goods like tins of dried paint, free gifts from Kellogg's cereal packets and wrappers that once contained cheese, on the thriving black market.

It will not take you long to realise that the city is falling apart. Alcoholism is rife at every level of society. (In fact, it is rumoured that whenever Yeltsin sends out an invitation to a cabinet meeting, he always adds 'PS. bring a bottle' at the end.) The streets throng with beggars. Afghan veterans, hopelessly addicted to falafel, stop you for chickpeas. Former top scientists sit in the streets holding up placards saying, 'will construct nuclear weapons for food'. Red Army generals hold out their caps next to signs saying, 'Please give generously. 600,000 mouths to feed.'

As you'd expect, violent crime is soaring too. Be sensible. Stick to brightly lit areas, never go out alone and never carry a lettuce. Keep any food you may have in the hotel safe. If you have a leather belt, lock this away too as it can be boiled down to make a popular soup.

At present, Moscow is the venue for a vicious turf war being fought between two rival gangs. This is because turf can also be boiled down to make a popular soup. Other gangs are at war with each other too. At night, the city echoes to the sound of gunfire from an illicit cauliflower deal that turned sour, or a bitter dispute over who can deal legumes in which area. An uneasy truce had been established between the warring gangs which ended when the 'East Side Mob' sensationally gained possession of a packet of Maltesers. This altered the balance of power forever and precipitated the open warfare witnessed today. It is easy to spot the local mafiosos and to keep out of their way – they're the ones arrogantly strutting around eating onions in plain sight.

Counterfeit food, made from industrial waste products and distributed through the black market, is also a growing problem. Insist on biting before you buy. Counterfeit bananas are a particular problem, but easy to spot for anyone from the West who is readily familiar with the fruit and who knows it is not usually blue and square. Likewise the orange, which, as every westerner knows, is not green (or four-foot long and triangular).

Visitors to Moscow are earnestly advised to avoid the cruel winter months. Instead, you should visit in high summer, when temperatures can soar to above zero. Despite the unyielding cold, you can still come home from your holiday with a tan. Just stand within a hundred miles of Chernobyl for ten minutes during your stay.

If you do wish to visit Chernobyl, or other equally attractive parts of the former Soviet Union, be aware that the country spans a truly staggering area, and the only practical way to get around is by air – so you may well be better off staying in Moscow. Air travel in the former Soviet Union is both exasperating and dangerous. Few planes ever take off at the advertised times and long delays caused by inconvenient crashes or planes disappearing off the radar in remote regions are not uncommon. When booking your ticket (which comes complete with a free St Christopher), a supplement of 100 roubles will buy you a guaranteed seat so you will not have to strap-hang for the entire flight. For a further supplement of 100 roubles you will be allowed to actually fly the plane. It is well worth paying the extra, because both pilot and co-pilot will be completely drunk, and you stand a far better chance of landing the plane than they do.

Finally, if you do decide to risk it and travel outside Moscow, avoid the irradiated sections of the country and never swim anywhere where there is a sign saying 'Warning! Nuclear submarine fleet slowly decaying at anchor'. Better still, put several hundred miles between yourself and the likely epicentre.

## EATING OUT

The swankiest restaurant in Moscow is McDonald's in Red Square. Few Muscovites can afford to eat here, but many come along to press their faces up to the glass and stare at the pictures on the menu. If you want to eat like a real Muscovite, try the cheap fast food restaurants like 'Turnip Czar' or 'Commissar Potato'. Alternatively, go hungry or search for scraps out of rubbish bins, which is what most Russians do.

## MONEY

The Russian rouble is worthless. The real currency in Russia today is food. Pack plenty of food when you go. (Avoid luxury items like tomato ketchup and scampi – Muscovites won't know what they are.)

## **CURRENCY CONVERSION TABLE**

*...What your food will buy.*

1 potato = car hire for a week

1 Mini Baby Bell Cheese = Double room in top two-star hotel for a year

1 pkt Rolos = Unlimited sex with the mayor's daughter

1 pkt chocolate digestives = Deeds for the Winter Palace

1 Birds Eye Boil in the Bag cod in cheese sauce = Soviet air force

PS. You can also get a personal 40-minute meeting with Boris Yeltsin for a Fray Bentos steak and kidney pie and a bottle of Thunderbird

# SAUDI ARABIA

The overwhelming majority of tourists who visit Saudi are Moslems making a pilgrimage to some of the Islamic world's most holy sites. Anyone else who goes there is an idiot and deserves all he gets.

Any tourist attraction worth seeing is strictly off-limits to non-Moslems. Non-Moslems are also not allowed anywhere near the holy city of Mecca – but don't worry. You're not missing much. People just swirl en masse around a big black thing and periodically crush each other to death.

The attractions you can see are, frankly, pitiful. If you like utter desolation, you could always visit the Rub Al'-Khali Desert, a vast tract of nothing the size of France. The only other wasteland of comparable size in the world is Radio 1 FM. Also try to miss the Jinadriyah National Festival held near Riyadh in February, as it features nothing you could possibly want to see.

Saudi is still very much in the grip of ancient Arab traditions. Half the population is still made up of wandering Bedouins who may invite you back to their traditional tents to partake of tea and male-on-male activities. Remember, it is rude to eat or drink with your left hand, point the soles of your feet at anyone or refuse to bend over if asked by the host. It is awkward to avoid such an invitation. If you wish to decline without giving offence simply say *'Shukran, alya al mudha Mahomet aqba al asharaim?'* which means 'Thank you but, oh look, isn't that the Prophet Mohammed over there?' and then leg it in the opposite direction.

It is worth remembering that almost everything is illegal in Saudi Arabia – including alcohol, tobacco, smiling, running, shouting, laughing, reading, writing, singing, dancing and everything beginning with a 'J', 'L' or 'M'. This is doubly true during Ramadan, when everything beginning with a letter from T to Z also becomes banned.

In the cities, keep a close eye out for the *Matawwa* or 'religious police' who are there to ensure that no-one has any fun. Fundamentalists to a man, the Matawwa have the powers to administer brutal on the spot punishments. These include twenty lashes for smiling, forty lashes for getting the giggles in public and one hundred lashes for attempting to tell a joke. Lashes are always carried out right-handed with the birch cane, while the left hand is, by tradition, used for simultaneous surreptitious self-gratification under the robes. Under the law, women can be beaten just for existing, but in practice this is seldom enforced as the Matawwa don't find it nearly as exciting.

Despite the Matawwa's lack of interest in women, it is advised that women should never venture out on their own. If they have to go anywhere, they must be accompanied by a responsible male with full ownership paperwork. Women found out on their own are considered 'lost property' and, if not claimed within 28 days are either put down or auctioned off.

Women are treated very much as property throughout the country. There are used-women showrooms in Jeddah and Riyadh where wives can be purchased for over £1,500 less than new ones. Test drives can be arranged, and your old wife may be taken in part exchange. Women can also be offered as security against bank loans and stored in the vault for the period of repayment.

As well as property, women in Saudi are also treated as commodities and as such are frequently traded on the Jeddah Commodities exchange along with oil, coffee and other consumables. Girl children are traded on a separate futures exchange. If you are considering investing in Saudi women, be advised that the value of women can fall as well as rise, and that you may not get back your original investment. Look for long-term potential, coupled with lack of growth.

## ILLEGAL ALCOHOL

Much of the illicit alcohol in the country is brewed in secret stills and is very potent. Be careful what you drink...

| NAME | PROOF | EFFECT |
| --- | --- | --- |
| **Siddiki** | 96-98% | Makes you behave like Gareth Hunt for a week |
| **Aziz Fizz** | 94-95% | Temporary insanity |
| **Faisal** | 94-95% | Genetic damage |
| **Ghansani** | 91-96% | Buildings seem sexually attractive |
| **Abdul's Ruin** | 95-97% | Blue spiders seem to eat your face |
| **Ansari** | 99-100% | Bobby Davro becomes amusing |
| **Buraydah Snakebite** | 140% | Giggles followed by brain death |

# SERBIA & BOSNIA

What can you say about Serbia that hasn't already been said about Adolf Hitler's Germany? What do you say about a country whose sole contribution to the world is the new phrase 'ethnic cleansing'? What do you say about a people so proud of the atrocities they perpetrated? How about, 'We hope you all die of slow syphilis'?

There is no good reason for normal people to visit Serbia. If, on the other hand, you live in Tower Hamlets, own two Rottweilers and call black people 'chocolate', you'll probably feel quite at home here. Hell, they'll probably make you prime minister. For those presently reading this paragraph and moving their lips at the same time, Serbia is open to tourists. Hotel rooms are basic, but most hotels host entertainment nights where ethnic Serbians perform traditional strutting, posing and clenched fists salutes.

If you do want to visit the region, and don't have a very small penis that requires you to wear leather and goosestep in order to bolster your self-confidence, try the neighbouring – and far prettier – state of Bosnia.

The conflict that recently rocked neighbouring Bosnia was a very 'green' civil war, conducted with both concern and respect for the land. Despite all the fighting, the Serb minority there adhered to a strict policy of environmentalism and filled in many unsightly quarries and open cast mines. This policy obviously met with the favour of the United Nations on the ground there, as they did nothing to prevent it.

The sweeping wooded hills and plunging ravines of Bosnia are still as beautiful today as they have ever been, but the population has fared less well. Today, many of the Bosnians you will come across are dead, especially if you like hiking in the woods or have an interest in school gymnasia. Those who are alive tend mainly to work in the construction industry, or in dentistry.

You can stay in many former top-class hotels in Sarajevo. All come with a huge hole in the wall and a pile of plaster on the bed. Entertainment is largely provided by passing units of the British Army singing vulgar rugby songs, or by watching ethnic Serbs trying to gain the moral high ground in post-war political debate.

It is probably best not to touch anything during your stay, as almost everything is still booby-trapped.

# SINGAPORE

The island's name means 'Lion City', so called because of a myopic Sumatran prince who thought he saw a lion when he landed there. (This creature was actually a mangy dog, so Singapore ought really to be called 'The Island of Mutt'.)

Providing visitors have 20/20 vision, the first thing they'll notice on arriving here is that the city itself is ultra-clean with no litter or graffiti. This is due to a repressive single-party government that's been in power since 1959. In Singapore it's illegal to drop litter or cigarette ash in the street, and spitting is a criminal offence taken so seriously that the Singapore police force have their own codes for it...

## PHLEGM-RELATED SINGAPORE POLICE CODES

124: Spitting on the pavement
127: Loitering with intent to roll sputum around your mouth
153: Hawking up phlegm with the intention to spit
156: Spitting with intent to do more spitting
162: Misdemeanour drooling
164: Expectorating without due care and attention
176: Aiding and abetting a spitter
186: Grievous bodily spitting

They also have 'stop and search' laws giving them powers to check the state of people's noses and throats to see if they're concealing a mucoid substance.

The price of a litter, smoke and phlegm-free city is high – a government that rules with an iron fist. This might be an attractive proposition to Julian Clary but to the average Singaporean it means press censorship and absolutely no public dissent. The Singapore government is the first in the world to only allow access to approved Internet sites. Visitors with laptops and modems hoping to access 'Busty Dusty' (http:/www.busty-dusty.com/) or 'Kayla Kleevage' (http:/www.kleevage. com/htm l/home. htm) will be in for a hard time (politically, not physically, of course).

Equally, people with scruffy clothes and men with long hair are viewed suspiciously if they enter the country. Those with facial hair are also regarded with distrust (particularly women).

## Shopping

Visitors to Singapore are bombarded with seemingly unrepeatable discounts on electrical goods and body parts of endangered species.

## Electrical Goods

Don't bother. Everything you buy might seem great value but when you discover that the NICAM Home Cinema system only works on Singapore voltage, or the 30-inch high definition TV packs up two minutes after plugging it in and has to be returned to Singapore for warranty work, then it won't seem like quite a bargain.

## Endangered Species

Singapore might be a thriving, progressive, affluent metropolis, but the people are still savages when it comes to believing that a snake's liver can cure baldness, a tiger's spleen is good for an itchy foot and bear's testicles will help impotence (not for the bear they won't). Apart from the trade in internal organs, you'll find a thriving market for animal skins and pelts – and a more than average chance of bumping into Brigitte Bardot protesting about something or other (have your camera ready – she's not the sex kitten she once was, but it will still impress your friends back home).

*Singapore is a real mix of cultures and you'll find clearly defined ghettoes:*

## The Colonial area:

You'll find this north of Singapore River and apart from various dull government buildings it's home to the famous Raffles Hotel. The tourist office suggests you drink a Singapore sling in the hotel bar, telling visitors it's part of the 'Singapore Experience'. It isn't. It's part of the 'getting ripped-off by adhering to a tourist cliché' experience.

## Chinatown:

This is an area north of the city centre, which is strange because the whole of Singapore is one big Chinatown...

## Little India:

The Indian district centres on Serangoon Road. Just follow your nose.

## Arab Street:

Where there's often a 124 and 153 in progress.

# SOUTH AFRICA

The ending of apartheid has brought mixed blessings for South Africa. On one hand, it has made the country more politically acceptable to visit. On the other hand, thousands of hard-line apartheid-supporting Afrikaners have been left twiddling their thumbs (and their trigger fingers) and this threat of new violence has discouraged visitors.

No longer able to inflict violence on the black population without fear of being fined, the Afrikaners have created a new kind of safari to satiate their deep lust for revenge against the victorious ANC. This package must rank as among the most politically incorrect vacations available anywhere in the world. Do try it...

### 2ND JULY

Arrived at Kruger National Park and after checking in to the Eugene Terre Blanche Dormitory, spent the evening going over strategy and plans for the safari. We were told that the animals we would be hunting were clever, cunning and would do everything they could to avoid capture and subsequent interrogation and torture.

### 3RD JULY

We made an early start and after three hours our guide told us he had picked up the characteristic spoor of a wildebeest known as 'Steve Biko'. This wily creature managed to elude us for several hours and seemed to double back at least twice. Our guide declared a State of Emergency. However, we eventually caught sight of 'Steve Biko' under a rocky outcrop. He was easily cornered here then hit numerous times on the head with a long-handled baton. We asked it a few questions then hit it again. It didn't get up and we drove off.

### 4TH JULY

Uneventful morning but one of the bearers saw 'Oliver Tambo', a graceful impala, silhouetted on the horizon. Splitting the party into two we used a pincer-movement to ambush this antelope. Surrounding it, we asked to see its Pass Book. On getting no reply one of the bearers swore at it, then beat it severely and threw it in a nearby detention centre.

### 5TH JULY

We chased 'Walter Sisulu' (a giraffe) for half a mile in the Land Rover before exhausting it. After a severe interrogation and beating we left it for dead on the parched veldt as a warning for any other wild animals who dare to cross our path.

Later that afternoon we were fortunate enough to sight 'Donald Woods', a white rhino at a water hole. We threatened him with a beating and he moved on.

### 6TH JULY

Around midday our guide pointed out a herd of zebras - or as he called them 'coloureds' - grazing on some arid scrub (their 'homeland'). As we approached they started to stampede. Fortunately some veterans from the Sharpeville Riots were in our party. They stood firm and averted danger by using their rifles; within a few minutes we'd bagged 257 of them.

### 7TH JULY

Tear gassed some meerkats in their squatter camp burrows and shot some monkeys in the back as they were running away.

### 8TH JULY

As dawn breaks, we heard rumours of Bishop Desmond Tutu nibbling on branches and drinking from a nearby water hole. We advanced silently through the long grass and watched through binoculars. We were horrified to see that it was indeed Bishop Desmond Tutu and not the Okapi of the same name we had been tracking, and so decided to move on in case he reported us.

### 9TH JULY

Encouraged by the ease with which we've been able to track and injure animals we decide to stalk the King of the Jungle - a rogue elephant called 'Nelson'. Just before sun down we saw it asleep by a creek. Creeping up, we managed to shackle it, topple its favourite tree and detain it without trial. Our guide says we'll break its spirit within a week...

## SUN CITY

This holiday resort near Cape Town has been described as 'Las Vegas meets Blackpool's Golden Mile'. Of course, the person who said this was mental. Or blind. Or born without any sense of smell. Or all three. Sun City is cosmopolitan and sophisticated – so you can see it's not like the Golden Mile at all.

------ **Cut out and keep guide:** ------

## HOW TO TELL YOU'RE IN SUN CITY AND NOT ON BLACKPOOL'S GOLDEN MILE

### CABARET

At Sun City:     Frank Sinatra, Tony Bennett, Julio Inglesias

On the Golden Mile:     The Grumbleweeds, Les Dennis, Sooty

### HOTELS

At Sun City:     The Sun City Hilton

On the Golden Mile:     Mrs Griddlesthwaite's B & B, at number 29 (no women in the room after 8pm)

### AVERAGE TEMPERATURE

At Sun City:     25°C

On the Golden Mile:     25°F

### GAMBLING

At Sun City:     Roulette, Black Jack, Poker

On the Golden Mile:     Bingo, unprotected sex with a Woolworth's shop girl

### SPORTS FACILITIES

At Sun City:     Twelve tennis courts, two 18-hole championship golf courses, wind surfing

On the Golden Mile:     A crazy golf course which has a windmill with a broken sail

**PEOPLE YOU'RE LIKELY TO MEET**

| | |
|---|---|
| At Sun City: | Cliff Richard, Cher, Henry Kissinger |
| On the Golden Mile: | Bobby Davro, some drunken plumber's mate who says 'Come on then, if you're hard enough' and lots of people who look like Bobby Davro |

**WHERE TO EAT**

| | |
|---|---|
| At Sun City: | Trader Vics |
| On the Golden Mile: | Harry Ramsden's |

**WHAT YOU'LL FIND LYING ON THE BEACH**

| | |
|---|---|
| At Sun City: | Jet skis and thousands of beautiful bronzed bodies |
| On the Golden Mile: | Donkey shit and dead seagulls |

**WHAT THE WOMEN WEAR**

| | |
|---|---|
| At Sun City: | Gucci sunglasses and not much else |
| On the Golden Mile: | Love bites and cellulite |

**WHAT'S WELCOME ON THE BEACHES**

| | |
|---|---|
| At Sun City: | Buckets |
| On the Golden Mile: | Buckets and spades |

---

# SPAIN AND ITS PROVINCES

It's ironic that for a country which ransacked all the gold of the Inca, Aztec and Maya dynasties in Central and South America, Spain today is a piss-poor country – but that doesn't stop hundreds of thousands of Brits travelling there each year singing:

*'This year I'm off to sunny Spain - I hate all the dagos*
*I'll get pissed before I'm on the plane - I hate all the dagos*
*In customs I will bare my bum - I hate all the dagos*
*All the locals, they will call me "scum"- España here I come!'*

And this sets the scene for the rest of the holiday. For Brits abroad, Spain has it all. Sun, sea, sand, sex and San Miguel.

---

## THE PERFECT ITINERARY FOR HOLIDAYMAKERS

---

SATURDAY

| | |
|---|---|
| 11.00am | Meet in Gatwick departure lounge. Start drinking duty frees |
| 2.00pm | Keep drinking |
| 4.30pm | Board chartered 737 to Algarve |
| 5.00pm | Realise you're on the wrong flight. Punch steward in frustration |
| 5.30pm | Board chartered 737 to Benidorm. Punch steward for the hell of it |
| 6.10pm | Grope stewardess. Inflate life jackets. Punch person behind you. Sing 'Champagne Supernova' over and over again |
| 7.25pm | Make unauthorised visit to flight deck. Vomit over co-pilot |
| 9.00pm | Arrive at Benidorm. Punch Spanish immigration staff |
| 10.20pm | Vomit over luggage carousel and watch it come round 28 times, giggling each time you see it |
| 10.55pm | Board coach to hotel. Punch driver. Moonie as coach drives past local convent on way to hotel |
| 11.20pm | Arrive at hotel. Punch manager. Punch hotel rep |
| 11.55pm | Visit local bar and drink your weight in Sangria |
| 2.00am | Back to hotel. Consume all of mini-bar. Punch yourself. Pass out. |

SUNDAY

| | |
|---|---|
| AM: | At leisure on the beach. Impromptu fight with party of German students |
| PM: | Sing rude song about the Pope outside the town cathedral. Vomit in hotel lifts. Punch manager |

MONDAY

| | |
|---|---|
| AM: | Organised farting contest in hotel lobby |
| PM: | Drinking games on beach. Punch each other. Yell abuse during Flamenco evening at hotel. Pick fight with head waiter |

TUESDAY

AM:  Alfresco fight with group of Brits wearing Manchester United football shirts in main shopping thoroughfare

PM:  Streak through convent gardens. Set fire to hotel bed. Vomit over hotel manager

WEDNESDAY

AM:  Rent car and drive on wrong side of the road shouting insults at young Spanish girls. Steal booze from hypermarket

PM:  Crash car. Punch man at rental company. Visit local disco. Punch any Spaniard that 'reckons himself'

THURSDAY

AM:  Visit local monastery. Successfully provoke monks into breaking their 500-year vow of silence

PM:  March through town shouting 'Keep Gibraltar British!' two hundred and twenty times. 'Drink yourself unconscious' competition

FRIDAY

AM:  Burn beach huts for a laugh. Urinate in public fountains Punch local mayor. Vomit over statue of Madonna and child

PM:  Running battle with Spanish riot police

SATURDAY

11.00am  Taken to airport under police escort. Drink yourself stupid in duty free lounge

1.00pm  Board chartered 737 to Gatwick airport

2.05pm  Let off fire extinguishers at 40,000 feet. Punch steward

3.40pm  Throw in-flight meals at each other

4.20pm  Try and open door at 38,000 feet

6.20pm  Land at Gatwick

8.00pm  Out with your mates, reminiscing about your great holiday

---

## Spanish Women

Spanish women are dark-eyed, raven-haired, passionate and tempestuous. So it's a bit of a pity you'll never meet one during your stay. Instead, you'll spend all evening pouring rum and cokes down the fat gullet of some overweight trainee hairdresser from Gala Shiels, only to see her go off with Pedro at the end of the evening, or else you'll throw up on a sun-burned, bleach-blonde, Kwik-Save supermarket checkout girl from Luton who didn't reckon you much in the first place.

## Spanish Hotel Staff

Spanish hotel staff exist for just one reason – to shag your girlfriend.
If going to Spain with your loved one, keep her in sight at ALL times. Five minutes is all they need (because five minutes is as much as most of the dago bastards can manage). It starts with the innocent kissing of hands over breakfast and being called 'an English rose', and ends with a knee trembler round the back of the hotel dustbins.

However, the truth will always out in the end (because six weeks later there won't be enough calamine lotion in the universe to stop your crotch from itching).

## Flamenco

This is what the Spanish gypsies call dancing; however, it is no such thing. Stamping your feet and wailing are more the antics of a spoilt child than a 'traditional art form'. That said, flamenco does help you relax – while the gypsies are dancing, you know they're not stealing your hire car.

## Sherry

The Spanish national drink originates in the region known as Jerez. If someone gives you a bottle it ends up in the region known as back of the booze cupboard.

## Spanish Art

It says a lot about the country when the finest exponents of Spanish art are Picasso and Salvador Dali. Picasso thought that people have both eyes on one side of their face and Dali was just plain loco.

---

## THE CANARY ISLANDS

---

### Lanzarote

*It's said that the volcanic landscape of this island resembles that of the moon. So does the atmosphere.*

### Gran Canaria

*Many people think of this as an exotic paradise (they're the ones that haven't been within 800 miles of the place).*

### Tenerife

*Scene of the world's worst aircrash – and the world's worst nightlife.*

### Fuerteventura

*Few people know this island even exists. Even fewer care.*

---

## THE BALEARIC ISLANDS

---

### Majorca

*Benidorm for snobs.*

### Minorca

*Majorca for snobs.*

### Mallorca

*This island doesn't exist. It's a pity the others do.*

### Ibiza

*Makes Eilat look exciting.*

### Formentera

*Robinson Crusoe would have rather drowned
than get washed up here.*

---

# SRI LANKA

No-one in their right mind chooses to visit Sri Lanka; tourists only end up there because they get to the end of India and forget to stop. Locals say the country resembles a teardrop or a pearl. Experienced travellers claim it owes more to a piece of phlegm or a rabbit turd – in both geographic shape and character. In defence of their nation, the Sri Lankan tourist office points out that Adam's Peak, east of the capital Colombo, is where Adam first set foot on earth. It's hard to believe that God, after creating man, would risk his finest achievement by setting him down anywhere this disease-ridden.

If you've been to India then you'll know just what to expect. If you haven't, then take this simple test to see if you really, really want to go:

---

❏ Do I want to visit a country declared by the World Health Authority as a 'no-go' area? (yes/no)

❏ Do I want to visit a country so dirty that even typhoid germs can't survive? (yes/no)

❏ Do I want to visit a country which pongs so much, you can smell it from Iceland? (yes/no)

❏ Do I want a more than 50 per cent chance of getting beri-beri? (yes/no)

❏ Do I want a more than 60 per cent chance of getting cholera? (yes/no)

❏ Do I want a more than 70 per cent chance of getting malaria? (yes/no)

❏ Do I want a more than 80 per cent chance of getting bacillary dysentery? (yes/no)

❏ Do I want a more than 99 per cent chance of getting diarrhoea so swift and intense that I wish I had beri-beri, cholera, malaria and bacillary dysentery instead? (yes/no)

❏ Do I want to share the streets with stray rabid dogs? (yes/no)

❏ Do I want to share my hotel room with stray rabid monkeys? (yes/no)

❏ Do I want to share my scalp with lice? (yes/no)

❏ Do I want to share my colon with a long thin, 20-foot long-worm? (yes/no)

---

If you answered 'yes' to any of the above then you'll get what's coming to you in Sri Lanka – plus chronic dehydration followed by the sweats and a long, lingering painful demise.

**If you answered 'no' to all of them, then think about going somewhere nicer, somewhere like Iran or Botswana.**

Apart from the risk to your health from disease, there's a good chance that your life expectancy might be severely reduced by getting caught up in the brutal and bloody civil war. The history is too convoluted to go into and the only thing you need to know is that the Tamil Tigers are not a basketball team but a group of mental Hindus who are fighting a group of mental Buddhists (the Sinhalese) because they have more religious holidays. Something like that. Anyway, lots of people get killed, but it doesn't matter because they get reincarnated and maybe the next time they'll get their shot in first.

Whatever the politics, it's important to know which parts of Sri Lanka are 'no-go' areas as far as the civil war's concerned.

THE NORTH   – dangerous
THE SOUTH   – very dangerous
THE EAST   – extremely dangerous
THE WEST   – wouldn't go there if I were you
THE MIDDLE   – bloody lethal

(There's a street in the southern town of Galle that's safe in daylight between the hours of 2 and 3.35pm. Mondays-Wednesdays only – but check with the British Embassy before visiting).

## WHAT TO WEAR

Despite Sri Lanka's humid climate tourists are advised to wear steel helmets, body armour and Kevlar flak-jackets.

## THE LOCALS

There's no Sinhalese world for 'thank you', making the Sri Lankans a bunch of ungracious bastards. If that wasn't bad enough, they nod their heads to say 'no' and shake it from side to side to say 'yes'. Twats.

### DID YOU KNOW?
*Apart from Colombo, there are a number of other cities around the world that are named after TV detectives:*

*Marples (Sumatra)*
*Poirot (The Maldives)*
*Clouseau (The Seychelles)*
*Morse (Western Samoa)*
*Sexton-Blake (Java)*
*Magnum PI (The Andaman Islands)*
*Secret Squirrel (Sicily)*

# SWAZILAND

'Africa's Best Kept Secret' is how the Swazis like to promote their country to visitors. Aware that you could get to see the traditional African way of life and exotic animals in dozens of other, more appealing African nations, Swaziland has veered completely the other way and proclaimed itself 'the most advanced nation on earth'. This is not 100 per cent true. Or 1 per cent true for that matter.

According to Swazi tourist bumpf, Swaziland has conquered space, settled the ocean floors and built the cities of the future.

Your holiday will start at the Mbabane Space Centre, just outside the capital, where Swazi missions to the stars blast off like clockwork the very day before you arrive. 'Mission Control' is off limits, but visitors can tour the souvenir shop or catch dysentery in the self-service cafeteria. You can also see the launchpad and marvel at the world's largest milk bottle.

Visitors to Mbabane can, for a modest sum, follow the progress of the Swazi space mission to the planet Jupiter by looking through the View-O-Scope on the side of the building. Offering crystal-clear pictures, the View-O-Scope reveals Jupiter to be covered in scrubby veld and populated by strange lion and gazelle-like animals. Astronauts apparently wear shorts and Oxfam 'Care Bear' T-Shirts during their missions.

The latest addition to the space centre's attractions is the 'Star Trek Simulator', where you can experience genuine space conditions. Apparently, being in outer space is remarkably like being blindfolded, spun around a few times and then hung upside down in a fridge by your ankles. Check your wallet.

'Future City' is another Swazi tourist attraction worth avoiding. Apparently, buildings of the future will use only renewable natural resources like wood, twine, mud and creepers, while energy-inefficient air conditioning will be replaced by special glass-free windows. Instead of using highly polluting fossil fuels, the Rapid City Shuttle Transport system will be powered by renewable ox technology, and ergonomically-designed Swazi 3000 Goat Carts will replace the family car.

Swazis also claim to have revolutionised air transport, making it noise and pollution-free. Catapult-launched passengers can be observed leaving the Swazi Future Air Centre in Manzini every hour, on the hour, in the direction of the swamp. A novel idea, but certainly not a solution to the problem of noise pollution, as there is a certain amount of screaming involved.

Swaziland's world domination of undersea exploration techniques has proved difficult to show its visitors as the country is entirely landlocked. However, at the Mhlume Oceanic Research Centre, you can see a typical Swazi deep-sea settlement by peering through observation ports in the side of an industrial water tank. Volunteer Swazi aquanauts can be seen tending tethered sea cows, performing strange thrashing tribal dances or beating traditional drum rhythms on the sides of the tank with their fists until they decide to take a rest break. (Working underwater is an exacting task, and Swazi aquanauts have been especially trained to conserve energy by floating face down on the surface of the water.)

Finally, Swazis say that the world of the future will be a cashless society – which explains why they haven't got any.

# SWEDEN

Think of Sweden and you think of blonde au pairs with pert breasts and small skirts who, as soon as your wife is out of the house, will show you how they keep their menfolk warm during the long arctic winters – a technique perfected over centuries and involving a tube of squirty cream and a sable glove. Well, that's what these writers think of.

For others, the country is synonymous with avant-garde furniture that's all flat-pack and primary colours, safe cars, pine forests, a multitude of lakes, clean cities, ABBA and that most magnificent of beasts, the elk.

Sweden is the country that most other nations envy. It boasts a clean and efficient public transport system, an effective national health service, a progressive social care system and some of the hottest pornography on the planet. This alone is sufficient reason to visit the country.

On the downside, the major cities and tourist attractions are all situated on the coast and unless your sense of smell was damaged as a child, the reek of herring is all too pervasive.

## EATING OUT

Sweden's culinary gift to the world is the smorgasbord. In theory this sounds like a good idea. For a fixed price you can help yourself to unlimited food from a buffet table. In practice it's not as good a deal as you might think – with the choices limited to cold fatty meats, dry crispbread, potatoes, eggs, rubbery cheese, more potatoes, meat that's even fattier than the first lot, black bread, even more potatoes, cheese that bounces when it falls on the floor, bitter tomatoes, meat that should technically be called 'fat' and, of course, the ubiquitous herring.

Swedes love the herring. They love looking at it. They love its company. They love its free spirit. And they love its taste – so much in fact that they have a special smorgasbord that just consists of herring called a sillbricka. The table positively groans under the weight of herring served in more ways than you'd imagine; marinaded, cured, smoked, poached, fried, grilled, baked, boiled, broiled, sauteed and steamed. The sillbricka, as you would imagine, stinks to high heaven.

## WHERE TO GO

### Stockholm

Located on the Baltic coast, this is the capital city. Surrounded by water, Stockholm combines an old town, a modern city, wide boulevards, well-thought-out parks and an enviable selection of adult book shops. In Stockholm it's difficult to turn a street corner without bumping into some museum or other. Many of these contain exhibits relating to sex:

❏ The Vibrationmuseet (an interactive history of the vibrator)

❏ The Pubeska Museet (pubic hairs through Swedish history including those from King Gustavus II Adolphus, Alfred Nobel, Dag Hammarskjöld, Olof Palme and Benny from Abba)

❏ Semenmuseet (everything you ever wanted to know about premature ejaculation under one roof)

❏ Buste Museet (museum devoted to all aspects of bosoms. At the time of writing, a special 'inverted nipple' wing was in the process of being constructed)

❏ Vaginamuseet (opening spring 1998)

## Gothenburg
Sweden's largest port, on the west coast and famous for its shipyards and herring processing plant. Not as many adult book shops here as Stockholm but still quite an exotic collection.

## Helsingborg
Another port. Once you've seen one herring factory you've seen them all. This city is across a narrow waterway from the similarly named Danish port of Helsingor – a cunning ploy on behalf of the Danish Tourist Board to get tourists to visit the wrong town. Four adult bookshops here, but at the time of writing one was closed for carpet cleaning and a further two were too crowded to get into.

## Malmo
Situated in the south, this city used to belong to Denmark. It contains a fortified castle, Malmohus, and only two adult books shops (one of which is a bit unsavoury and specialises in magazines about donkeys).

## The Baltic Islands
Oland and Gotland are two small islands in the Baltic that Swedes visit for beach holidays. However, unless you have a particular liking for windmills (there are 400 of them on Oland) or medieval churches (Gotland boasts nearly 100) the absence of any adult bookshops makes a visit questionable. In an emergency, the newsagents in Visby, Gotland's capital, keeps a few copies of the Swedish language version of 'Asian Babes' under the counter).

## Suicide & Divorce
Sweden has one of the highest suicide and divorce rates in the world, probably down to the high incidence of pornographic magazines, and the failure of men to match the sexual perfomances described in these magazines. Many disappointed Swedish women call their husbands 'herring' – the nearest English equivalent being 'tiddler'.

### DID YOU KNOW?
*The Norwegians might have discovered America, but the Swedes discovered the clitoris. (As an aside, it was the Moroccans who discovered the North-West Passage).*

# SWITZERLAND

It's difficult knowing where to go in Switzerland. Does Berne have more banks than Zurich? Does St Moritz have more expensive shops than Lugano? Where can you purchase the most tacky cuckoo clock – in Locarno or Montreux? Is Lake Lausanne any more interesting than Lake Geneva? Where are the best-looking nuclear shelters, Basel or Zermatt?

Ask the Swiss Tourist Office these questions and you'll be fobbed off with 'it depends' or 'I couldn't really say'. This is a classic example of Swiss neutrality – and it permeates every aspect of Swiss life.

Swiss soccer matches are decidely quiet affairs, as spectactors support both teams equally and a no-score draw is encouraged by being awarded 3 points, whereas teams only get one point for a win. No-one has ever won the Swiss version of *Opportunity Knocks* – not even Ferdinand Hodler and his yodelling cheese. No-one's ever lost either. Everything – and everybody – is neutral. No-one is ever found guilty in a Swiss court of law, every single Swiss play displays exactly the same review outside the theatre ('It's all right') and there are no opinion columns in any of the nation's five newspapers.

Switzerland is not just judgementally neutral – it is also morally neutral, which explains why Nazis, terrorists and drug barons deposit their money here – and why so many multinational pharmaceutical companies choose to make Switzerland their home.

Swiss banks are among the most competitive in the world. Any terrorist organisation opening a new deposit account can choose between an 'Our Price' record token, personal organiser, two cinema tickets or money saving vouchers off their next Pizza Hut meal.

They also offer some very special services. During the war years, the Nazi regime took advantage of their 'High Yield Art Treasure 90-Day Deposit Account', which promised good interest in the form of a Canaletto miniature for every 50 plundered paintings sequestered.

Despite their history of rank collaboration, the Swiss are intensely proud of their banking facilities and many tourist attractions are banking related. Try 'The Museum of the Deposit', 'Musee de PEP' or 'The Gallery of Banking Slips' in Zurich. 'Banking World' in Berne offers no less than 30 different banking and financial-management-related rides, including a spectacular rollercoaster based on the Italian lira. The Swiss Tourist Board describe it as 'Fiduciary fun for the whole family!' It is not.

Apart from their interest in banks, the Swiss enjoy the art of useless inventions. Since they've had no wars, border disputes or civil unrest to keep them stimulated in hundreds of years, they have to do something to keep themselves occupied...

## Yodelling

For years, people the world over have got by with shouting, but the Swiss had to invent a particularly stupid way of doing this. Even in city centres it's the only way the Swiss know how to communicate, and asking 'What time is the next train to Zurich?' is likely to invoke the reply, 'At a quarter past two-ooo-ooo-ooo-ooo-ooo...'

## Fondue

In Switzerland, fondue is a culinary experience. For the rest of the world it's an unwanted wedding gift.

## Cuckoo Clocks

Why? If we wanted to watch a small unpopular bird come out of a house, we'd hang around outside Teresa Gorman's place.

## The Swiss Army Knife

With a weapon like this in its arsenal it's not surprising Switzerland remains neutral.

## Cheese with Holes in it

Few people realise that Swiss cheese can not only be eaten, it can also be played. Just like a flute. James Galway has recorded a number of albums on the Swiss cheese, against the advice of his management.

## The Red-Light District

The only vaguely interesting place in Switzerland is Zurich's red light district that runs along Bahnhofstrasse. This was established primarily for the bankers and stockbrokers in this financial centre, and services offered by the prostitutes reflect their clientele. The sex is very business-like with no refunds given under any circumstances (remember, erections can go down as well as up).

### Services offered

| | |
|---|---|
| Quick withdrawal: | 80 Swiss francs |
| Rapid growth followed by liquidity: | 160 Swiss francs |
| Large endowment: | 110 Swiss francs |
| Making a deposit: | 70 Swiss francs |
| Tit fucking: | 90 Swiss Francs |

# SYRIA

There are many things about Syria which make it unique. This is marvellous, because if you don't go there you will never have to witness them.

For example, Syria is the only country in the world to host a goat beauty contest. 'Miss Goat Syria'. Regional heats to decide Miss Aleppo, Miss Al Furat etc. are decided in February, and the grand final is staged in Damascus in the last week of June. Be warned – tickets are sold out months in advance for any goat-related event and this is the country's premier show.

Should you be lucky enough to score a ticket, you will be privy to one of the strangest shows this side of *Starlight Express*. The audience love it, cheering and making 'goat whistles' (which are just like wolf whistles except you say 'come by' at the end) throughout the night's proceedings. The show itself starts with the contestants parading down the catwalk to the sound of Charlie Rich singing 'The Most Beautiful Girl In The World'. After a brief interview with each, the goats reappear in the swimsuit and evening wear rounds before the judges go off in a huddle. After the judges have finished in the huddle, they smoke a cigarette and then discuss the contestants.

The winning goat is crowned 'Miss Goat Syria'. The actual prize – a bramble bush – is quite modest, but the lucky winner can expect to go on to receive a lucrative modelling contract, generous fees for personal appearances and to have its name romantically linked with several top Syrian soccer players.

If you want to know something about the Syrian national character, visit a Syrian cinema. It doesn't matter which one. They're all showing *The Sound of Music* anyway. Don't watch the film. Watch the audience (not too much of a hardship). You'll see the most macho of Syrian men dissolve into floods of tears and bang their heads against the seat in front at the pivotal moment when Julie Andrews tells them, 'high on a hill stands a lonely goat...' Often, the projectionist has to stop the film, while grief turns to anger and Israeli flags are openly burned in the aisles.

What is going on? Julie has reminded them of the biggest tragedy in modern Syrian history – the loss of the Golan Heights. Middle-aged Syrian men still grieve for their lost loves, trapped behind Israeli lines never to be seen again. Younger Syrians mourn for a Utopian past when they didn't have to sleep with women. It is all very sad. While negotiations over the return of the Heights continues, young Syrians regularly brave the Israeli patrols and mine-fields to find true love. The carnage is appalling, as it is hard to run away from a tank with your trousers wrapped around your ankles.

## One Final Footnote:
Compared to many surrounding Arab countries, Syria is surprisingly liberal at present. However, here, as elsewhere, fundamentalism is on the rise, and there is increasing pressure on goats to take the veil; so the heady days of 'Miss Goat Syria' may soon be over...

# THAILAND

Thailand has so much to offer the traveller: The Grand Palace – a fabulous city within a city, the astounding Wat Arun – the Temple of Dawn, stunning scenery, dazzling pageants, tropical beaches, unique food and some of the nicest people on earth. So it's a bit of a pity that people only ever go to Thailand for a cheap shag.

The only other time you might find yourself visiting Thailand is as a stopover on a flight to Australia. Time will be short and most passengers barely have enough time to deplane and catch something atrocious before having to get back on board and carry on to their eventual destination. Thailand is worth more than that.

Unfortunately it is not easy to have a normal holiday in Thailand. If you're white and male, everyone assumes you're a sex tourist. Give up any hope of ever eating a meal in peace, as some complete stranger will invariably sidle over and stick part of her anatomy in your *Tom Yam*. Try and have a nice pint by yourself and – before you know it – some brazen young hussy has poured it down her cleavage and is inviting you to reclaim it. Order a cheese sandwich from room service in your hotel and it comes complete with a double jointed oriental nymphet who wants to show you a trick with a Marlboro.

We say, if you can't beat them, join them. You may feel guilty about exploiting these women, but you really shouldn't. If they weren't hostesses, they'd be working a twenty-hour day in some firetrap Bangkok sweatshop for pennies – so they get screwed either way.

Nor should you fall in love with them. This may be the only time in your life when the girl you're with refers to you as 'my number one top gun big boy love hammer', but this does not mean you've found the girl of your dreams. This is probably the only English she knows, except for

'Please don't do that – I've just washed my hair' and 'Please don't smear me with Bovril. I'm a Buddhist'.

No matter what you feel, you cannot save her. The life of a bar girl is fixed right from the start. She begins as a dancer and an 'escort' in seedy nightclubs. After a few years, when she is too old, sick or too drug-addled to be appealing, she eeks out a living performing unnatural acts in illegal stage shows behind closed doors. From there it is only a matter of time before whoring for pennies in the rat-infested street markets and then finally, the greatest indignity of all – an arranged mail-order marriage to some lonely middle manager from the West Midlands.

No-one should need to be warned about the dangers of sexually transmitted diseases, but there is a new infestation in Bangkok which is now causing extreme alarm – Channel 4 film crews. Be aware. At any one time, there are probably at least five Channel 4 crews filming in the bars, making bleeding-heart stories about the plight of the bar girls. If they film you, there's nothing you can do about it. The tape goes straight back home – and your face gets plastered in close-up on the nation's screens, which will probably result in cries of, 'Isn't that your Dave with his head up that girl's Wotsits? I thought he was in Pwllheli!' in your household or versions thereof.

Worse, once they've filmed you, you're in the TV archive forever after, under the heading 'British Pervert in Bangkok'. Then, whenever there's a report about the upsurge in VD in Thailand, they'll pull that clip out again and show it on *News at Ten*, basically declaring you uncrowned king of gonorrhoea to all who watch. This has an uncanny knack of coinciding with the first time you meet your girlfriend's parents, or on the eve of your speech to the Conservative Party Conference.

Finally, a word about drug smuggling – do. Officially, the penalty for drug smuggling is death or life imprisonment. In reality though, this means less than three months in jail while the British press wage an impassioned campaign on your behalf and a triumphant return to Blighty with a six-figure cheque for your exclusive story and a further offer of a BBC miniseries about you. Believe that and you'll believe anything.

## THE RED-LIGHT DISTRICT

For those who fancy playing 'Thai Roulette', the girly bars are to be found on Sukhumvit Road, Soi Nana, and Pat Pong Roads I and II.

Try: Madame Za-Za's House of Aids
The Syph & Sceptre English Pub
Madame Rosie's Bar 'n' Dose
Humpy-Boy of Soi Nana
Girlie XXX STD
The Happy Herpe
Club Epidemic
Shags R Us

---

## WARNING

---

Kok Lik Suk      Phuk Bang Nob      Kok Chu      Bum Prik Bum

Despite their salacious – sounding names, these are not brothels. They are upmarket department stores – and buying a girl here is likely to cost you twice as much.

## WHAT HAVE I CAUGHT?

The fleshpots of Bangkok are home to so many different strains of social disease that your GP may have difficulty in diagnosing you. Here are the symptoms of some of the more obscure diseases

| | |
|---|---|
| Pain, rainbow-coloured penis that moves of its own accord | Sub-Epidermal Cockworm |
| Sweating, palpitations, day-glo discharge | Thai Goat Palsy |
| Uncontrollable sobbing, soreness | GI's Gonad |
| Banging your head against a wall and squealing in agony | Viper crab infestation |
| Wishing you were dead | Patpong Urethra |
| Taking sandpaper to your testicles | Phuket Scrotal Measles |
| 100 per cent loss of all genitalia | Farang Genital Leprosy |
| Incredible pain, loud screaming | Bangkok Rot |
| Testicular swelling to the size of a family Volvo, followed by a loud bang | Bangkok Exploding Testes Virus |

NOTE – Crabs are considered as wildlife by HM Customs. On return, any part of your anatomy found to be carrying them may have to spend up to six months in quarantine.

## SHOPPING

Don't bother shopping around for presents for your wife or girlfriend. You're probably already bringing them something back.

## TIPS

Do not get involved with any British women you meet out here. They are invariably smuggling heroin for some dodgy geezer they met in a Solihull night club.

### DID YOU KNOW?
*Bangkok is actually called Krungthepmahanakhornbowornrattanakosonm-ahintarayuthayama-hadilokpopnopparatratchathaniburiromudomratchhariwetmashasathan – but it's not in Wales!*

# TRINIDAD & TOBAGO

For people who like to really get to know the natives while on holiday, the twin island paradises of Trinidad and Tobago are something of a non-starter. Never mind that the people here don't understand the Queen's English. They don't even understand each other's English. This is because the islands are home to the most individual English-based creole dialects on earth – so individual in fact that no two Trinidadians or Tobagans actually speak the same language.

Consequently both islands are in a state of perpetual confusion. Attempts have been made to develop a shared sign language. This has failed, as signs have acquired many individual meanings. Shaking the head can mean 'yes', 'no', 'I don't know', 'I need the toilet' and '51'. Nodding the head can mean 'yes', 'no', 'perhaps', 'goodbye', 'hello', 'cheese' and 'there are sharks in that water'. More disturbing for first time visitors, islanders employ the traditional 'wanking' gesture to convey such things as 'yes', 'no', '4 o'clock', 'craft fair', 'scampi in a basket' and 'Philip Schofield'. Even the good old traditional two-fingered salute can sometimes mean 'that's the best idea I've ever heard!'

This inability to communicate deeply pains the islanders, who are a very friendly people, so, in place of trying to make themselves understood, they just smile a lot. It's considered more polite than saying 'you what?' God, how they smile. Everywhere you go people smile at you with big beaming toothy grins. Even this can be misinterpreted, especially by sexually insecure young white men with hair-trigger tempers.

Trinidad and Tobago have good reason to apologise to the world of music. The islands share the distinction of being the spiritual homes of both the calypso and the limbo. Go to Port o' Spain in June for the annual limbo contest if you want to be on disability benefit for the rest of your working life, or visit Scarborough on Tobago if you like calypso (not a very likely eventuality, you'll agree, and the town is normally deserted during the 'calypso jamboree' as even native Tobagans can't stand it). Trinidad is also where the tradition of the steel drum band began, a particularly monotonous way of making music now forced on innocent schoolchildren in many inner London boroughs.

Trinidad is also home to over four hundred different species of tropical bird, so being shat on is a common problem for tourists to contend with. Many of the species are hummingbirds. These are known as 'politician birds' because of their incessant droning.

## DID YOU KNOW?
*Amongst the Caribs (the originally islanders), men and women spoke two entirely different languages – just like in Britain today!*

# TUNISIA

Tunisia has long enjoyed a reputation of being the most liberal of all Arab countries not just in political and religious terms, but in freedom of sexual expression too. Whereas most westernised countries would be satisfied with progressive attitudes towards prostitution and homosexuality, the Tunisians go one step further, and this is evident to users of public phone boxes not only in the capital Tunis, but in most towns. Like the UK, these kiosks are plastered with cards offering sexual services. However, unlike the UK, these cards offer the services of camels, justifying Tunisia's unofficial title as 'the Bangkok of North Africa' (that, and 'Camel-Shagging Centre of the World').

At a loose end? You could be, with my camel cavalcade. Eight to choose from. All pretty and all with sexy walk! Phone Hussein – Kebili 7762

My camel might be able to go without water for two weeks but she's desperate for you NOW! Phone Ahmed on Beja 72974 now!

Mustapha Fuck? No problem with my prize Dromedary, Clara. You try? Ali, Tamerza 5524

FOR THE BEST HUMPING NORTH OF TUNIS
CALL: 65221 AND ASK FOR HABIB.

---

## DEALING WITH THE LOCALS

Most package holidays to Tunisia fail to mention the above aspect, but if you look beyond the beautiful beaches of Bizerte and Hammamet, the calm oasis at Nefta and the Carthaginian ruins outside of Tunis, you'll see a country where camel humping is more than the sexual aberration of a twisted minority – it's a way of life.

The warmth and hospitality of the Tunisians is legendary, but if you do strike up a conversation, be aware that the friendliness and apparent hospitality is just a charade. What seems like an innocent chat will soon turn out to be a standard business pitch...

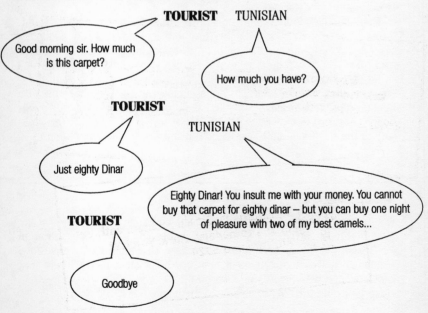

**TOURIST**    TUNISIAN

Good morning sir. How much is this carpet?

How much you have?

**TOURIST**

TUNISIAN

Just eighty Dinar

Eighty Dinar! You insult me with your money. You cannot buy that carpet for eighty dinar – but you can buy one night of pleasure with two of my best camels...

**TOURIST**

Goodbye

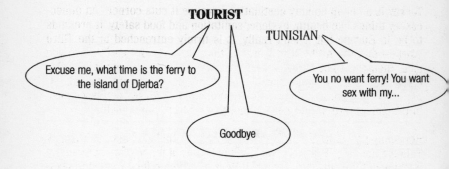

## Carthage

This was the mighty capital of the ancient Carthaginian Empire, a city founded nearly 2,800 years and rebuilt by Julius Caesar as the second city and cornerstone of the Roman Empire. Today, it is the cornerstone of the Tunisian 'rip off tourists' industry, as what little is left of the site is promoted as a glorious wonder.

Don't be taken in by sightseeing tours – the remains resemble a building site more than a once-mighty city and looking at a few randomly placed rocks and the odd broken pillar does not justify a £25, three-hour excursion. There is something that looks like an amphitheatre, but which could just as easily be a landfill site. There's also a broken wall and a statue without a head that Tunisians claim is a 'stunning example of a Roman villa', four bricks ('a prime example of a senator's palatial residence') and a lagoon of stagnant water that smells ('the Punic Port, gateway to the Carthaginian Empire and a symbol of world domination').

# TURKEY

The home of Turkish delight, doner kebabs and incurable diseases of the intestinal tract, Turkey has unaccountably become a popular destination for British tourists in recent years. In part, this must be because food and lodgings are cheap but, as anyone who has visited Turkey in the past knows all too well, what you save on meals and hotels, you more than make up for on the cost of diarrhoea medicine.

Turkey is a cheap holiday destination because it cuts corners on unnecessary things like health, hygiene, sanitation and food safety. It pretends to be in Europe but it isn't really. It is firmly entrenched in the Third World – and the Arab Third World at that. If the food doesn't make you sick, then the sight of sweaty burly moustachioed men openly slipping each other their tongues surely will. If you are taken sick on holiday, expect little help, as 95 per cent of all doctors in Turkey only specialise in proctology and 45 per cent of those won't treat non-blondes.

For many years, in fact, Turkey was known as the 'sick man of Europe'. This did not refer to its economy or the health of its people – although it could well have. Instead, commentators were referring to the sick sexual practices of its population.

Most tourists start off their holidays in Istanbul. Look out for the Arab-style architecture encrusted with precious stones and centuries of grease and the marketplaces, which are some of the busiest and dirtiest in the world today. Pay particular attention to the carpets, which are of remarkable quality considering they are woven by five-year-olds working twenty-hour days for a pittance. Examine goods surreptiously, and do not stop to admire them. If you pause to examine goods, the stallkeeper will greet you in the traditional way by pulling your trousers down and performing vigorous oral sex on you. You will be expected to reciprocate before bargaining can begin. You may well think that a handwoven carpet is not worth it. You would be right.

Outside of Istanbul, in the country, you will find yourself warmly welcomed, especially if you have blonde hair and tight jeans. Be polite but firm. Mutual masturbation might be above board in their culture but it is not in yours – especially not in the back seat of a crowded bus or in front of twenty chain-smoking close relatives. As a British tourist, you may also find yourself something of a novelty, especially in remote regions, where few have ever seen a human being before.

---

## 8 TURKISH PUBLIC HOLIDAYS TO AVOID AT ALL COSTS

---

**MARCH 23: RIGOR ANKARA DAY** Named after the national hero who introduced the sheep into Turkey in 1161. For this deed, the capital city was named in his honour

**APRIL 16-23: TURKISH INTERNATIONAL FESTIVAL OF THE BOTTOM**  For a whole week, Turkey plays host to one of the most unusual celebrations in the world

**JUNE 6: GLANS DAY**  A celebration dating back to the Middle Ages when there was very little to do. Young men of the town take their members in their hands and storm the local town hall with them, vigorously slapping senior public officials around the ears, nose and throat, crying *'Khafjuh Hufrica Turkiscka!'* – literally, 'My manhood, I pledge for public service'

**JULY 30-31: FESTIVAL OF THE TREES**  Turkish males between the ages of 14 and 65 sneak off into the woods and are not seen by their womenfolk for 48 hours

**AUGUST 16: RIGOR ANKARA REMEMBRANCE DAY**  Commemorates the death of Rigor Ankara after his failed attempt to introduce the mountain cougar into Turkey as the demand for sheep had outstripped supply. During the day, people gather in the village square to hear a stirring rendition of the Turkish national anthem, *Strapping Young Men of the Balkans (How You Glisten As You March By)*

**OCTOBER 18: TAPEWORM DAY**  In every village a maiden is crowned 'Queen of the Tapeworms' and everyone then avoids her for a whole year

**NOVEMBER 5-19: SMEGMA HARVEST FESTIVAL**  Peasants still harvest their smegma to make candles to see them through the winter months ahead. By tradition, peasants must present one tenth of their produce in tithe to the mayor of the village who, by tradition, runs away when he smells them coming

**DECEMBER 6: ST BARDOLPH'S DAY**  The happiest day in the Turkish calendar, when young and old alike paint their bottoms in bright, festive colours and display them on horse-drawn carts paraded through the town for all to see and admire

**DID YOU KNOW?**
*The Black Sea is black because Turks swim in it?*

---

## PRINCIPAL ACTIVITIES OF THE TURKISH POPULATION

*by percentage*

- Agriculture, forestry and fishing — 6%
- Manufacturing — 4%
- Making Turkish delight — 10%
- Working in kebab shops — 17%
- Wrestling — 12%
- Sheep worrying — 14%
- Men holding hands with other men in public — 27%
- Looking swarthy — 98%
- Belly-dancing (female) — 48%
- Belly-dancing (male) — 34%
- Getting behind one another and committing vileness — 43%
- Smoking 'substances' — 26%
- Talking in the world's ugliest language — 100%
- Emigrating to open a Wimpy Bar — 39%
- Things we won't go into — 59%
- Washing 'down there' — 4%
- Clubbing starving Kurdish refugees with rifle butts — 14%

## THE MAIN EXPORTS OF TURKEY

Foul-tasting coffee

Foul-tasting cigarettes

Foul-tasting Turkish delight

Foul-tasting hashish

Foul-tasting doner kebabs

Smegma

Ear wax

Lice

Grease

Sheep that walk funny

A really unpleasant smell when the wind's blowing the wrong way across the Bosphorus

## THE MAIN IMPORTS OF TURKEY

Diarrhoea medicine

Vaseline

Flea powder

Copies of Locker Room Bottom Bonanza magazine

Dresses in suspiciously large sizes

Sheep aphrodisiacs

## TURKEY'S PRINCIPAL CONTRIBUTIONS TO THE INTER-NATIONAL COMMUNITY

❑ Inventing the Turkish baths, so that men of dubious practices may meet under cover of steam clouds, hidden from the all-seeing eye of God
❑ Dishonesty and deception in commerce
❑ Several sexual acts you now only ever see in strange German porno movies
❑ The invasion of Cyprus
❑ Moustachioed women
❑ A town called Batman (south west of Lake Van)
❑ Food poisoning (Istanbul Tummy, Ankara Sphincter, Izmir Colon, Silvas Gut, Kaysen Ploppy, Denizh's Revenge and the Erzurum Shits)
❑ First recorded pubic hair to be found in an hors d'oeuvre (1546)
❑ Inspiring the film *Midnight Express*

# U

## UGANDA

Uganda is not at all what you would expect. In many ways it is worse. It is certainly stranger.

Since the Asian community was forcibly ejected by Amin, there are no doctors, no lawyers, no accountants and it is virtually impossible to buy an extortionately priced pint of milk and a packet of semi-stale Wagon Wheels anywhere in Kampala after 6pm.

Decades of being ruled over by lunatics like Idi 'Big Dada' Amin, have left the Ugandans with an unnatural reverence for mental illness. Amin's antics, which included appointing himself as the leader of the Scottish Provisional Government and establishing a 'Suicide Regiment' clad in bright canary yellow uniforms, are now the standard by which all would-be Ugandan leaders are judged.

The sad truth is that, in Uganda today, the more mental you are, the more respected you are. A virtual caste system is in effect, with all the sane people doing the dirty menial jobs and the lunatics getting all the most prestigious appointments, like running the economy and vital public services. This probably explains why all the bus services in Kampala go around in a tight circle without stopping, why shops are open from 9 in the morning until 9.01 precisely and why the chief export of Uganda is bright orange shoes with no soles, made entirely of cheese with human pubic hair laces. Senior lunatics are sent for duty as part of Uganda's delegation to the United Nations, where their attempts to start a Mexican wave in the council chamber has been met with no little dismay.

Ambitious Ugandan parents can be seen repeatedly hitting their children around the head for not being stupid enough, and if you meet a pregnant woman you should greet her with the phrase *'Mbunto ite ite n'doungite t'tare jing ding'* which means 'may your first-born have to be taken away and sedated'. Parents make every effort for children

– particularly sons – to grow up mental. This they do by allowing them to go head-first down makeshift slides onto hard concrete and to watch as many American cartoons as they like. Wealthier Ugandans send their sons to school in Britain, where they can experience life in an inner-city comprehensive and breathe in all the lead fumes in preparation for life as an idiot.

There is not much for the tourist to see in Uganda. The most spectacular attraction is Lake Victoria which boasts one of the most terrible smells in the world today, especially for several weeks after one of Uganda's frequent ferry disasters. Never ever get on board a ferry. (Piloting a ferry on Lake Victoria is seen as very prestigious and consequently is a job reserved for the most seriously mentally-challenged.)

Far more entertaining are the Ugandan elections, held every four years, when ambitious Ugandan politicians get up on the hustings, bare their buttocks and shout obscenities until they pass out. If you book ahead, you can buy tickets for the swearing-in of the Prime Minister, a solemn ceremony which includes the presentation of the 'Straightjacket of Office' and no little kicking and thrashing. Sit towards the back, where you stand less chance of getting bitten.

## GETTING SERVED IN A UGANDAN RESTAURANT

Unless you appear to be deranged, you will not receive good service. Diners who turn up naked or smeared with their own faeces are guaranteed the best table in the restaurant. If you do not want to go this far, just pretend to be mad to your waiter. Try saying:

*'I want to eat your head'*

*'When the rest of my fellow dribbling psychotics turn up, please direct them to this table'*

*'I used to play the bagpipes until gorillas stole my nightlight'*

*'Iboiboiboiboibo blaah bibble'*

Unfortunately, Ugandan staff must also pretend to be crazy if they want to get on. The cross-dressing waiter who tips soup in your lap while doing a Carmen Miranda medley is probably angling for promotion. Or he could indeed be mental. It's so hard to tell in modern-day Uganda!

### DID YOU KNOW?

*The most popular film star in Uganda is Jim Carey – but at least they have an excuse.*

# UNITED STATES
# East Coast

To many people, the Eastern United States means just one thing – New York City – the self-proclaimed 'Big Apple'.

New York became 'The Big Apple' in 1926, after a city-wide vote to decide which fruit it should name itself after. While many of the city's poor preferred 'The Colossal Pomegranate' or 'The Outsize Pineapple', influential City councilmen lobbied hard for 'The Big Apple' and won the day, beating 'The Humungous Banana' and 'The Enormous Avocado' into second and third place respectively. It has remained 'The Big Apple' to this day, despite the work of ethnic pressure groups trying to have it changed to 'El Grande Satsuma'.

Apart from being known as 'The Big Apple', NYC is also known as the rudest city in the world, with good reason. New Yorkers pride themselves on being as rude and abusive as possible to natives and tourists alike. From La Guardia, be prepared for roadsigns saying 'Route Fucking 101' and 'The Cocksucking New York Expressway, 2 miles'. At your hotel, be prepared for the doorman to greet you with a terse, 'go home, ya bum!' This is a perfectly normal New York greeting and should be responded to with the odd phrase, 'your momma wears army boots!' and a tip of approximately $1 per case.

The rudeness of New Yorkers may take some getting used to, like any strange foreign customs. Whereas we shake hands as a greeting, they push you off the sidewalk. Whereas we wave upon recognising someone, they flip them the finger and shout sexually impossible suggestions. If you want to survive in Manhattan, you've got to be as rude and abrasive and insensitive as the natives. Practise before you go. Take a Saturday job at Dixons or write a gossip column in a down-market Sunday supplement.

Every year, Broadway sees one of the most spectacular events staged in the city, the 'Celebration of Rudeness' parade where New Yorkers march through the streets hurling abuse at the onlookers, who throw bottles back at them. The parade has floats, many showing grossly outsize papier mâché depictions of the human genitals, and is feted with ticker tape, every single tiny piece of which has the word 'asshole' printed on it. The parade goes on until nightfall, or until shots are fired, whichever comes first.

The city also boasts several world-class museums and art galleries reflecting its obsession with discourtesy and all things offhand. The

'Gallery of Modern Insults' (8th Avenue) has a stunning collection of twentieth century abuse on display, from the priceless 'kiss my ass!' to several highly acclaimed 'fuck yous'. Be sure to visit the 'Gesture Gallery'. The 'Metropolitan Museum of Rudeness' (5th Avenue) is home to more important international works of intolerance and brusqueness, and boasts the finest race hate collection outside Japan. For more avant-garde art lovers, the 'Manhattan Gallery of the Living Insult' (8th Avenue) allows you to interact with many of the pieces on display, either by spitting on them or writing rude words in spray paint across them.

Visit The Battery or Central Park to see shows by young performing arts students, who will vigorously abuse you and your ethnic identity for just a few quarters in the hat. It's a unique experience if you can hold your temper.

Also while you are in New York, be sure to visit the top of the Empire State Building. At least while you're up there, people can't spit down on you from the observation gallery. Many tourists also take the ferry out to Liberty Island. More fool them. Here you can stand in line for hours for the opportunity to climb up inside the Statue of Liberty which reeks of the puke of small overfed schoolchildren and whose tiny observation deck faces out to sea away from anything of even remote interest.

It is perhaps ironic that the woman who posed for the Statue of Liberty was a prostitute. So, every time you see Lady Liberty from now on, don't forget that this symbol of everything American probably had her lips around the sculptor's todger on more than one occasion. Perhaps the sign should read 'Give me your huddled masses – $60 for a half and half, $20 hand relief'...

It is by night that New York truly comes alive – there are an estimated 60 million cockroaches in the city. Stay in your hotel room with a good book – a thick hardcover you can thump them with.

The only other city worth mentioning in the area is Washington DC. You can visit the White House provided you are a representative of a murderous terrorist movement or can donate at least $500,000 in campaign funds to the Democrats (add an extra $4,000 if you want sex with Chelsea Clinton while you're there – or an extra buck fifty if you want to make it with Socks). Washington also boasts some monuments to dead American presidents you've probably never heard of and the largest collection of call girls outside Bangkok. Book ahead if Congress is in session.

## HAILING A CAB

Don't try and get around by subway. You'll be murdered in cold blood by someone who wants your tie. Instead, travel everywhere by yellow cab. To hail one, simply stand at the corner of a main road and give passing yellow cabs the finger. If one is free, he will stop and ask you, 'where to, asshole?' to which you should reply, 'none of your goddamn business, dinky-dick' and get in. This will leave your driver none the wiser as to your destination but, even if you told him he wouldn't know where you meant. Empire State Building? Where's that? Wall Street? Never heard of it! This is because almost 70 per cent of the city's taxi drivers come from Lagos, and the other 30 per cent from outer space, if their strange language and personal odours are anything to go by. None of them know their way around Manhattan, so be prepared to give them directions out of a street map. They won't have one, so buy your own before setting out. Allow twice as long for your cab journey as you would normally. This is partly because of the gridlocks that plague the city and partly so that your driver can suddenly stop the cab in the middle of the street and get into an alarming fist fight with another cabbie.

## HOW TO SAY HELLO TO A NATIVE NEW YORKER

GREETING: Fuck you!
RESPONSE: Yeah? Your mother, buddy!

## NICKNAMES OF EAST COAST CITIES

**NEW YORK** - THE BIG APPLE

**BOSTON** - THE TRANSLUCENT GORILLA

**WASHINGTON DC** - THE HAPPY POTATO

**JERSEY CITY** - THE EXPLODING THRUSH

**PITTSBURGH** - THE ITCHY LOBSTER

**PHILADELPHIA** - THE SPREADABLE CHEESE

# THE UNITED STATES
## Florida

Florida is a popular holiday destination for Brits abroad, who regard it as an English-speaking home away from home but we say it's less of a holiday and more of a battle for survival. Before you leave, check that your insurance covers you for 'acts of crackheads'. Many don't, and major facial reconstructive surgery does not come cheap in America.

Muggers are on the lookout for tourists, and the trick is not to look like a tourist in your shiny hire car. As soon as you get the keys to your rental car, throw several pots of paint over it and chisel large lumps of metal away to imitate corrosion. Put on the dirtiest clothes you can find, strap a bandana around your head and play Hispanic pop music on the car stereo, jacked up as loud as you can stand it. Then drive at twenty miles an hour, eyeing up all the other drivers and making tongue-waggling gestures at their female passengers. If you have a passenger in the back seat, ensure they spend the entire journey with their bare bottom pressed up against the rear window. You will now look like any other car on the road in Miami and will not draw attention to yourself. Provided you follow this simple advice, you have a greater than fifty-fifty chance of making it from Miami International to your hotel with all your vital organs unpunctured.

There is little to do in Miami itself if you don't smuggle cocaine or enjoy strutting around aimlessly in tight trousers and an open Latin shirt. You can visit 'God's Waiting Room', a strip of apartment blocks around Palm Beach where elderly retirees sit around and look at you with fear, or take in a Cuban nightclub show, which usually features a singer, two dancers and a brutal stabbing.

The real action takes place in Orlando – and Disneyworld. Disneyworld is OK, if you don't mind being subjected to violent motion sickness on the rides and violent pricing in the restaurants and souvenir shops. Avoid the 'Small World' ride, where ugly and ill-conceived puppets sing of racial harmony and togetherness. This is a gentle ride but still likely to induce vomiting. Especially avoid in high season, as the 'Small World' ride fairly reeks of puke from unsentimental Brits. If travelling with small children, avoid Mickey Mouse if you see him, as he is usually pursued by gangs of drunken Brits with their penises hanging out yelling, 'go on, take a photo of this!' Also be on the look out for counterfeit Goofys. These are really other drunken Brits in stolen Goofy costumes. You can readily spot them by the persistent 'wanking' gestures they make at other popular children's characters in the park. The real Goofy would not do this.

Orlando is also home to the educational Epcot centre, which has bored children for many years now, and the Universal Studios tour, which vividly recreates some of the movies you found only moderately entertaining twenty-five years ago.

The only other major tourist attraction in Florida is the Everglades. The Everglades are worth visiting if you like vast tracts of stagnant water and unappealing wildlife. December is the best month, because many parts of the Everglades are inaccessible.

# UNITED STATES
# Midwest

Here, for USA, read UFO. This whole region is home to the most UFO-related places of interest anywhere in the world. Believers in this phenomenon think that UFOs choose to land here because they know they won't be seen — either because it's so sparsely populated, or due to the fact that the population are a bunch of stupid corn-chewin', field-workin', finger-pickin' yokels who wouldn't know a flying saucer from a banjo. Others claim that the region is so dull that all the UFO sightings are made up just to attract tourists. The truth? Well, it's out there...

### Nevada

For UFO buffs, Area 51 is the top secret military installation that the government refuses to admit exists. The site where highly sensitive captured alien spacecraft are examined and tested. A place where the greatest secret of the twentieth century is hidden. A place so secret that thousands of tourists go there every year in the hope of catching a glimpse of a UFO.

However, visitors to the base are more likely to have a close encounter with a uniformed guard who jumps up and down on their camera, than any extra-terrestrial craft. Their Nikons ruined, most tourists go away happy. This is probably just done for show, because as everybody knows, the real action goes on at Area 52...

## New Mexico

The same UFO fans who trek to Area 51 show up in force at the town of Roswell, site of the alleged UFO crash of 1947. Since this incident has become famous, the locals are all keen to cash in on their experiences. Everyone you meet claims to have witnessed the crash and several say that they were personally responsible for causing it. It's impossible to walk down the street without someone offering to show you their own autopsy film or selling you a bit of alien wreckage kept in their garage (which will probably look suspiciously like part of an old washer/dryer painted silver).

Look out for the Roswell UFO Crash Museum. As no part of the supposed saucer or any trace of its occupants has ever turned up, you have to wonder what it's got in it...

## Kansas

According to the comic book, when Superman was rocketed to Earth from Krypton, he crash landed in Topeka, Kansas. Local residents claim that this is the God's honest truth and point out a large depression in a cornfield just off the Topeka Turnpike that looks like it may have been caused by a crashed rocket (that or a car driven by a drunk that spun off the road). The same locals claim to have witnessed the tornado that plucked Dorothy and Toto from their farm before depositing them in Oz.

## Wyoming

Here you'll find Devil's Tower, instantly recognisable as the object reconstructed out of mashed potato by Richard Dreyfuss in *Close Encounters*. It's not worth the effort of climbing to the top since you won't find a secret UFO landing area, just some used condoms and old Coke cans.

## Nebraska

The only mystery about this place is why Bruce Springsteen decided to make a dreary album of the same name.

## Colorado

Many locals claim to have seen extra-terrestrial beings wearing silvery one-piece suits and some form of face covering. Reliable witnesses say they seem to glide over the ground without making a sound. The skiing resort of Aspen is in Colorado. Make up your own mind.

## Oklahoma

What this state claims to be a rash of 'horrifying alien abductions' is, in reality, just loads of people leaving this godforsaken middle America state.

Seeing someone being teleported out of their bed in a searing flash of light at 2am is likely to be an alien abduction. Finding them gone the next morning with a note saying 'I've had enough of this middle America shit-hole' is probably not.

# UNITED STATES
## South

Wish you were in Dixie?

Believe us, you'd be much better off humping an obscure cartoon mouse than visiting the Southern United States.

The South is a community still fiercely divided, where old hatreds run deep. Total segregation is still the order of the day, and it is the ultimate sin to become romantically involved with anyone 'different'. In practice, this translates to only being allowed to have sex with your own close relatives, which explains all kinds of things.

So fierce is segregation that today, many Southerners are inbred to the extent that they are their own parents. This has led to many hereditary illnesses, congenital idiocy and a strong love of country music. Many play the banjo. The most inbred are banished to the Louisiana swamps where they become Cajuns. Many are so badly addled that they eat raccoons and speak French. It is a modern tragedy. Those not even capable of making it as Cajuns turn to the last refuge – the Ku Klux Klan, an idiot's self-help group where members can put bedsheets over their heads and then set fire to things.

Most visitors to the Southern United States make a pilgrimage to Gracelands, the one time home of Elvis Presley and decorated in the style of early senile dementia. 'Tacky' does not do the place justice. 'Vile' comes close. If anyone needs any convincing that drug abuse and interior design do not mix, they need look no further than 'Gracelands'. The surrounding area is devoted almost entirely to the 'Elvis Industry' and souvenirs of 'The King'. Be warned, most of the toenails on sale are undoubtedly fakes. You can also pick up bootleg copies of Elvis's earliest recordings which betray his true Southern roots. Tracks worth adding to your collection include 'You're a-havin' my Baby, Ma', 'Kissin' Cousins' and 'Since Ma Sister Dun Left Me'.

No visit would be complete without a trip to Elvis's grave. Of course, as every Southerner knows, Elvis isn't really in that grave. He's off having Bigfoot's baby.

There are many things you will only find in the Southern United States. This is good news because, as long as you never dip below the Mason-Dixon line on your travels, you are hardly likely to encounter them.

This is particularly true of the great Southern tradition of tobacco spitting. Here, the politically correct brigade have had their way as they have in so many other parts of America. The spitting contests continue on, but the evil tobacco is now banned.

Despite the absence of any actual tobacco in contests, World Series Tobacco Spitting remains a far more popular sport than either football or baseball in the Southern States. Several TV channels are devoted to bringing live coverage of major spitting contests, and spitting scholarships are available at most Southern colleges for students who show spitting promise during their high school years. Southern children collect and trade bubble gum cards of their spitting heroes, just as their more normal Northern counterparts do baseball stars.

Many clapped-out English footballers also find a new sporting career here. Ex-Arsenal striker Charlie George has been spitting for Atlanta for almost a decade now, alongside Peter Storey and against Martin Chivers of the Charlestone Llamas.

Spitting contests are traditionally family affairs held on Sundays after Church, and there is little in the way of hooliganism like you would expect to find at a match back home. The whole affair is packed with razzmatazz from start to finish, with huge illuminated scoreboards and gorgeous young cheerleaders clad in oilskins. If you decide to take in a match during your stay, you are advised not to watch. You are certainly advised not to try to attempt to eat a hot dog while the match is in progress, or to sit in the cheap seats downwind of the 'spitter's plate'. The highlight of the entire season is the 'Superbowl', which is usually more than halfway filled up by the end of the game.

*Courting in the South has its own unique charm...*

## DIXIELAND DATING

Alright, ah'm a sick a sittin' at home nights interfering with chickens. Ah want to meet someone and have me a whole passle a' babies!

### MY IDEAL PARTNER WOULD BE

[  ] Cousin Jake          [  ] My half sister Ellie-Mae

[  ] Ma                   [  ] Pa

[  ] Uncle Billy-Bob      [  ] Auntie Billy-Bob

[  ] Granny               [  ] Grandpa Moses

### THE THING I LOOK FOR MOST IN A PARTNER IS

[  ] Blood relations      [  ] Same surname

[  ] Same parents

[  ] Willing to stand behind me and say
'squeak piggy squeak!'

### SHARED INTERESTS

[  ] Drooling             [  ] Spitting

[  ] The Grand Ole Oprey  [  ] Klan membership

[  ] Banjo-plucking       [  ] Elvis Worshipping

[  ] Trailer parks        [  ] Moonshine

[  ] Lynchings and burnings

[  ] Walking in small circles, muttering 'uh-huh'.

[  ] None of this book-learnin' stuff

# THE SPITTING CHANNEL

**3.30 FAMILY FLOBS** Fun quiz show combining general knowledge with spitting to win valuable cash prizes

**4.00 THE LONG SPIT.** Spitting action from overseas. Today's guest is, from Britain, Spit the Dog

**5.00 THEY THINK IT'S ALL OVER (THEIR SHIRTFRONTS)** Light-hearted look at the world of spitting and mucous

**5.30 SPITTING IMAGE.** Close-up slow-motion action

**6.00 SPITBALL ROADSHOW.** Live from Hazard County

**6.30 CUSSIN' AND SPITTIN'** Topical spitting-based panel show. Tonite. Should players be allowed to throw back their heads?

**7.00 VARSITY SPITTING ROUND-UP.** All the best phlegm action from the week, plus your chance to vote for 'Spit of the Day'

**8.00 THE BIG MATCH.** Live coverage from the Nashville Phlegm-offs. Houston Hawks vs. St. Louis Spitballers. Saliva-based mayhem you can't afford to miss!

**10.00 PRO-CELEBRITY SPITTING.** Garth Brooks and Crystal Gayle team up with 'Gobby' Smith and 'Splashdown' McCoy for a no-holds barred spit-off of champions for the prestigious Robert E Lee Trophy Shield

**12.00 TEAM PROFILE.** This week, the Memphis Expectorates

Also growing in popularity are pro-celebrity spitting events, usually held in aid of charity. Kenny Rogers was once a seemingly permanent fixture on the circuit until he took a closer look at his beard, while Southern belle Julia Roberts can always be relied upon to add a touch of very badly needed glamour to proceedings.

# UNITED STATES
# West Coast

To most holidaymakers, the West Coast is synonymous with Los Angeles. Believe us when we say that the best thing about Los Angeles is that it is positioned squarely on the wrong side of the active San Andreas fault line and it will only take a few raised voices or a few visiting Masai dancers to pitch the entire stinkhole of a town into the Pacific and be rid of it once and for all.

In creating his 'inferno', Dante could not have envisaged Los Angeles. This is because he was a master of imagination and whoever built this slum town had none whatsoever. The city has no heart, geographically or spiritually. It is composed entirely of suburbs which range from 'drab' to 'presently under martial law'. Cold, heartless and empty, Los Angeles is the original 'town without pity'. It is also the town without adequate public transport, water supplies, police or any sense of community.

It is not that LA is a poor city. Poverty here is relative. Everyone in the ghetto has a VCR, colour TV, mobile phone and laptop computer. However, it's been over three years since the Rodney King riots and many are now starting to break down or exceed their warranties – so it could be a long, hot summer...

Los Angeles is a dangerous city. Going for a stroll at night is roughly equivalent to going walkabout naked in Longleat Safari Park with a liberal coating of Bovril. Police response times are poor – if the LAPD bother to come out at all. They've been sulking since the OJ verdict and many 911 emergency calls for assistance are now met with a petulant 'shan't!' However, you can be sure that the police will still turn out for really serious crimes like smoking in a public place and being black in a residential zone.

Despite all this, Brits continue to flock to LA for the glamour. Many make the mistake of visiting Malibu beach where, unless you look like

Pam or Arnie, you are pointed out and jeered at until you wrap your beachtowel around your inferior body and beat a hasty retreat. Others come to Hollywood in the hope of seeing the stars. Will you see a celebrity at the very next table? Not if they let you in, matey.

Other ports of call include Disneyland, Universal Studios, Grummans Chinese Theatre where you can see the star and handprint of your favourite movie star provided you're prepared to scrape away the conjealed junkie vomit, and the Galleria shopping mall, where teenagers gather from all over LA to be hateful and to make you wish the time period for legalised abortion could be raised to fourteen years.

San Francisco, the other big city in the region, is another kettle of fish altogether. Make no bones about it. San Francisco is a gay city. The politicians are gay, the residents are gay, the shopkeepers are gay, the tram drivers are gay, the fire brigade are gay – even the police are gay.

San Francisco is traditionally a tolerant city, but in recent years certain right wing elements have been on the rise in the community, leading to a backlash against heterosexuals or 'straight hate' as the crimes have become known. Despite this, the only serious trouble you are likely to get into is with the SFPD. Remember, you can be arrested for wearing plaid, and not being able to colour-co-ordinate your socks and singlet is a felony. as is possession of cheap aftershave. Sections of the SFPD have been known to discriminate against 'straights' so watch your step, and do not display any overt signs of straightness, like whistling at women or buying a sports magazine. It is better not to hold hands with your partner in the open. Remember, heterosexual kissing is still offensive to many.
   The straight community is largely underground, but if you know where to go you can find a few straight clubs where the police won't hassle you. There is also a weekly newspaper for straights, *The Hetero Herald*, giving you details of straight-related arts, dance, social events and toilets. If you're straight, you may wish to avoid such overtly gay events as 'Mineral Water World' and 'EXPO Gym '97'.

Aside from Los Angeles and San Francisco, the region boasts a number of other attractions including San Diego – home of Seaworld and 20,000 illegal Mexicans crouching in the bushes; Yosemite Park – famous for featuring in the worst of all the *Star Trek* movies; Las Vegas, which is better avoided if you have an IQ over 100; and Seattle, Washington State, which is justly famous for not being worth visiting.

# WBSF SAN FRANCISCO

5.30 THE LOVE DOCTOR
     Is heterosexuality incurable?

6.00 SPOTLIGHT ON TRUCKERS.

6.30 MR AND MR
     Quiz show

7.00 FABRICS ROAD SHOW
     Live from Oakland

8.00 FILM: FIRST FIST OF SUMMER:
     Romantic drama

9.30 OUCH!
     Pro-celebrity body piercing

11.30 LATE MOVIE; STRAW DOGS.
      All-felching version of 'Reservoir Dogs'

1.40 FREE WILLIE.
     Not the whale, but 101 useful money-saving
     tips to meet... your dream guy!

2.30 THE STRAIGHTS OF SAN FRANCISCO
     Police drama starring Karl Malden
     and Michael Douglas, back when he was
     young and scrummy

## WALES

Cross the Severn Bridge and suddenly you're in the Third World. Visiting Wales is like stepping back in time about 600 years. It is also like stepping in a fresh cowpat. Why do it?

The problem with Wales isn't just the Welsh, although they don't help matters, it's with the country itself. Wales has little to offer the discerning tourist (or indeed the one who's not fussy), unless you like poxy little narrow guage steam trains that go from Lllyggrlly y Llobbb (Nowhere in Particular) to Lyylllgrubbly yl Llren (Nowhere That Matters) twice a day, precarious slag heaps and grubby sheep pasture. Even the country's most distinct natural feature, the mountain of Snowdon would, if it were in any other country, be truthfully called a hill and arouse little interest.

Because the country is so lacking in genuine natural beauty, attempts have been made to attract tourists interested in decaying industrial sites. The campaign to lure tourists to the collieries, which boasted the slogan 'Wales is the pits', failed to generate much interest, but did at least win the 'Truth in Advertising' award in 1988. (The Welsh Tourist Board won the same award the following year with their follow-up campaign to attract tourists to mining spoilage heaps with its slogan 'Wales – home of the slag')

In a country where electric light is regarded as a tool of the devil and the wheel wasn't known before 1957, it is not surprising that you will feel you have very little in common with the people. All over the world, people proudly declare their descent from Scots or Irish stock. Have you noticed that no-one ever claims Welsh descent? Interesting, isn't it?

It doesn't help that there are probably only three surnames in the whole of Wales – Jones, James and Evans. To help the Welsh tell each other apart, they used to label people by their profession, e.g. Jones the Post,

Jones the Milk, Jones the Colliery Supervisor. Nowadays, this system has largely broken down, because everyone is called 'Jones the Unemployed'. To outsiders, it doesn't matter who's who. You won't want to get on speaking terms with anyone during your visit.

As you travel, you will notice that many signs are in English and Welsh. The Welsh are fiercely protective of their unique language which, when spoken, sounds like the speaker is either mad or dying. Do not worry. They are not dying. However, they might well be mad, so give them a wide berth just in case.

Aside from the roadsigns, the other great manifestation of Welsh is the annual Eisteddfod, where Welsh culture is put on prominent display as a warning to others. The Eisteddfod is open to visitors. Allow at least ten minutes to view it if you have a high boredom threshold.

May sees the 'Yllyrd Yl Ylllllll Festival', in which the Welsh pit their wits against the sheep they tend in a series of quickfire general knowledge rounds. The winner of the last six events, Fluffy Boy, is now a bona fide Welsh celebrity. He opens supermarkets, makes charity appearances and was recently voted 'Sexiest Man in Wales'.

The only other thing that goes on in Wales, apart from witch-duckings, are performances by the country's famous male voice choirs. Although thought to be an old tradition, Welsh male voice choirs were in fact first developed by Winston Churchill in 1940 as a way of annoying the Germans should they invade. When the threat of invasion was lifted, male voice choirs were used overseas to good effect, irritating the Germans at Tobruk and mildly pissing them off at El Alamein and Monte Cassino. Subsequently banned by the Geneva Convention, male voice choirs have not been used in anger since, but still unofficially form part of Britain's wartime deterrent.

### DID YOU KNOW?
*Welsh has 47 different words for 'sheep' but no word for 'washing'.*

### DID YOU KNOW?
*Welsh Scrabble has 54 Ls, 75 Ys, 2 Es and 2 Ns.*
*However, no-one ever buys the game because the Welsh are*
*almost 100 per cent illiterate.*

### DID YOU KNOW?

*Cardiff is the size of Birmingham – but only half as interesting.*


### DID YOU KNOW?

*Since 1987 over 68,000 Welsh miners have lost their jobs. Good.*


### DID YOU KNOW?

*'Welsh Rarebit' originally meant a virgin.*

## ZAMBIA

Zambians are intensely proud of their Southern African nation.

*This is totally without justification.*

Some anthropologists have attributed the Zambian's professed admiration for his homeland as evidence of a deeply rooted inferiority complex. Others have just labelled Zambians as deeply stupid. Either explanation is equally convincing.

Because he is friendly and proud, it is hard not to like the Zambian. But do try.

The official language is English (not that you can recognise it, given the atrocious accent), and the typical Zambian can make himself just well enough understood to annoy you.

Because the Zambian is deeply proud of his homeland, he wants to show you all the wonderful things that abound in his land. Any tourist unwise enough to walk the streets of the capital, Lusaka, is sure to be accosted by some beaming toothy idiot saying, 'Come I show you where you can see drainpipe!' or 'Quick, take a photo of that pane of glass!' After half an hour of having assorted twigs, fencing, lightbulbs, pavements, trees and assorted dead animals pointed out to you on the streets of Lusaka, you will realise that there are no sights to see here whatsoever, a fact which doesn't deter the Zambian one jot. You *will* admire his ramshackle country.

The embittered tourist may wish to deliberately point things out which contradict the Zambians' Utopian view of their country. Don't bother. The average Zambian has an explanation for everything. Point out the emaciated, starving poor huddled in alleyways and your companion will say something like, 'Aha! Glad you have noticed this. Today Zambia is host to all-Africa supermodel symposium. All eyes on Zambia for slinky togs.' Point out the shanty towns sinking into their own filth and the average Zambian will just grin and say,'Very latest in corrugation housing. Zambia lead, world follow'. Point out the greasy mongrels ferreting in the garbage heaps and the rats thronging the gutters and your friendly guide will smile and boast, 'Zambia have wildlife all the world flock to see. Have jumbo safari without even leaving town!'

Once Zambians find out that you are in town, the hotel is no refuge. If you do not emerge, they will bring you Zambian wonders to see, like mouldy cardboard boxes, long sticks and bread. More patriotic and healthy Zambians will shin up the drainpipe and briefly waggle a child's colouring book or a car tyre outside your window before inevitably falling to their death as the rusty, decrepit ironwork crumbles into oxidised powder in their grasp. Do not blame yourself for the pile of dead Zambians that will inevitably grow under your window. They brought it on themselves.

Do not try to escape by venturing out into the countryside. It is worse there. The people have absolutely nothing. They will tell you about entirely imaginary events. 'I saw a can of beans last week,' they will say, or 'My grandfather once saw a car,' hoping to impress you. You can try offering them money to leave you alone, but they will inevitably refuse it. 'We have money in Zambia,' they will tell you. 'I saw a man with a coin when I visited the splendours of swanky Lusaka last year!'

The best way to avoid the attentions of Zambians is not to go to Zambia. Failing that, you could pretend to be dead for the duration of your visit. This is a proven method of Zambian-avoidance which works, and there is no danger of premature burial because in Africa no-one cares about dead bodies lying in the street. This is fortunate, because few of the dead bodies are in fact dead. Most are fellow tourists playing possum.

## MAKING FRIENDS

### TRY SAYING

\# Zambia is number one place for food utensils!

\# My, that's a fine oil drum you live in!

\# I went to Acalpulco last year and it wasn't half as nice as this place

\# So this is where Lassa fever started — you must be so proud

\# I wish I could stay here for ever and ever

\# I wish I had a second-hand 'Teenage Mutant Ninja Turtle' T-Shirt like the one you're wearing

## DON'T SAY

\# Cats aren't considered edible where I come from

\# I have seen a toilet roll before, thank you – and that one had some paper left on it...

\# A puddle of dog's piss is not worth taking me all the way across town to see

\# Where I come from, a scab is not a status symbol

\# When's the next plane out of this hellhole?

\# I spit on Zambia. Ptoi!

---

## TOP TEN POSTCARD SLOGANS FROM ZAMBIA

**ZAMBIA** - IT'S NICE

I SAW A RAT IN **ZAMBIA!**

**ZAMBIA** - HOME OF LASSA FEVER!

**ZAMBIA** - SANITATION BY 2010 OR BUST!

YABA-DABA-**ZAMBIA!**

**ZAMBIA** - HEAVEN ON EARTH AND SOME SHOPS TOO!

**ZAMBIA** LAST IN THE ATLAS EXCEPT FOR ZIMBABWE AND SOME OTHER PLACES-
BUT FIRST IN THE HEART

LIFE'S A PARTY IN **ZAMBIA!**

**ZAMBIA, ZAMBIA, ZAMBIA** - SO GOOD WE NAMED IT THREE TIMES!

OOH-AAH-**ZAMBIAHHH!**

# ZIMBABWE

Zimbabwe has gone through far fewer changes than you might think over the past two decades or so. Once it was ruled by a vicious and oppressive white government. Now it's ruled by a vicious and oppressive black government. *Plus ça change* as the Zimbabweians would say if they had any culture (which they don't).

The chief tourist attraction is the newly re-named Hwange National Park, better known to schoolboys the world over as Wankie. Quite how Wankie got its name is still something of a mystery. Some say the park was named after a local Ndebele chief – Chief Wankie, son of the great war chief King Tosso M'Risti. Others say that Cecil Rhodes himself gave the place its name when he first set eyes upon it, declaring, 'this place is Wankie!' This is the more likely explanation, as Rhodes had a habit of naming places as he travelled through Africa. He almost certainly provided the name for Shitole in Burkina Faso and Dump in Tanzania, for example.

Despite its natural beauty and abundance of spectacular wildlife, it has proved difficult for the Zimbabweans to attract tourists to Wankie. In part, this is because the tourist board came up with a number of off-putting tourist slogans including 'It's Wankie this year!', 'Make mine Wankie!', 'Wankie – it's wankadaciously good!' and 'Wankie, Wankie – so good they named it twice!' No-one wanted to spend a thousand pounds on a holiday and then come back and tell everyone they'd been to a place called 'Wankie'. In 1989, plans to build a theme park there – 'Wankieworld' – were abandoned when it was discovered that this breached the copyright of 'Legoland'. Now Wankie is officially called Hwange – but it's still wanky.

If you're going on an organised tour to Hwange or one of the other game parks, chances are you'll be staying in one of the new treetop hotel complexes. These are built high up in the branches of magnificent old trees. This is partly to stop guests making off before they've paid, and partly to stop leopards making off with the guests before they've paid. The drawback of this design is that it attracts the baboons.

Baboons get *everywhere*. In your room. In your closet. Under the bed. Down the toilet. Behind the shower curtain and in your trousers. Baboons are noisy, nosy, ugly, destructive, loud and manic. It's as if someone has cloned Shane Richie and let the results loose to plague you. If you like aggressive monkeys with huge red arses (or Shane Richie) then you will be in heaven. If not, Hwange and Zimbabwe may not be the place for you.

The other tourist attraction for which Zimbabwe is famed are the Victoria Falls. They're alright if you like watching water falling off the side of a big rock, but in that case you'd be better off going to see Niagara Falls where there are 4,000 Burger Kings and a brace of *Guinness Book of Records* museums all within easy walking distance.

## DID YOU KNOW?

*One president of Zimbabwe was called Canaan Banana. Other holders of the post include Zion Cucumber, Ur Tangerine and Ashdod Pomegranate.*